EL ARSENAL

UNKNOWN ENEMY

El Arsenal created by & ©2010 Salvador Vázquez & Ferrán Daniel

W9-AZG-555

Written by
SALVADOR "MUDO" VÁZQUEZ

Art by
FERRÁN DANIEL

Arse Crew:
TATTO CABALLERO (Color Asst.)

Editor in Chief
SEAN O' REILLY

www.elarsenal.com

Translated by
CARLOS GARCÍA CAMPILLO

Additional Crew:
MARCO FABELA (Colors)
TERESA MARTÍNEZ (Art- Godzukee Dream Sequence)
ABURTIX, LOCOJON, EDZ, HOMER (Color Flats)
DAVID CURIEL (Color Asst.)

PROTO
BUNKER
www.protobunker.com

TPB Crew:
EVA CABRERA (Design)
JOSH CANDIA (Design/Copy Editor)
ARMANDO VALENZUELA (Copy Editor)

www.arcana.com

CEO and Owner	VP of Operations	VP of Marketing
Sean O'Reilly	Mark Poulton	Tyler Nichol
VP of Special Projects	Senior Editor	General Manager
Nick Schley	Mike Kalvoda	Michelle Meyers

PURAS PINCHES CHINGADERAS

Whazzup, ése? Is this your first contact with El Arsenal? Well, let me warn you, this is not your average science fiction comic book. If you're not new around, you already know that this is the sequential art's equivalent to Mexican mud.

'Cause, you know? This is heavy stuff. The kind of science fiction you seldom come by. Dangerous visions, ideas with sharp teeth, as Harlan Ellison would say. And boy, do they bite.

So first off, yeah, there's Mexican science fiction and yes, El Arsenal is one of its finest examples. This is a comic book Bruce Sterling may enjoy to read. It's simple: world's economy is been blown to debris. A multinational corporation, The System, rules whatever remains of the so called free world. Among other things, in a world without law and order, The System provides mercenaries to whoever requires them. Nasty hijos de la chingada.

And this is where it all begins. Somewhere someone has the ultimate bioweapon. Somewhere else someone else wants it badly. That's when our antihero comes to scene. Meet Simón Templas Masiosare. The ultimante merc. The man to get the job done. Snake Plisken and Pedro Infante rolled into one.

Sounds weird? It's only the start.

On the next pages you're about to meet mercenary assasins, genetically modified whores, iraqi astronauts, living dead shamans, chilango drug lords, deadly beautiful Zazil, corrupt entrepreneurs, a mercenary-hiring pope, Ragnarok-carrying cockroaches and among all these madmen, beer gulping Simón swearing chingaderas.

An extreme ride south of the border. Are you brave enough to join or are you a puñetas?

My carnal Salvador Vázquez's writing has created an eerily dystopia set in an uncomfortably plausible future, set right at the turn of the corner. Good ol' cyberpunk writers used to set their stories twenty minutes in the future. El Arsenal seems to be happening five minutes from now.

And Ferran Daniel's awesome artwork will make you say "¡Ah, cabrón!" for the elegantly rendered brutality of El Arsenal's world. I re read several times the exquisitely detailed images on every page, subtlely colored to create an atmospheric storytelling.

So, get yourself comfortable. Pop open an ice cold Tecate and join the ride.

You'll love it.

After all, it's safer than cruising Tijuana, loco.

Bernardo Fernández, *Bef*
SF/Crime novelist and comic book artist

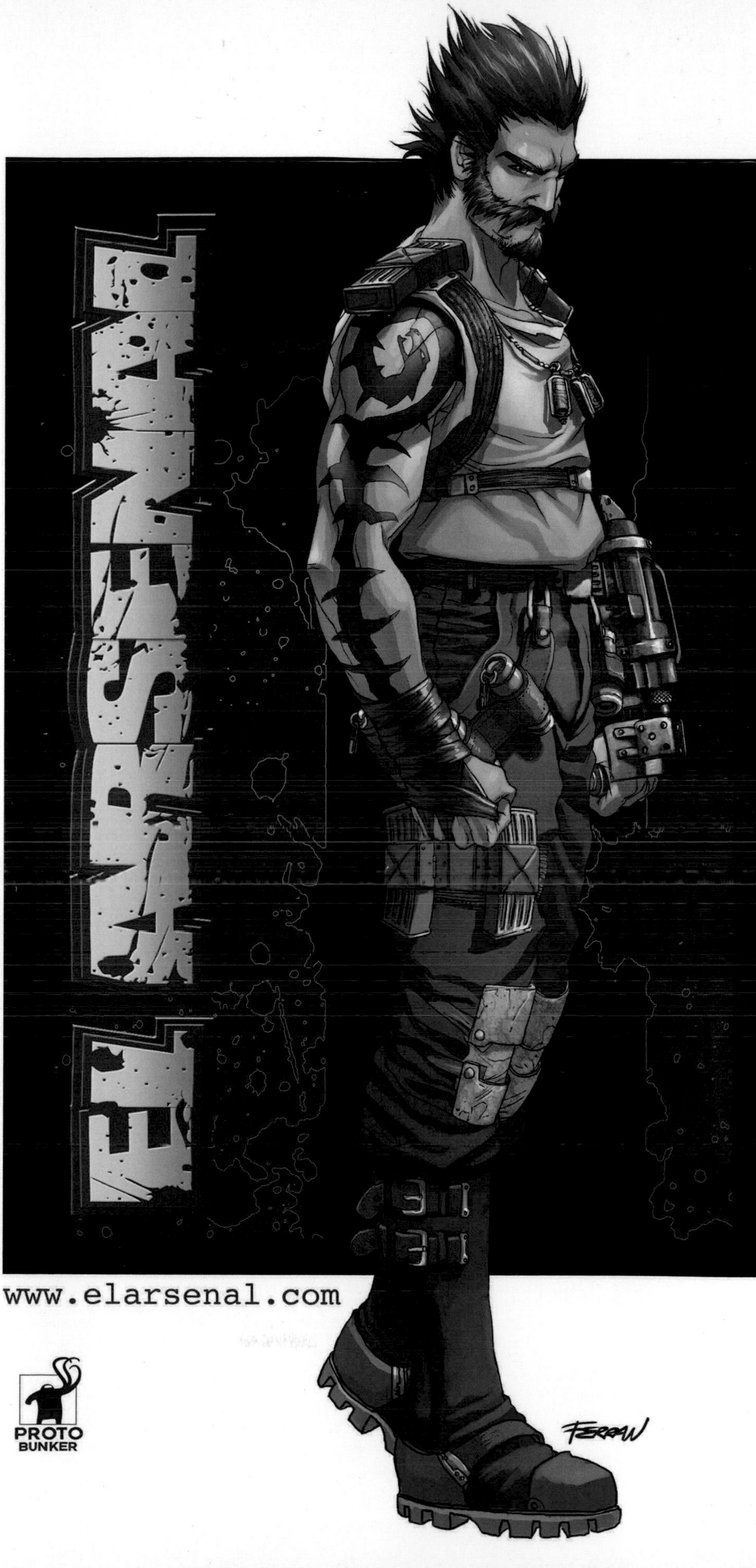
EL ARSENAL
FERRAN

www.elarsenal.com

PROTO BUNKER

"In this land of strangers,
   there are dangers,
   there are sorrows..."

                    -Silver by the Pixies.

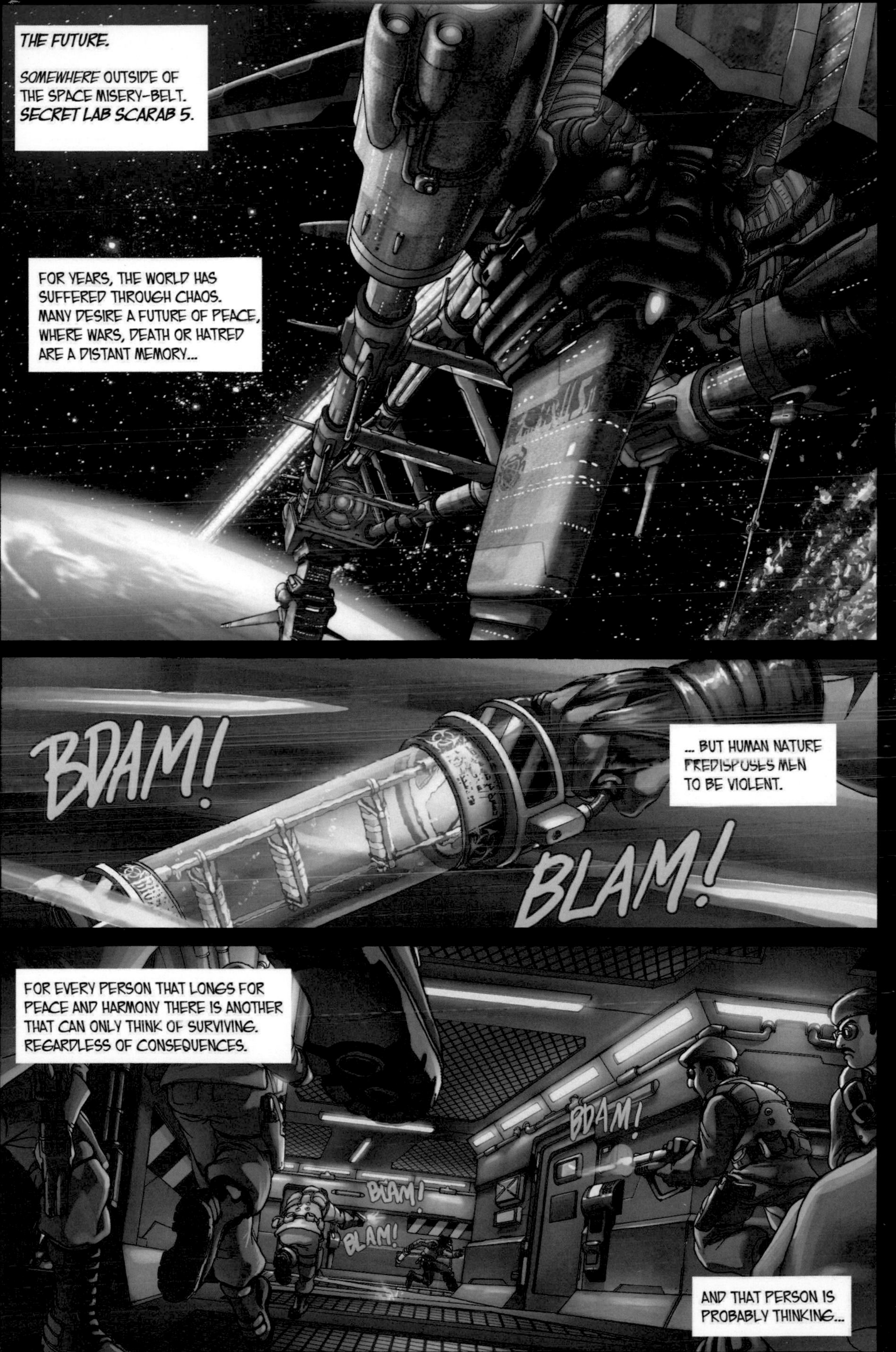
THE FUTURE.
SOMEWHERE OUTSIDE OF THE SPACE MISERY-BELT. SECRET LAB SCARAB 5.
FOR YEARS, THE WORLD HAS SUFFERED THROUGH CHAOS. MANY DESIRE A FUTURE OF PEACE, WHERE WARS, DEATH OR HATRED ARE A DISTANT MEMORY...
BDAM!
... BUT HUMAN NATURE PREDISPOSES MEN TO BE VIOLENT.
BLAM!
FOR EVERY PERSON THAT LONGS FOR PEACE AND HARMONY THERE IS ANOTHER THAT CAN ONLY THINK OF SURVIVING. REGARDLESS OF CONSEQUENCES.
BDAM!
BLAM!
BLAM!
AND THAT PERSON IS PROBABLY THINKING...

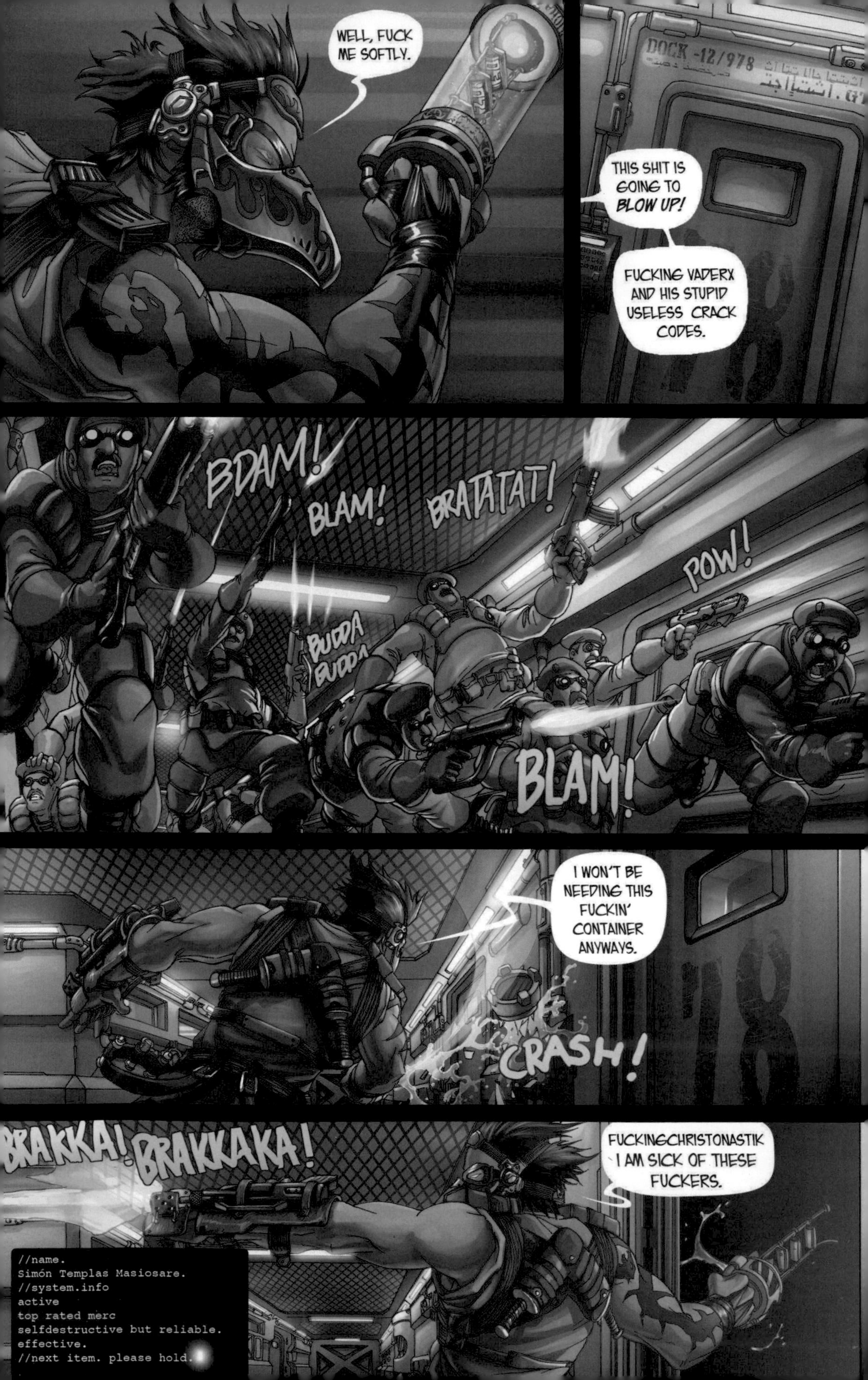
WELL, FUCK ME SOFTLY.
DOCK -12/978
THIS SHIT IS GOING TO *BLOW UP!*
FUCKING VADERX AND HIS STUPID USELESS CRACK CODES.
BDAM!
BLAM!
BRATATAT!
POW!
BUDDA BUDDA
BLAM!
I WON'T BE NEEDING THIS FUCKIN' CONTAINER ANYWAYS.
CRASH!
BRAKKA! BRAKKAKA!
FUCKINGCHRISTONASTIK I AM SICK OF THESE FUCKERS.
//name.
Simón Templas Masiosare.
//system.info
active
top rated merc
selfdestructive but reliable.
effective.
//next item. please hold.

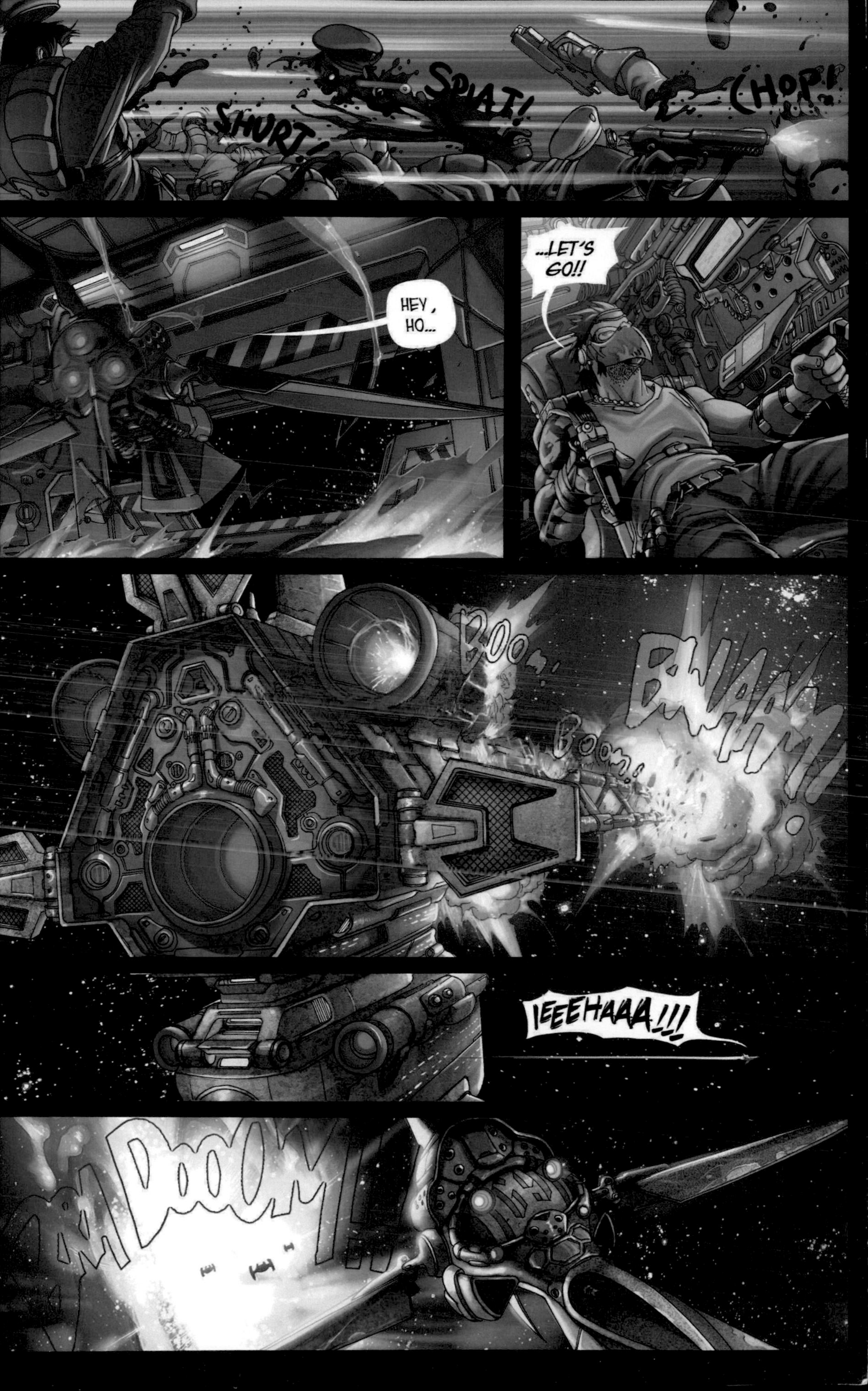
SHURT!
SPLAT!
CHOP!
HEY, HO...
...LET'S GO!!
BOOM!
BWAAAM!
BOOM!
IEEEHAAA!!!
BRADOOM!!

The end of the world as we know it.

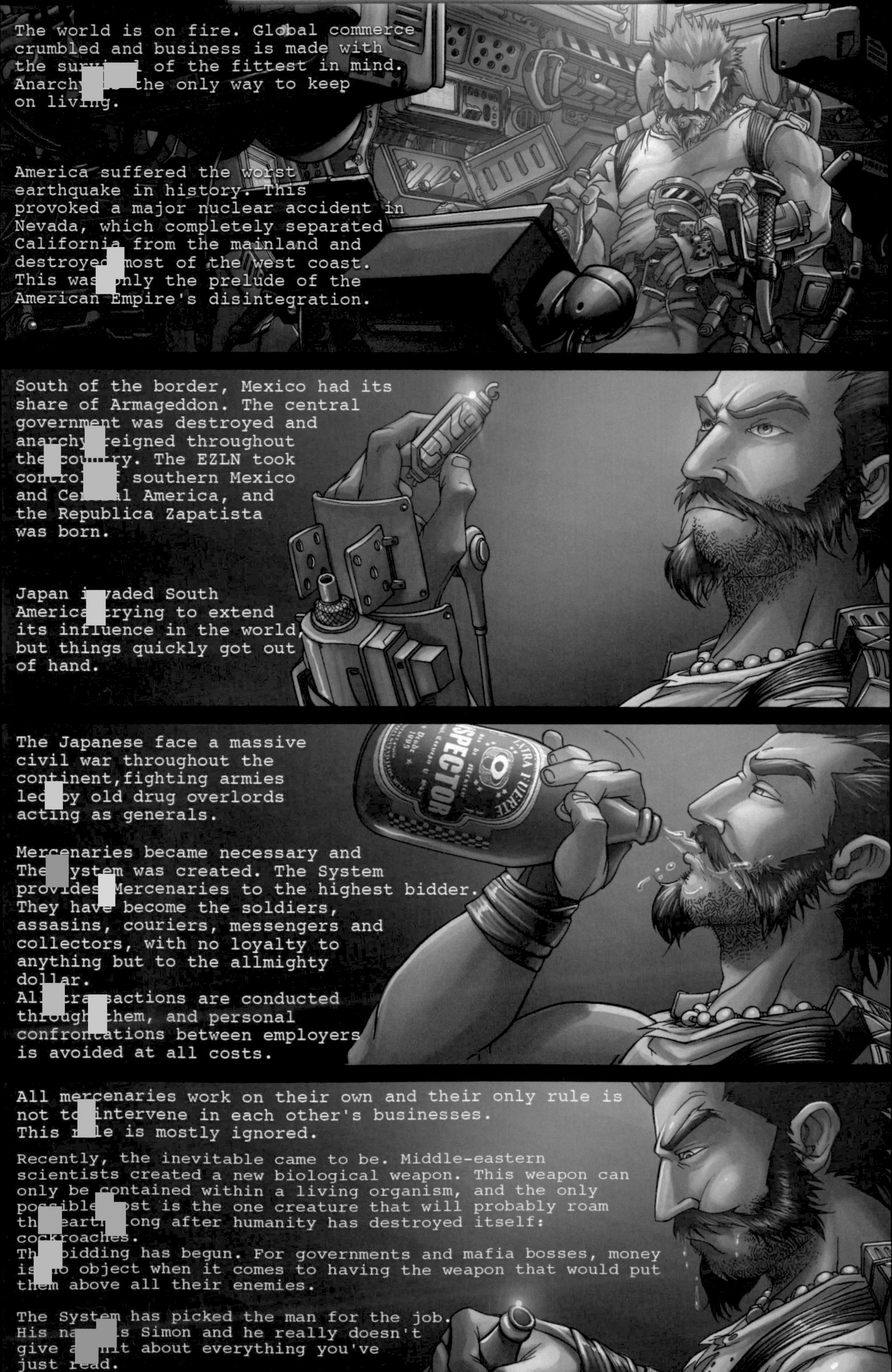
The world is on fire. Global commerce crumbled and business is made with the survival of the fittest in mind. Anarchy is the only way to keep on living.
America suffered the worst earthquake in history. This provoked a major nuclear accident in Nevada, which completely separated California from the mainland and destroyed most of the west coast. This was only the prelude of the American Empire's disintegration.
South of the border, Mexico had its share of Armageddon. The central government was destroyed and anarchy reigned throughout the country. The EZLN took control of southern Mexico and Central America, and the Republica Zapatista was born.
Japan invaded South America trying to extend its influence in the world, but things quickly got out of hand.
The Japanese face a massive civil war throughout the continent,fighting armies led by old drug overlords acting as generals.
Mercenaries became necessary and The System was created. The System provides Mercenaries to the highest bidder. They have become the soldiers, assasins, couriers, messengers and collectors, with no loyalty to anything but to the allmighty dollar.
All transactions are conducted through them, and personal confrontations between employers is avoided at all costs.
EXTRA FUERTE
All mercenaries work on their own and their only rule is not to intervene in each other's businesses. This rule is mostly ignored.
Recently, the inevitable came to be. Middle-eastern scientists created a new biological weapon. This weapon can only be contained within a living organism, and the only possible host is the one creature that will probably roam the earth long after humanity has destroyed itself: cockroaches.
The bidding has begun. For governments and mafia bosses, money is no object when it comes to having the weapon that would put them above all their enemies.
The System has picked the man for the job. His name is Simon and he really doesn't give a shit about everything you've just read.

0.2 Blitzkrieg bop.

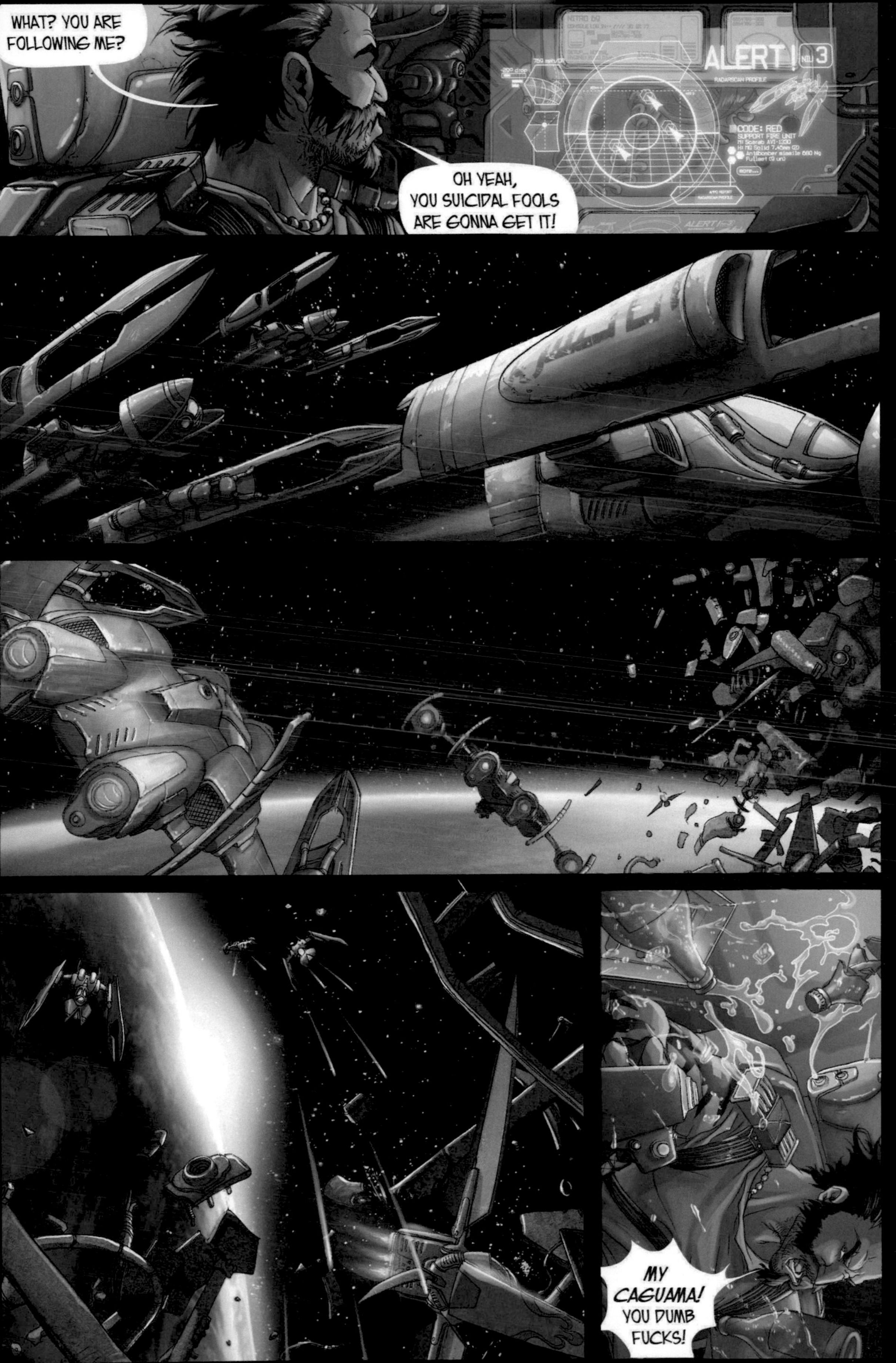
WHAT? YOU ARE FOLLOWING ME?
ALERT! NO. 3
RADARSCAN PROFILE
CODE: RED
SUPPORT FIRE UNIT
OH YEAH, YOU SUICIDAL FOOLS ARE GONNA GET IT!
MY CAGUAMA! YOU DUMB FUCKS!

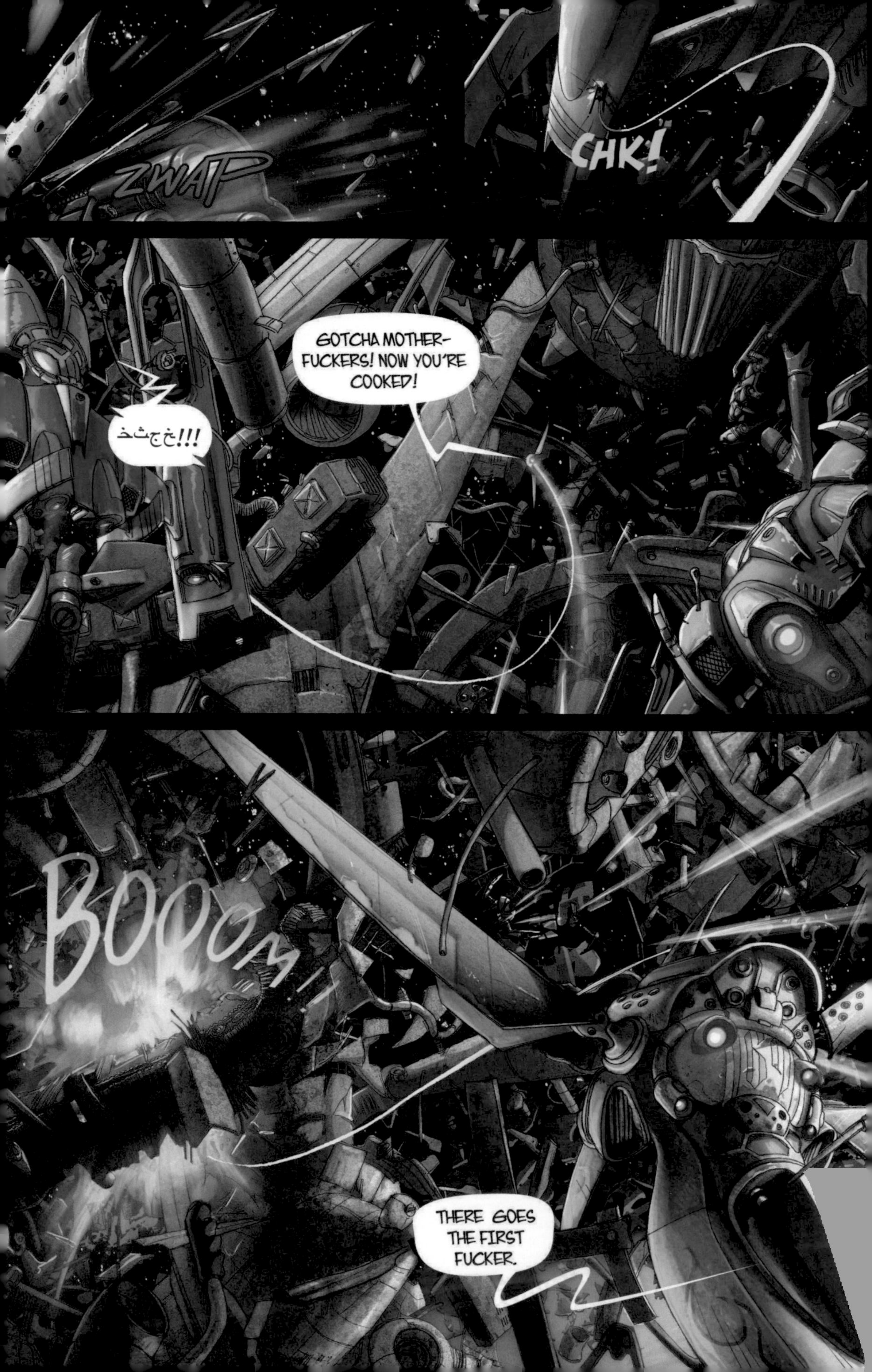
ZWAP
CHK!
GOTCHA MOTHER-FUCKERS! NOW YOU'RE COOKED!
خجثخ!!!
BOOOM
THERE GOES THE FIRST FUCKER.

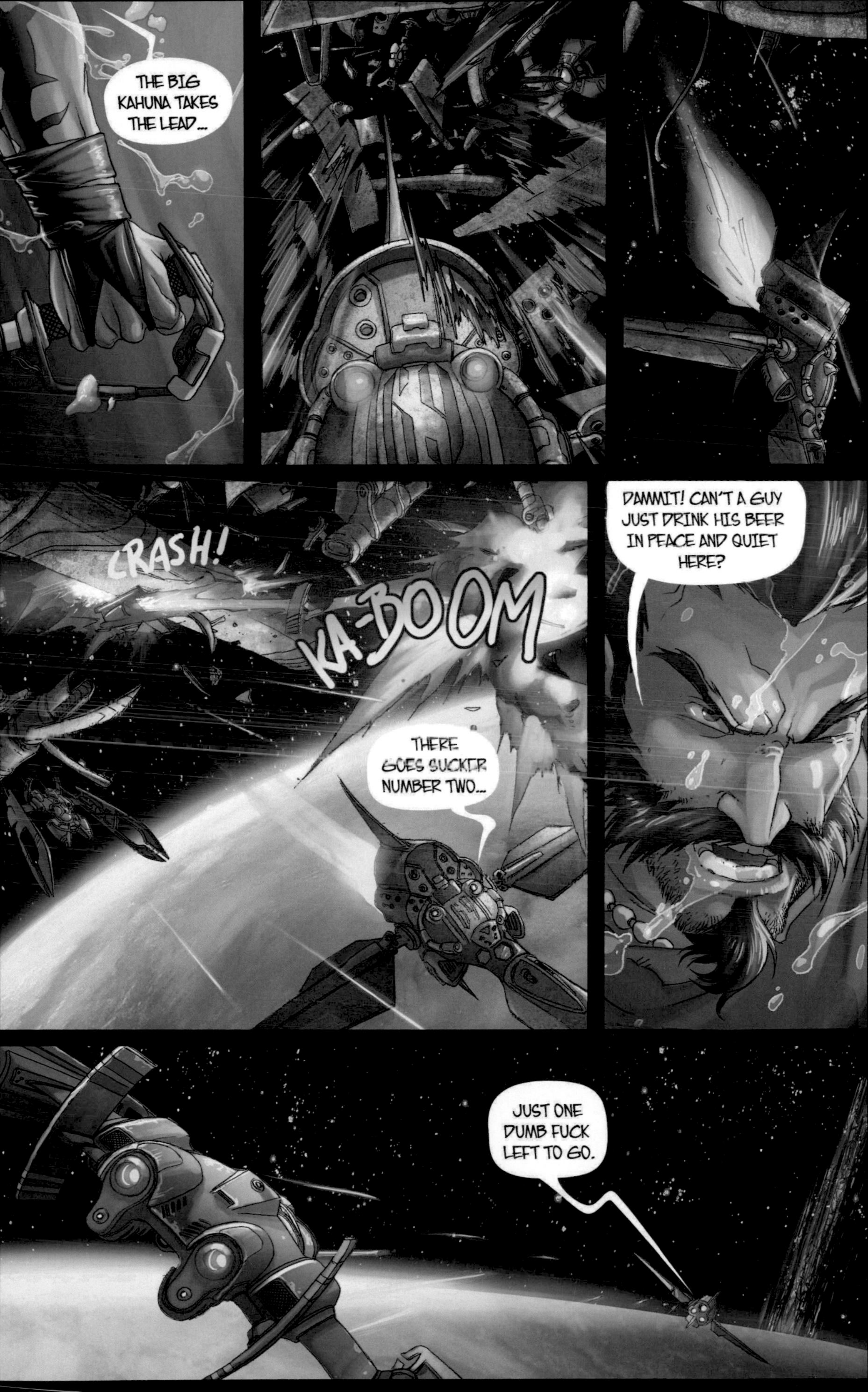
THE BIG KAHUNA TAKES THE LEAD...
CRASH!
KA-BOOM
THERE GOES SUCKER NUMBER TWO...
DAMMIT! CAN'T A GUY JUST DRINK HIS BEER IN PEACE AND QUIET HERE?
JUST ONE DUMB FUCK LEFT TO GO.

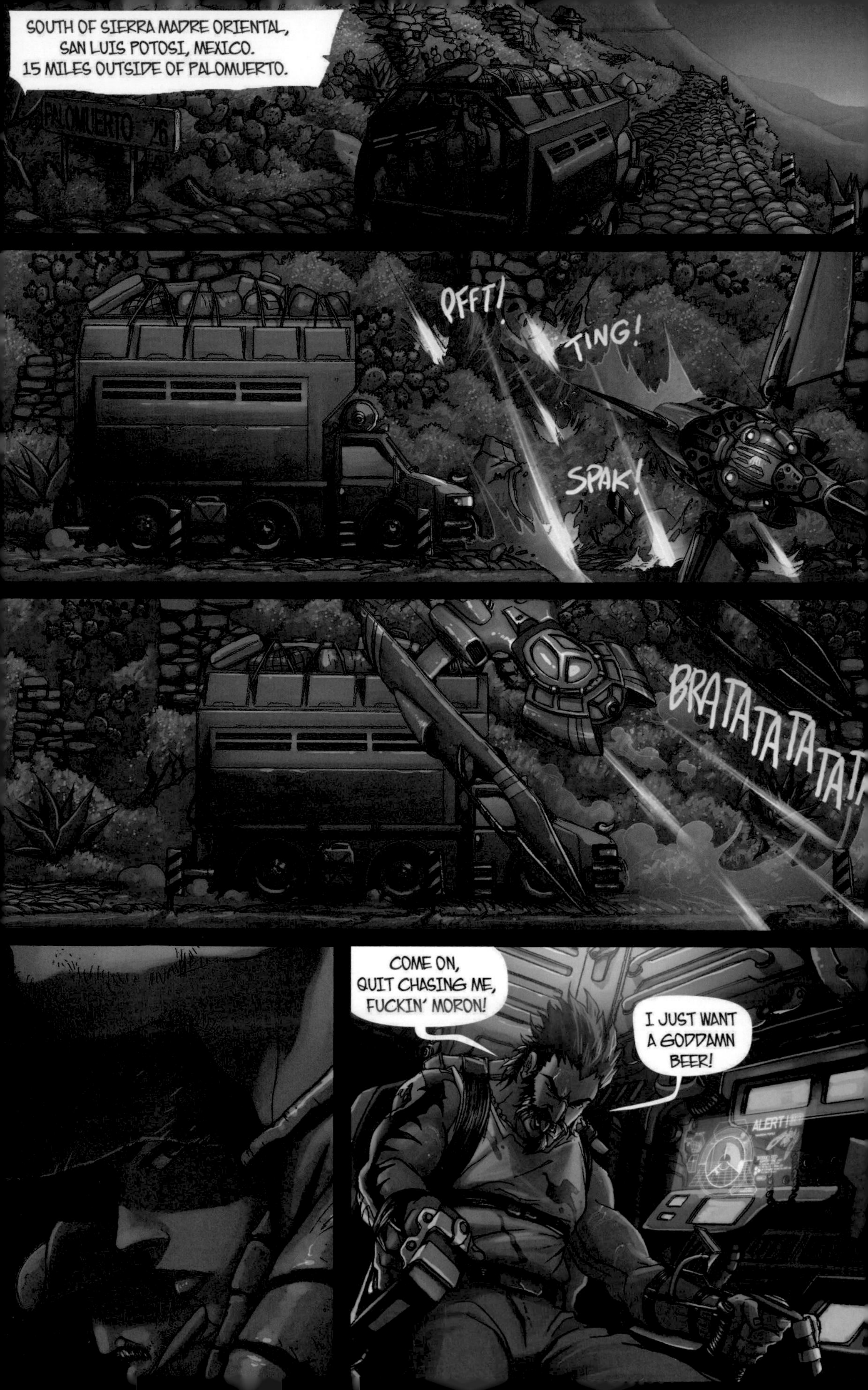

SOUTH OF SIERRA MADRE ORIENTAL, SAN LUIS POTOSI, MEXICO. 15 MILES OUTSIDE OF PALOMUERTO.
PALOMUERTO 26
PFFT!
TING!
SPAK!
BRATATATATATA
COME ON, QUIT CHASING ME, FUCKIN' MORON!
I JUST WANT A GODDAMN BEER!
ALERT!

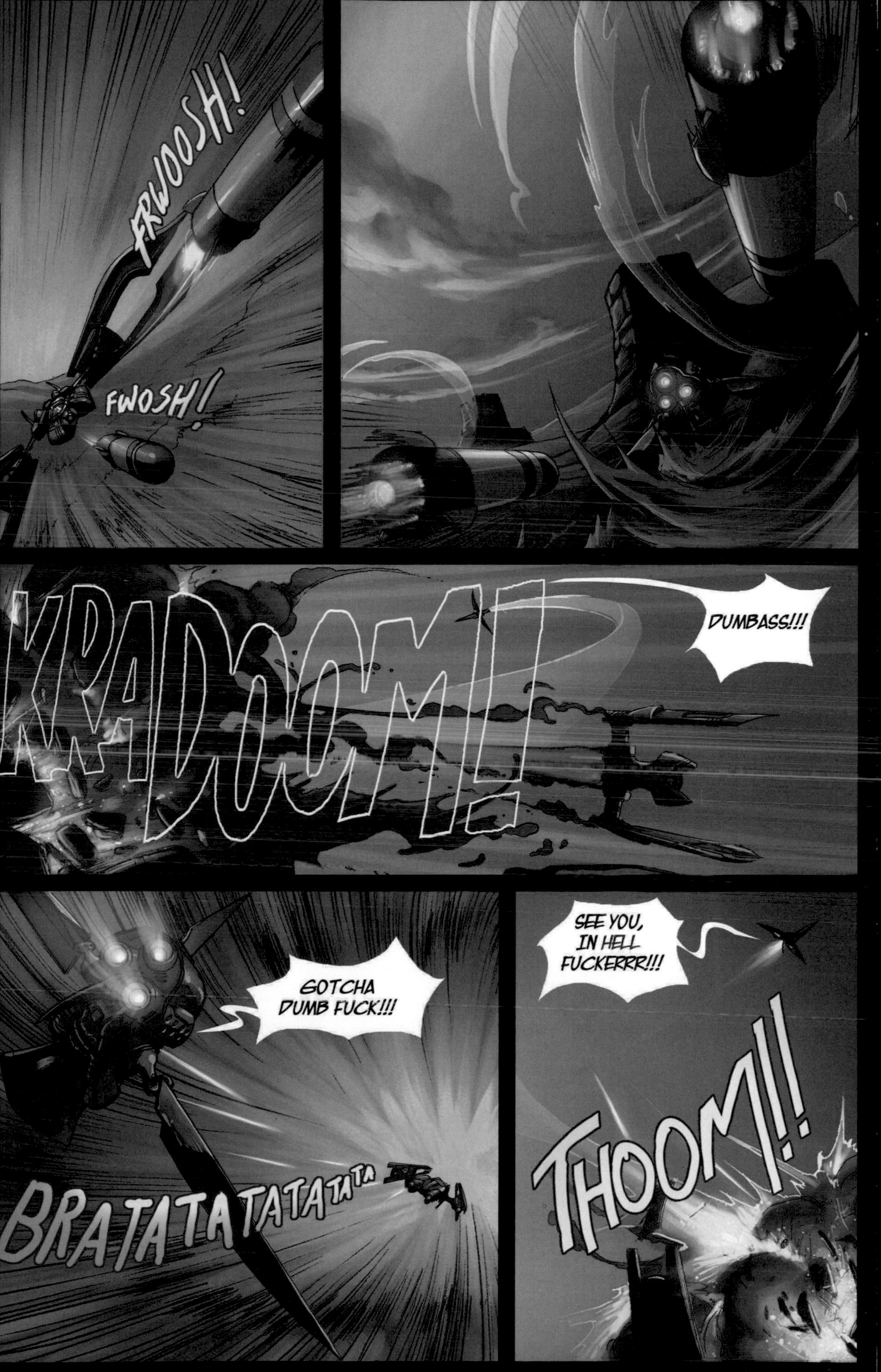
FRWOOSH!
FWOSH!
KRADOOM!!
DUMBASS!!!
GOTCHA DUMB FUCK!!!
BRATATATATATATATA
SEE YOU, IN HELL FUCKERRR!!!
THOOM!!

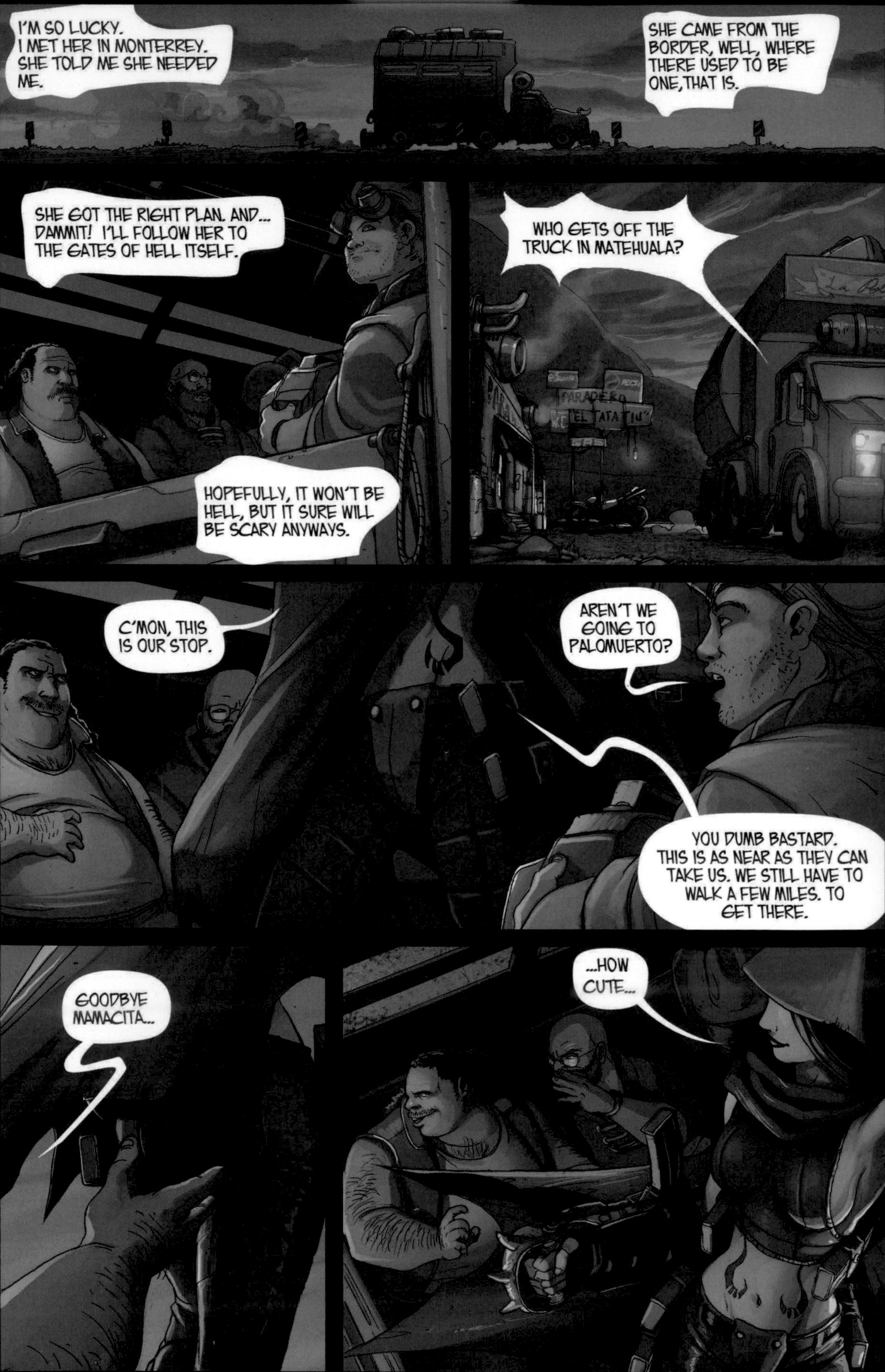
I'M SO LUCKY. I MET HER IN MONTERREY. SHE TOLD ME SHE NEEDED ME.
SHE CAME FROM THE BORDER, WELL, WHERE THERE USED TO BE ONE, THAT IS.
SHE GOT THE RIGHT PLAN. AND... DAMMIT! I'LL FOLLOW HER TO THE GATES OF HELL ITSELF.
HOPEFULLY, IT WON'T BE HELL, BUT IT SURE WILL BE SCARY ANYWAYS.
WHO GETS OFF THE TRUCK IN MATEHUALA?
PARADERO "EL TATATIU"
C'MON, THIS IS OUR STOP.
AREN'T WE GOING TO PALOMUERTO?
YOU DUMB BASTARD. THIS IS AS NEAR AS THEY CAN TAKE US. WE STILL HAVE TO WALK A FEW MILES. TO GET THERE.
GOODBYE MAMACITA...
...HOW CUTE...

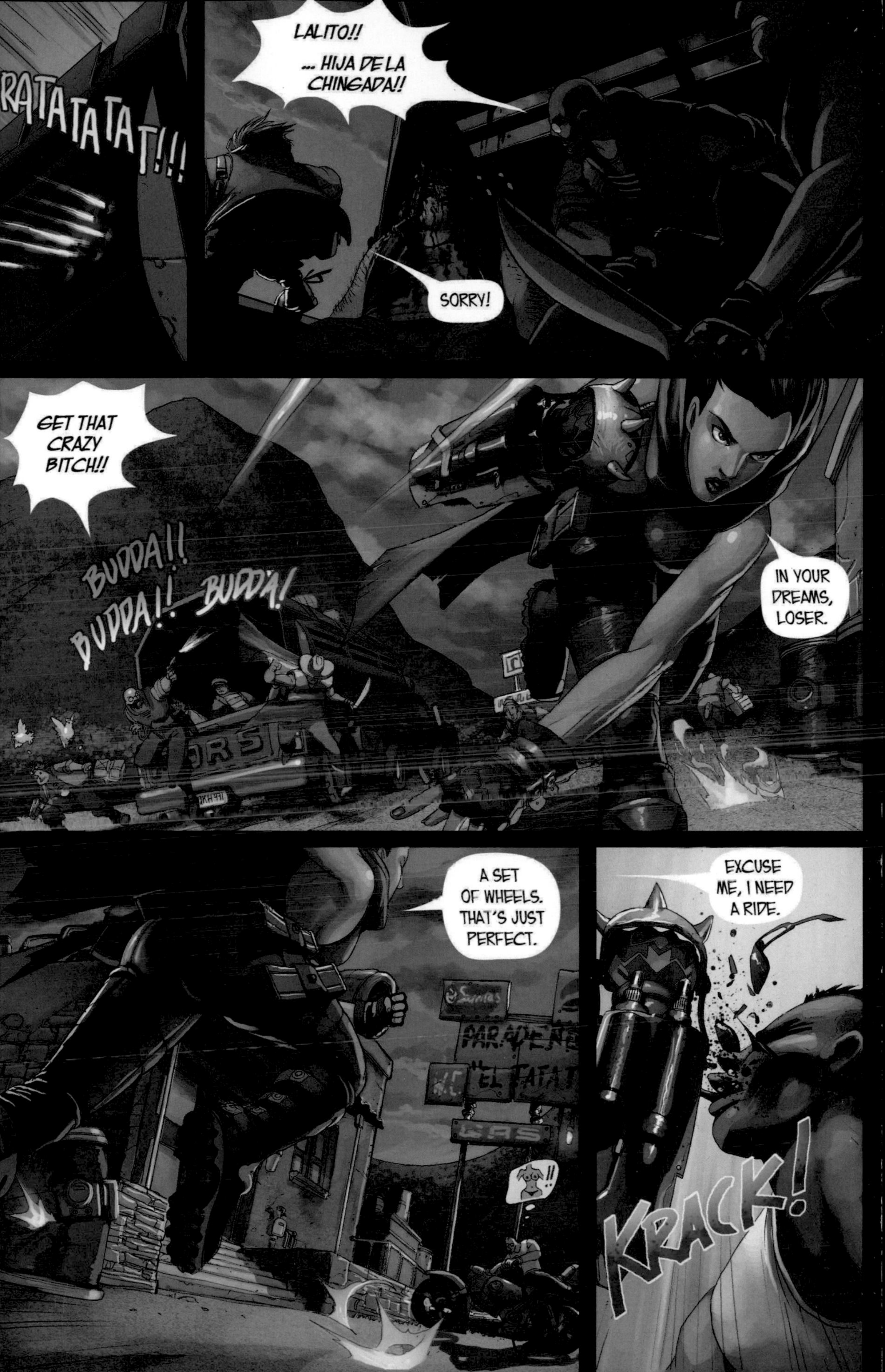
RATATATAT!!!
LALITO!!
... HIJA DE LA CHINGADA!!
SORRY!
GET THAT CRAZY BITCH!!
BUDDA!! BUDDA!! BUDDA!
IN YOUR DREAMS, LOSER.
A SET OF WHEELS. THAT'S JUST PERFECT.
GAS
EL TATAT
EXCUSE ME, I NEED A RIDE.
KRACK!

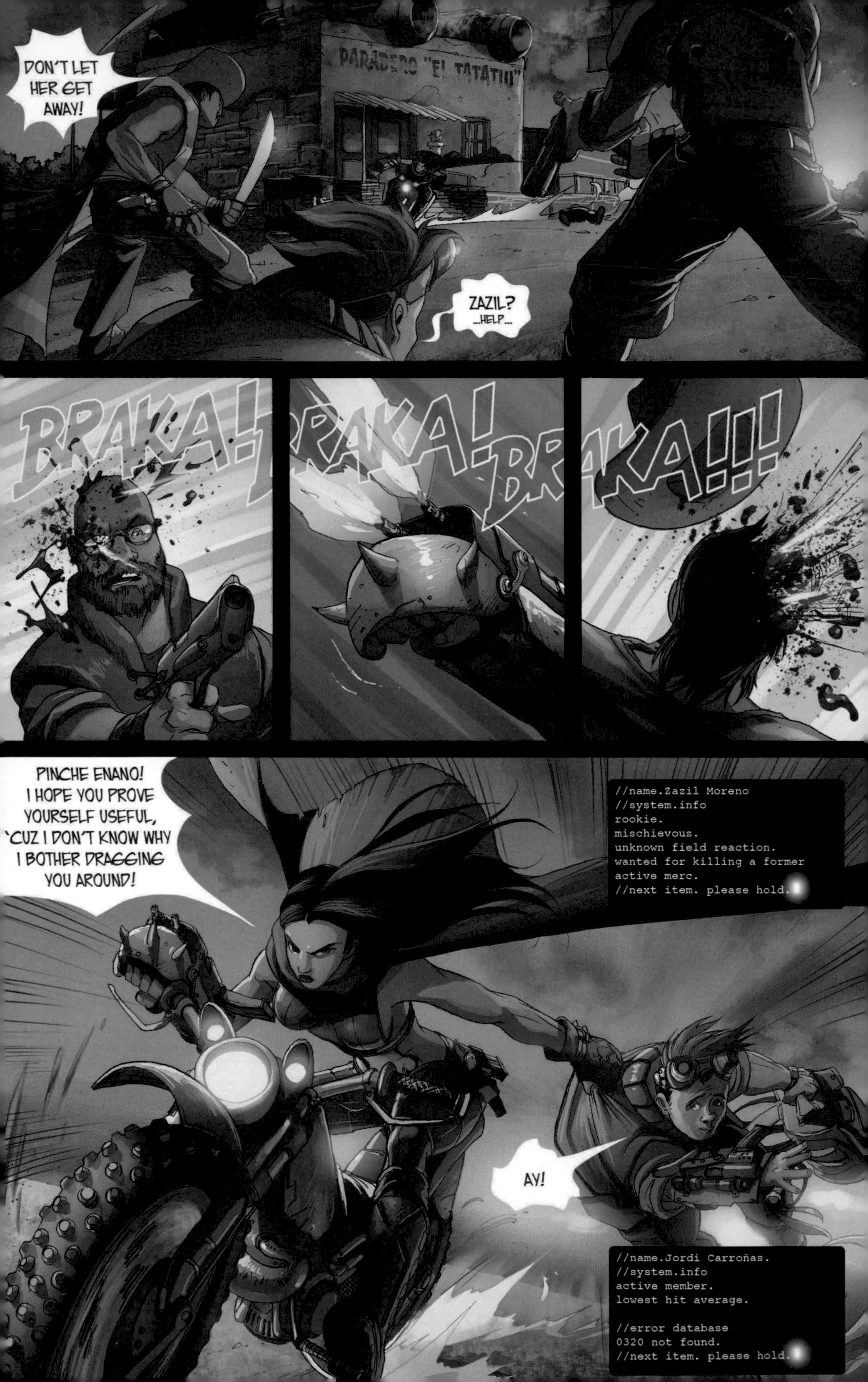

DON'T LET HER GET AWAY!
PARADERO "EL TATATIU"
ZAZIL? ...HELP...
BRAKA!
BRAKA!
BRAKA!!!
PINCHE ENANO! I HOPE YOU PROVE YOURSELF USEFUL, 'CUZ I DON'T KNOW WHY I BOTHER DRAGGING YOU AROUND!
//name.Zazil Moreno
//system.info
rookie.
mischievous.
unknown field reaction.
wanted for killing a former active merc.
//next item. please hold.
AY!
//name.Jordi Carroñas.
//system.info
active member.
lowest hit average.
//error database
0320 not found.
//next item. please hold.

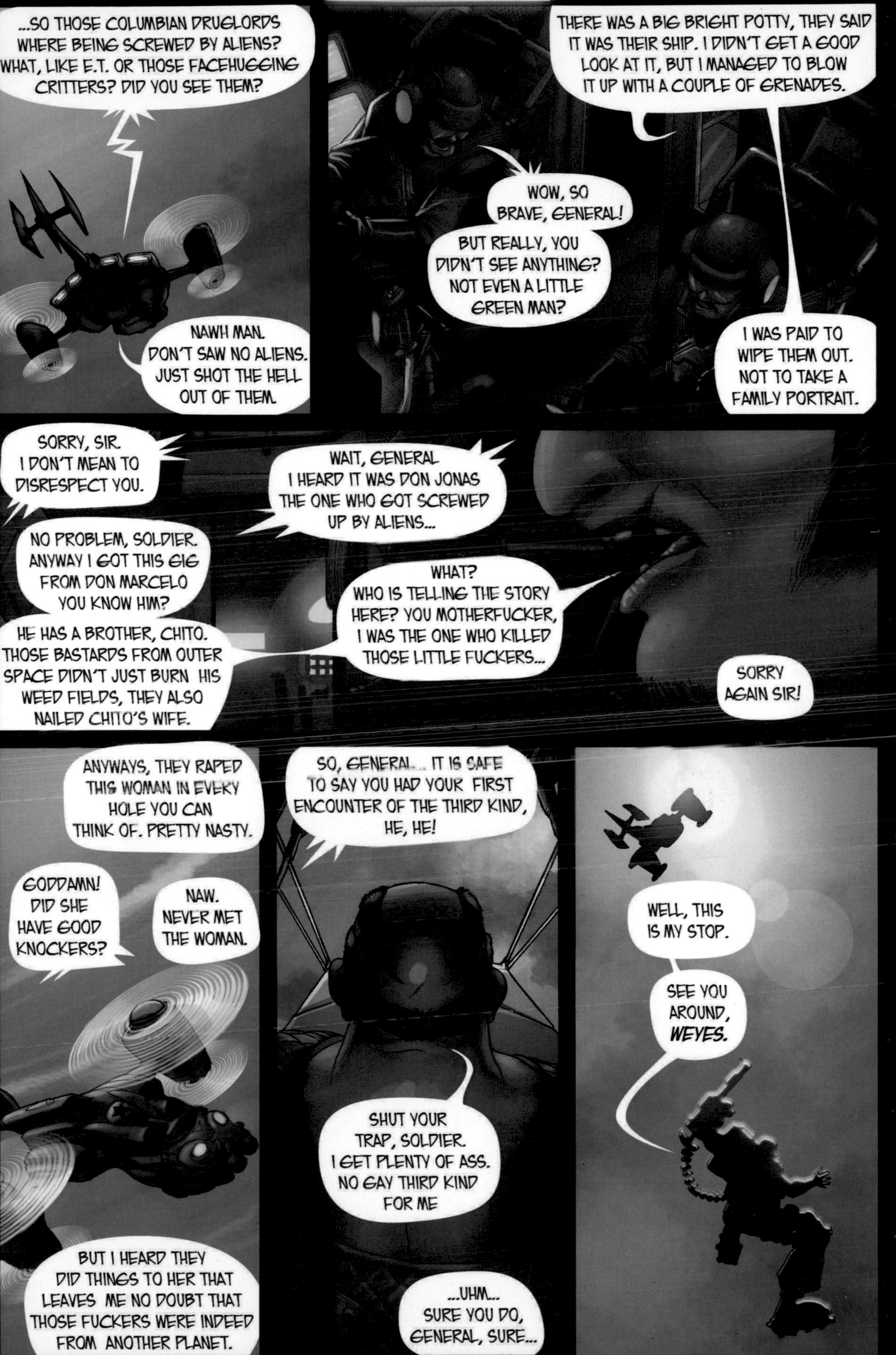
...SO THOSE COLUMBIAN DRUGLORDS WHERE BEING SCREWED BY ALIENS? WHAT, LIKE E.T. OR THOSE FACEHUGGING CRITTERS? DID YOU SEE THEM?
NAWH MAN. DON'T SAW NO ALIENS. JUST SHOT THE HELL OUT OF THEM.
THERE WAS A BIG BRIGHT POTTY, THEY SAID IT WAS THEIR SHIP. I DIDN'T GET A GOOD LOOK AT IT, BUT I MANAGED TO BLOW IT UP WITH A COUPLE OF GRENADES.
WOW, SO BRAVE, GENERAL!
BUT REALLY, YOU DIDN'T SEE ANYTHING? NOT EVEN A LITTLE GREEN MAN?
I WAS PAID TO WIPE THEM OUT. NOT TO TAKE A FAMILY PORTRAIT.
SORRY, SIR. I DON'T MEAN TO DISRESPECT YOU.
NO PROBLEM, SOLDIER. ANYWAY I GOT THIS GIG FROM DON MARCELO YOU KNOW HIM?
HE HAS A BROTHER, CHITO. THOSE BASTARDS FROM OUTER SPACE DIDN'T JUST BURN HIS WEED FIELDS, THEY ALSO NAILED CHITO'S WIFE.
WAIT, GENERAL I HEARD IT WAS DON JONAS THE ONE WHO GOT SCREWED UP BY ALIENS...
WHAT? WHO IS TELLING THE STORY HERE? YOU MOTHERFUCKER, I WAS THE ONE WHO KILLED THOSE LITTLE FUCKERS...
SORRY AGAIN SIR!
ANYWAYS, THEY RAPED THIS WOMAN IN EVERY HOLE YOU CAN THINK OF. PRETTY NASTY.
GODDAMN! DID SHE HAVE GOOD KNOCKERS?
NAW. NEVER MET THE WOMAN.
BUT I HEARD THEY DID THINGS TO HER THAT LEAVES ME NO DOUBT THAT THOSE FUCKERS WERE INDEED FROM ANOTHER PLANET.
SO, GENERAL... IT IS SAFE TO SAY YOU HAD YOUR FIRST ENCOUNTER OF THE THIRD KIND, HE, HE!
SHUT YOUR TRAP, SOLDIER. I GET PLENTY OF ASS. NO GAY THIRD KIND FOR ME
...UHM... SURE YOU DO, GENERAL, SURE...
WELL, THIS IS MY STOP.
SEE YOU AROUND, *WEYES.*

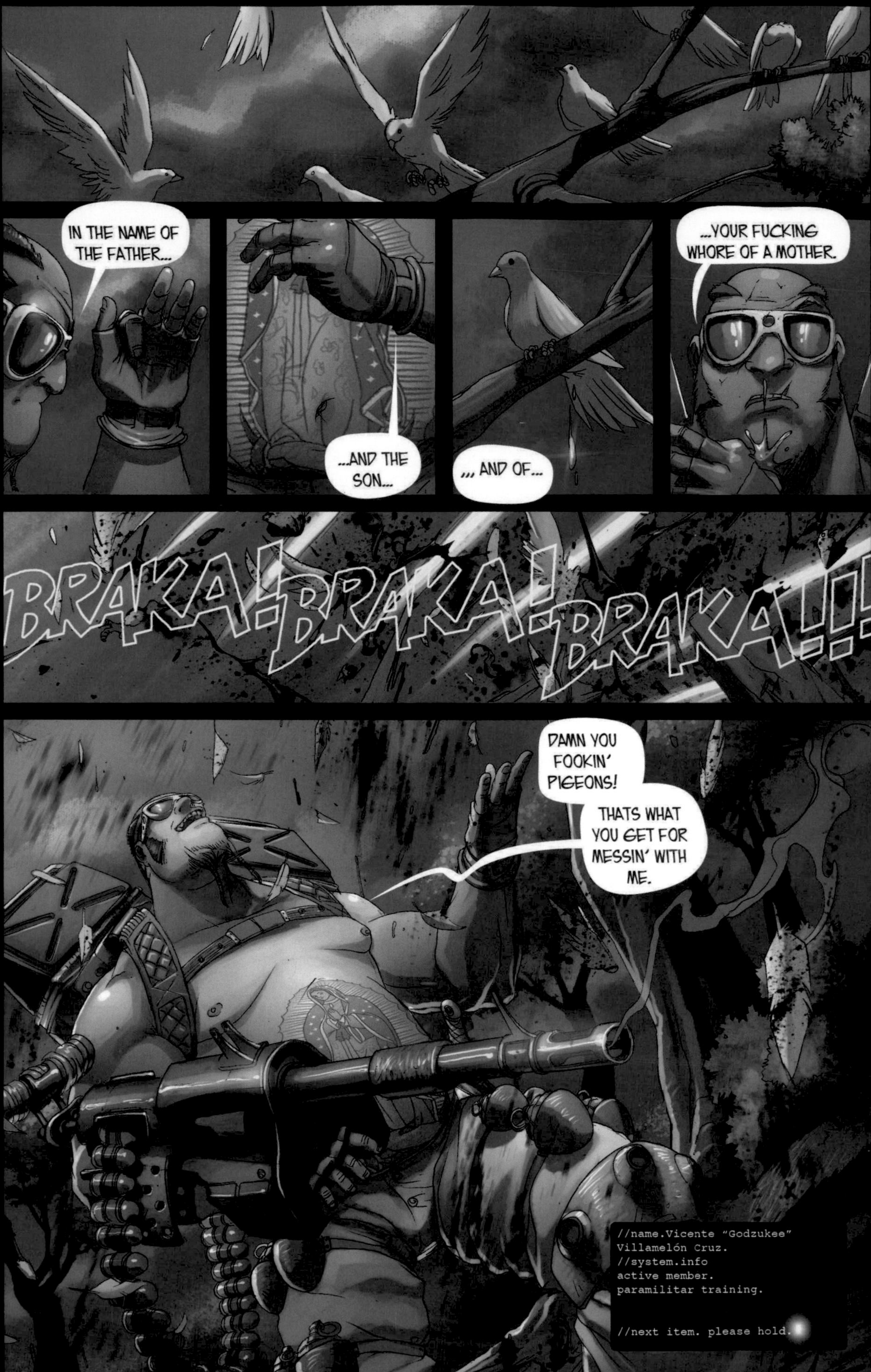
IN THE NAME OF THE FATHER...
...AND THE SON...
,,, AND OF...
...YOUR FUCKING WHORE OF A MOTHER.
BRAKA! BRAKA! BRAKA!!!
DAMN YOU FOOKIN' PIGEONS!
THATS WHAT YOU GET FOR MESSIN' WITH ME.
//name.Vicente "Godzukee" Villamelón Cruz.
//system.info
active member.
paramilitar training.
//next item. please hold.

Otro alcohol, más rocanrol y una hembra.

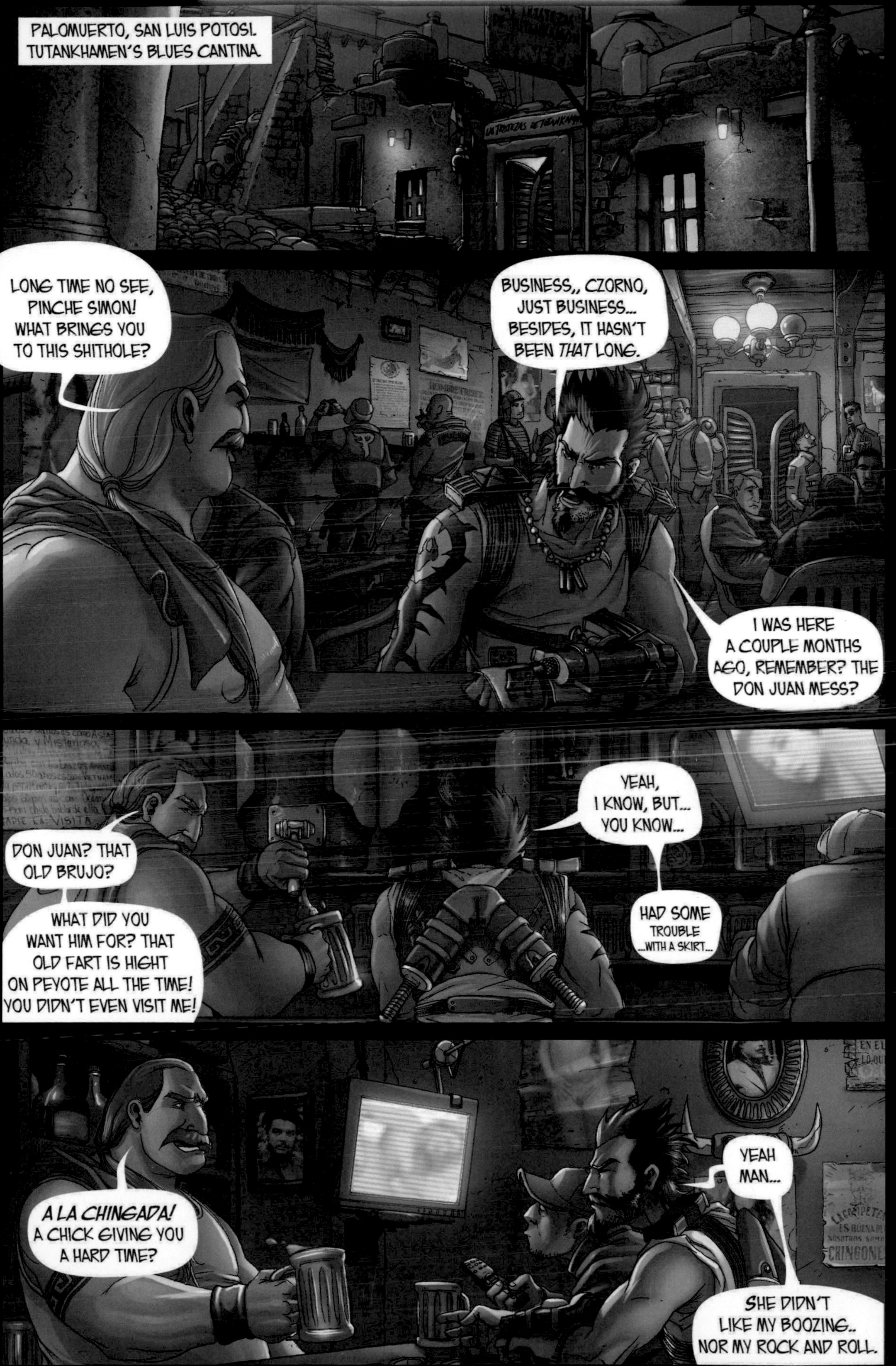
PALOMUERTO, SAN LUIS POTOSI.
TUTANKHAMEN'S BLUES CANTINA.
LONG TIME NO SEE, PINCHE SIMON! WHAT BRINGS YOU TO THIS SHITHOLE?
BUSINESS,, CZORNO, JUST BUSINESS... BESIDES, IT HASN'T BEEN THAT LONG.
I WAS HERE A COUPLE MONTHS AGO, REMEMBER? THE DON JUAN MESS?
DON JUAN? THAT OLD BRUJO?
WHAT DID YOU WANT HIM FOR? THAT OLD FART IS HIGHT ON PEYOTE ALL THE TIME! YOU DIDN'T EVEN VISIT ME!
YEAH, I KNOW, BUT... YOU KNOW...
HAD SOME TROUBLE ...WITH A SKIRT...
A LA CHINGADA! A CHICK GIVING YOU A HARD TIME?
YEAH MAN...
SHE DIDN'T LIKE MY BOOZING.. NOR MY ROCK AND ROLL.

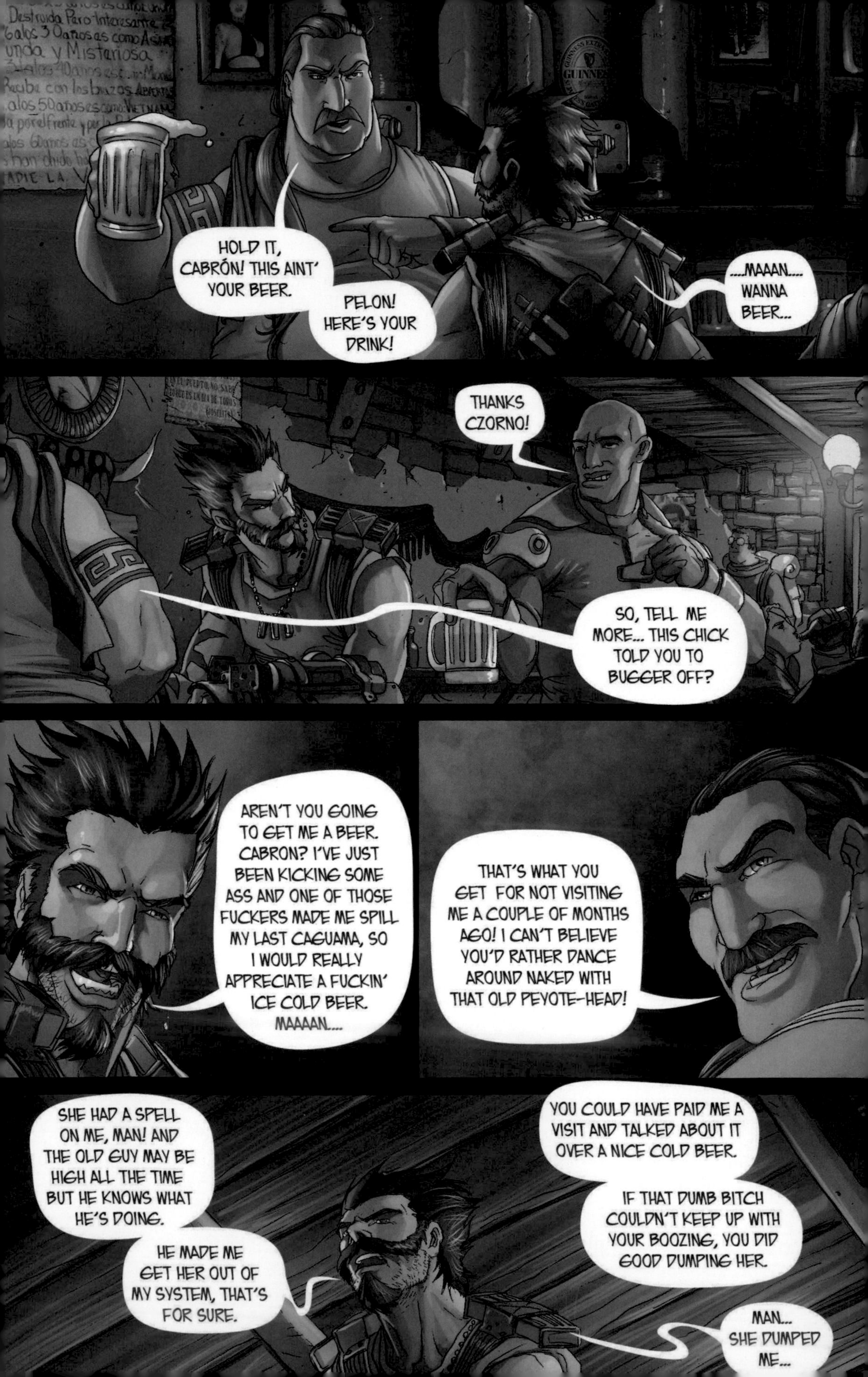
HOLD IT, CABRÓN! THIS AINT' YOUR BEER.
PELON! HERE'S YOUR DRINK!
...MAAAN.... WANNA BEER...
THANKS CZORNO!
SO, TELL ME MORE... THIS CHICK TOLD YOU TO BUGGER OFF?
AREN'T YOU GOING TO GET ME A BEER. CABRON? I'VE JUST BEEN KICKING SOME ASS AND ONE OF THOSE FUCKERS MADE ME SPILL MY LAST CAGUAMA, SO I WOULD REALLY APPRECIATE A FUCKIN' ICE COLD BEER. MAAAAN....
THAT'S WHAT YOU GET FOR NOT VISITING ME A COUPLE OF MONTHS AGO! I CAN'T BELIEVE YOU'D RATHER DANCE AROUND NAKED WITH THAT OLD PEYOTE-HEAD!
SHE HAD A SPELL ON ME, MAN! AND THE OLD GUY MAY BE HIGH ALL THE TIME BUT HE KNOWS WHAT HE'S DOING.
HE MADE ME GET HER OUT OF MY SYSTEM, THAT'S FOR SURE.
YOU COULD HAVE PAID ME A VISIT AND TALKED ABOUT IT OVER A NICE COLD BEER.
IF THAT DUMB BITCH COULDN'T KEEP UP WITH YOUR BOOZING, YOU DID GOOD DUMPING HER.
MAN... SHE DUMPED ME...

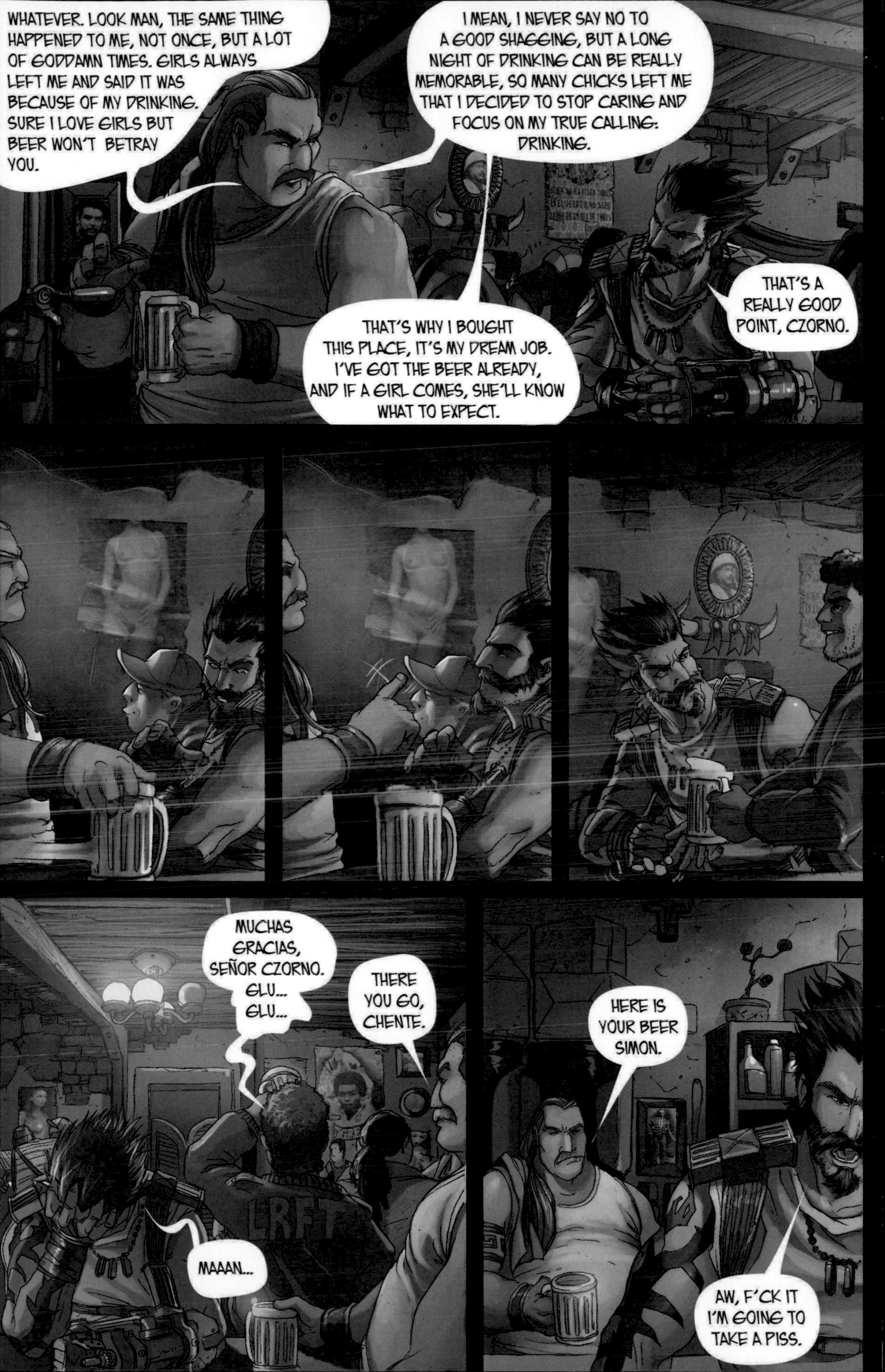
WHATEVER. LOOK MAN, THE SAME THING HAPPENED TO ME, NOT ONCE, BUT A LOT OF GODDAMN TIMES. GIRLS ALWAYS LEFT ME AND SAID IT WAS BECAUSE OF MY DRINKING. SURE I LOVE GIRLS BUT BEER WON'T BETRAY YOU.
I MEAN, I NEVER SAY NO TO A GOOD SHAGGING, BUT A LONG NIGHT OF DRINKING CAN BE REALLY MEMORABLE, SO MANY CHICKS LEFT ME THAT I DECIDED TO STOP CARING AND FOCUS ON MY TRUE CALLING: DRINKING.
THAT'S WHY I BOUGHT THIS PLACE, IT'S MY DREAM JOB. I'VE GOT THE BEER ALREADY, AND IF A GIRL COMES, SHE'LL KNOW WHAT TO EXPECT.
THAT'S A REALLY GOOD POINT, CZORNO.
MUCHAS GRACIAS, SEÑOR CZORNO. GLU... GLU...
THERE YOU GO, CHENTE.
MAAAN...
HERE IS YOUR BEER SIMON.
AW, F'CK IT I'M GOING TO TAKE A PISS.

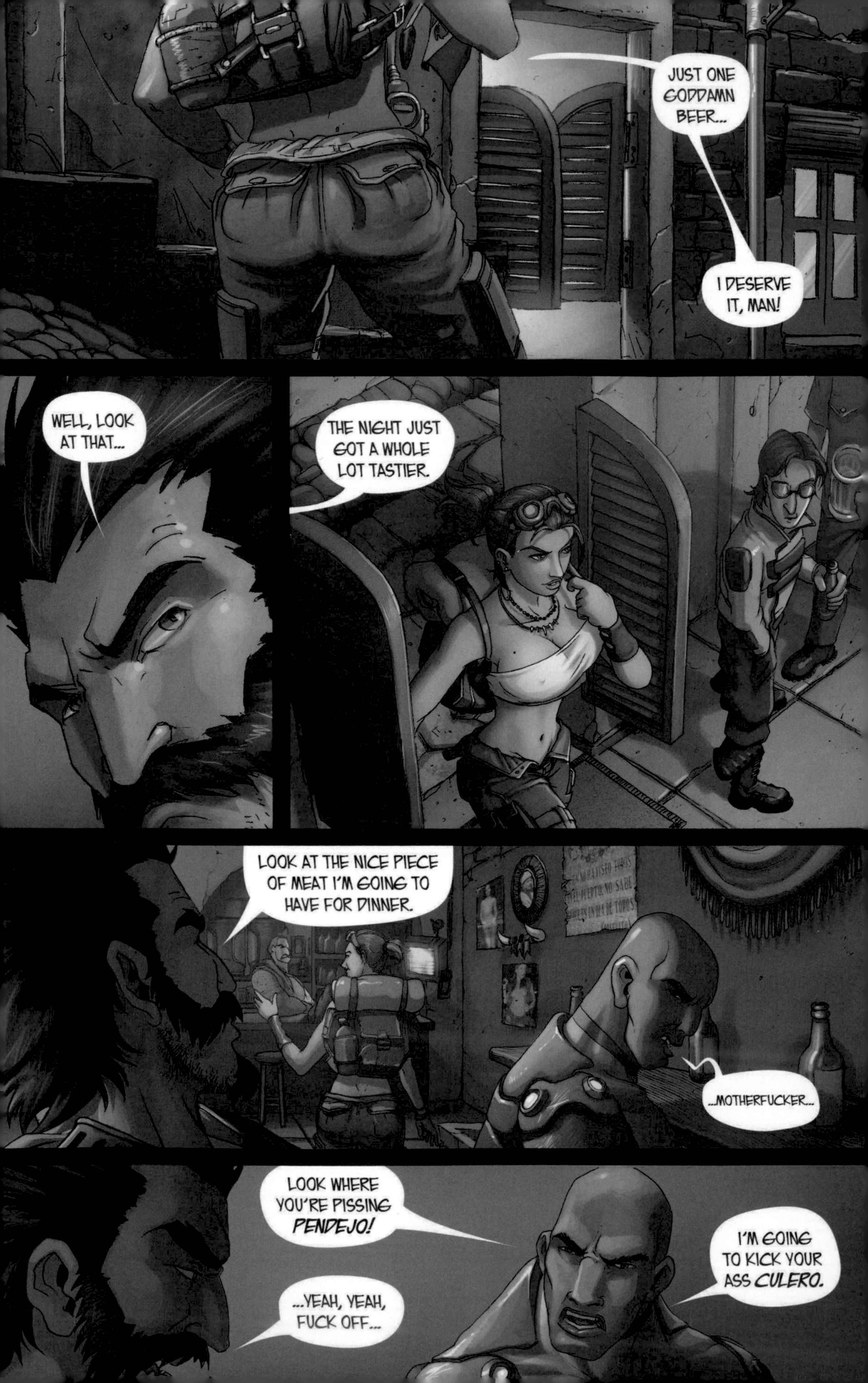
JUST ONE GODDAMN BEER...
I DESERVE IT, MAN!
WELL, LOOK AT THAT...
THE NIGHT JUST GOT A WHOLE LOT TASTIER.
LOOK AT THE NICE PIECE OF MEAT I'M GOING TO HAVE FOR DINNER.
...MOTHERFUCKER...
LOOK WHERE YOU'RE PISSING *PENDEJO!*
I'M GOING TO KICK YOUR ASS *CULERO.*
...YEAH, YEAH, FUCK OFF...

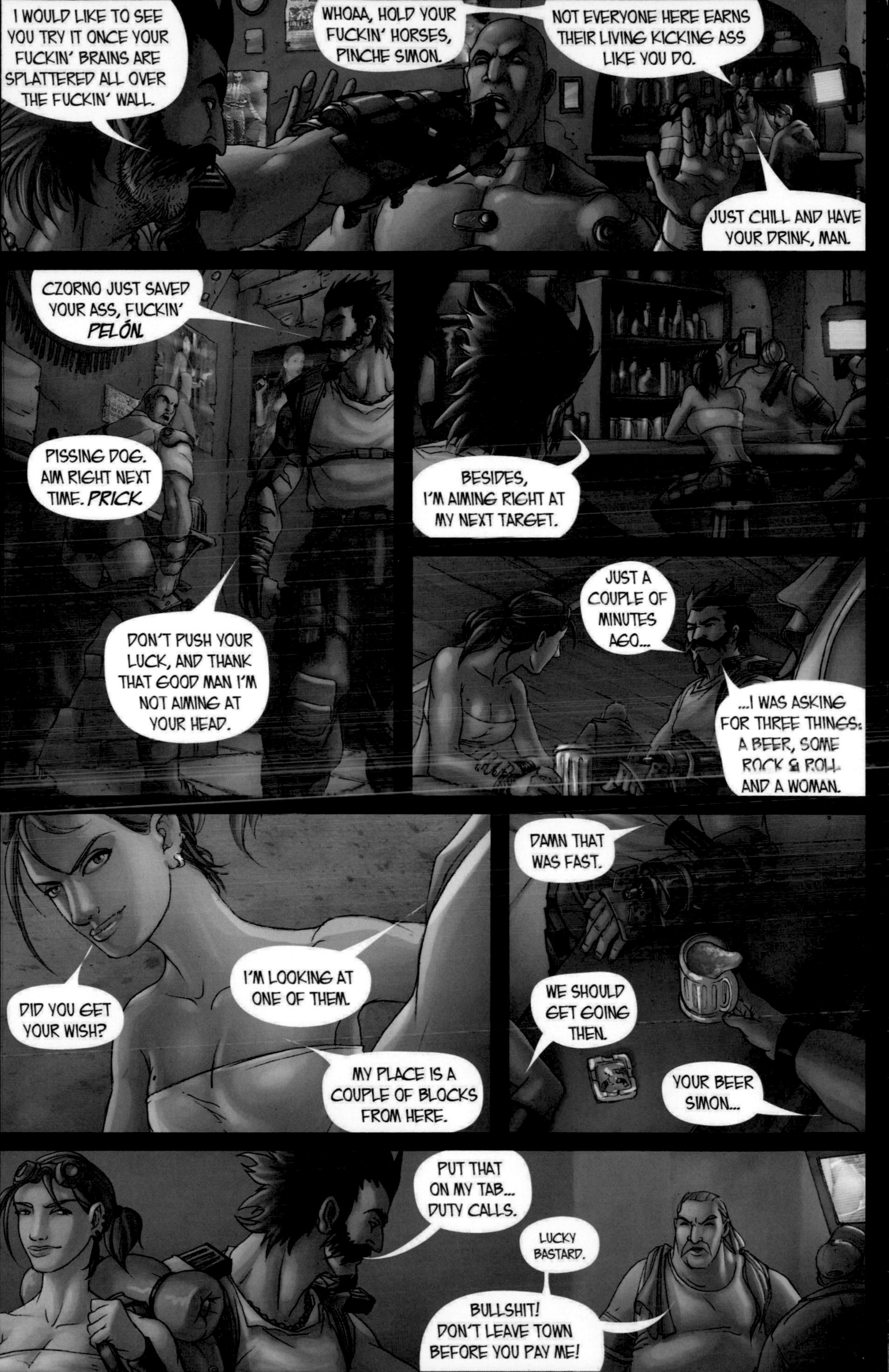
I WOULD LIKE TO SEE YOU TRY IT ONCE YOUR FUCKIN' BRAINS ARE SPLATTERED ALL OVER THE FUCKIN' WALL.
WHOAA, HOLD YOUR FUCKIN' HORSES, PINCHE SIMON.
NOT EVERYONE HERE EARNS THEIR LIVING KICKING ASS LIKE YOU DO.
JUST CHILL AND HAVE YOUR DRINK, MAN.
CZORNO JUST SAVED YOUR ASS, FUCKIN' PELÓN.
PISSING DOG. AIM RIGHT NEXT TIME. PRICK.
DON'T PUSH YOUR LUCK, AND THANK THAT GOOD MAN I'M NOT AIMING AT YOUR HEAD.
BESIDES, I'M AIMING RIGHT AT MY NEXT TARGET.
JUST A COUPLE OF MINUTES AGO...
...I WAS ASKING FOR THREE THINGS: A BEER, SOME ROCK & ROLL AND A WOMAN.
DID YOU GET YOUR WISH?
I'M LOOKING AT ONE OF THEM.
MY PLACE IS A COUPLE OF BLOCKS FROM HERE.
DAMN THAT WAS FAST.
WE SHOULD GET GOING THEN.
YOUR BEER SIMON...
PUT THAT ON MY TAB... DUTY CALLS.
LUCKY BASTARD.
BULLSHIT! DON'T LEAVE TOWN BEFORE YOU PAY ME!

0.6 Innagada da vida.

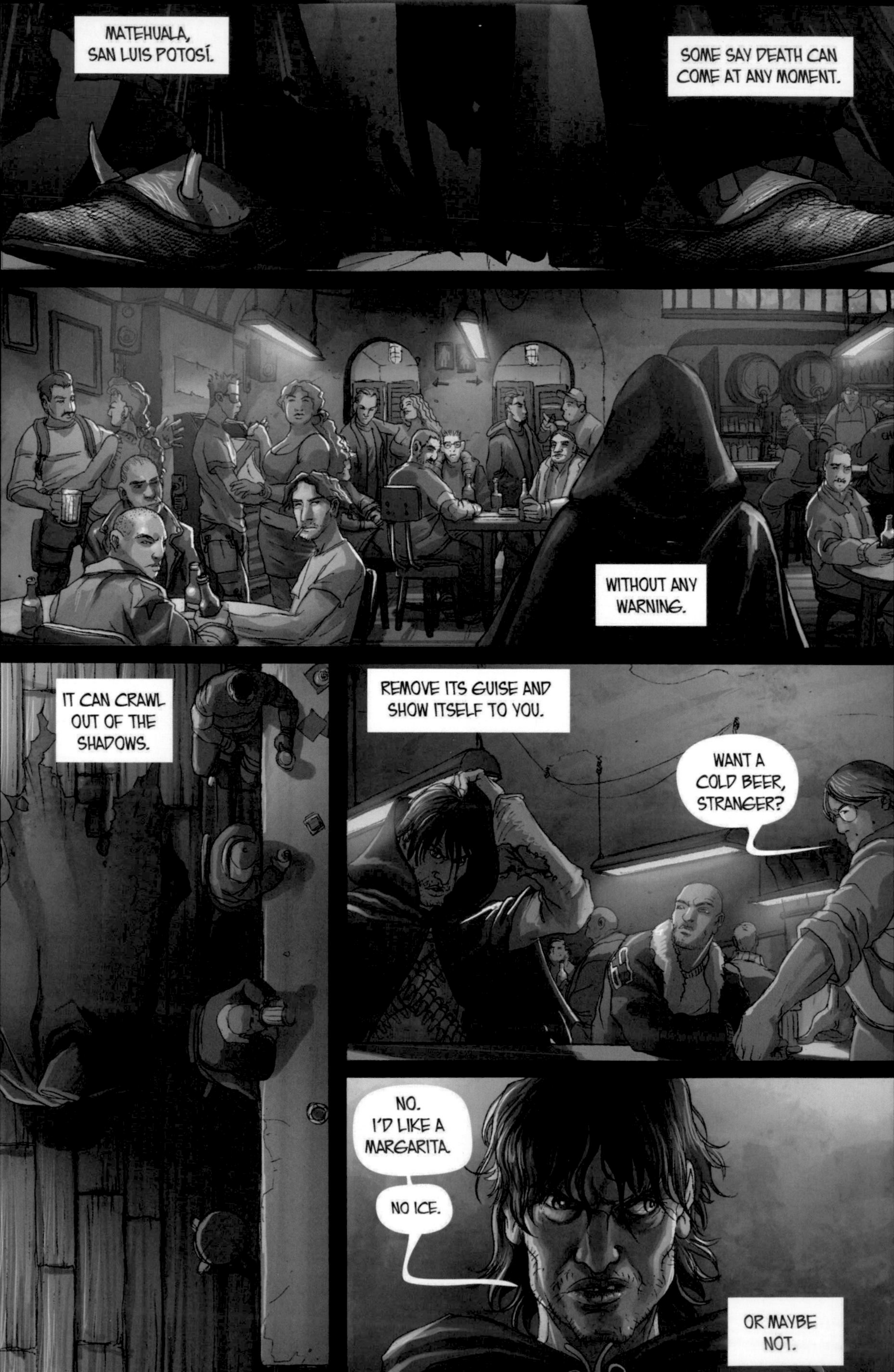
MATEHUALA, SAN LUIS POTOSÍ.
SOME SAY DEATH CAN COME AT ANY MOMENT.
WITHOUT ANY WARNING.
IT CAN CRAWL OUT OF THE SHADOWS.
REMOVE ITS GUISE AND SHOW ITSELF TO YOU.
WANT A COLD BEER, STRANGER?
NO. I'D LIKE A MARGARITA.
NO ICE.
OR MAYBE NOT.

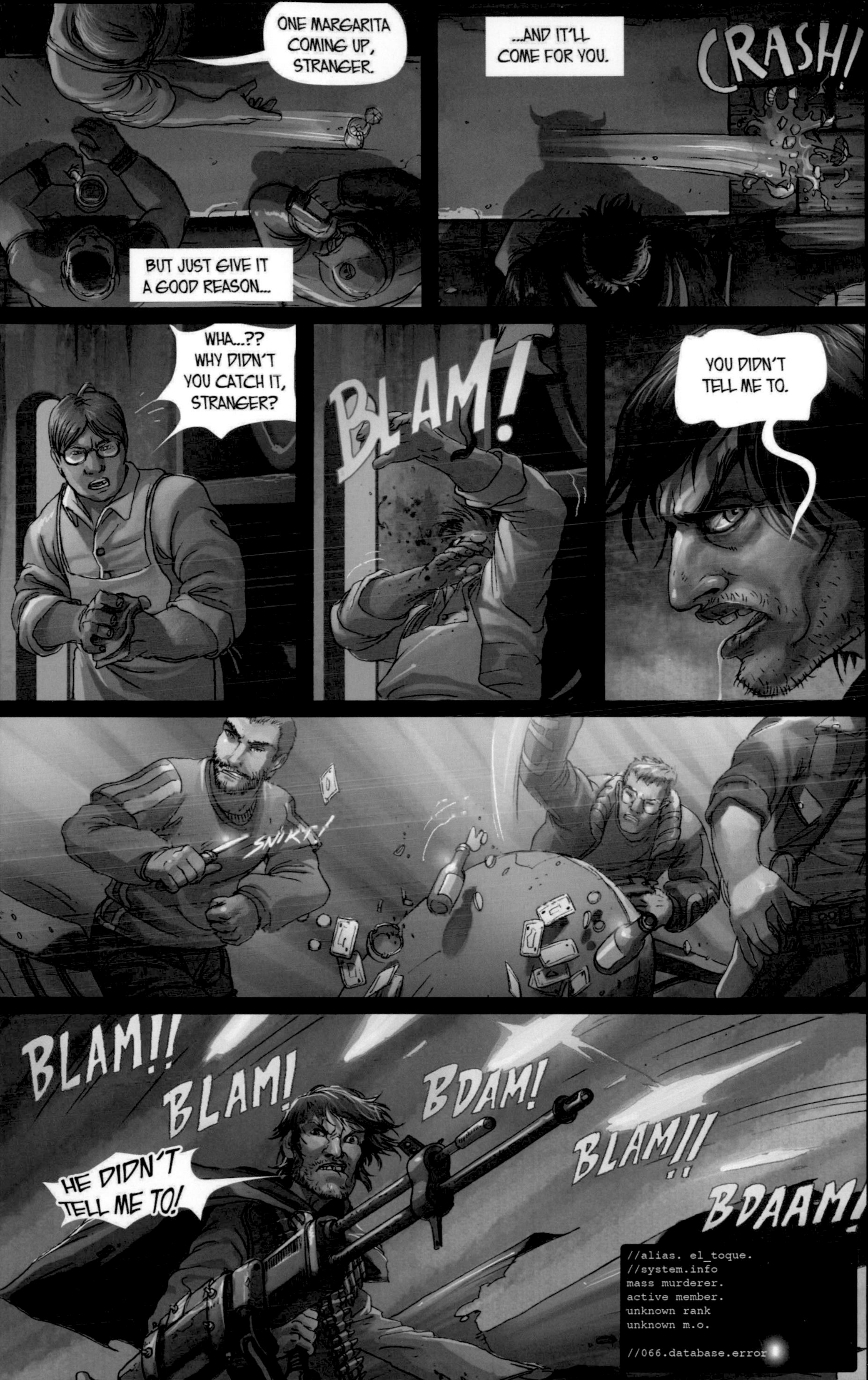
ONE MARGARITA COMING UP, STRANGER.
BUT JUST GIVE IT A GOOD REASON...
...AND IT'LL COME FOR YOU.
CRASH!
WHA...?? WHY DIDN'T YOU CATCH IT, STRANGER?
BLAM!
YOU DIDN'T TELL ME TO.
SNIKT!
BLAM!!
BLAM!
BDAM!
HE DIDN'T TELL ME TO!
BLAM!!
BDAAM!
//alias. el_toque.
//system.info
mass murderer.
active member.
unknown rank
unknown m.o.
//066.database.error

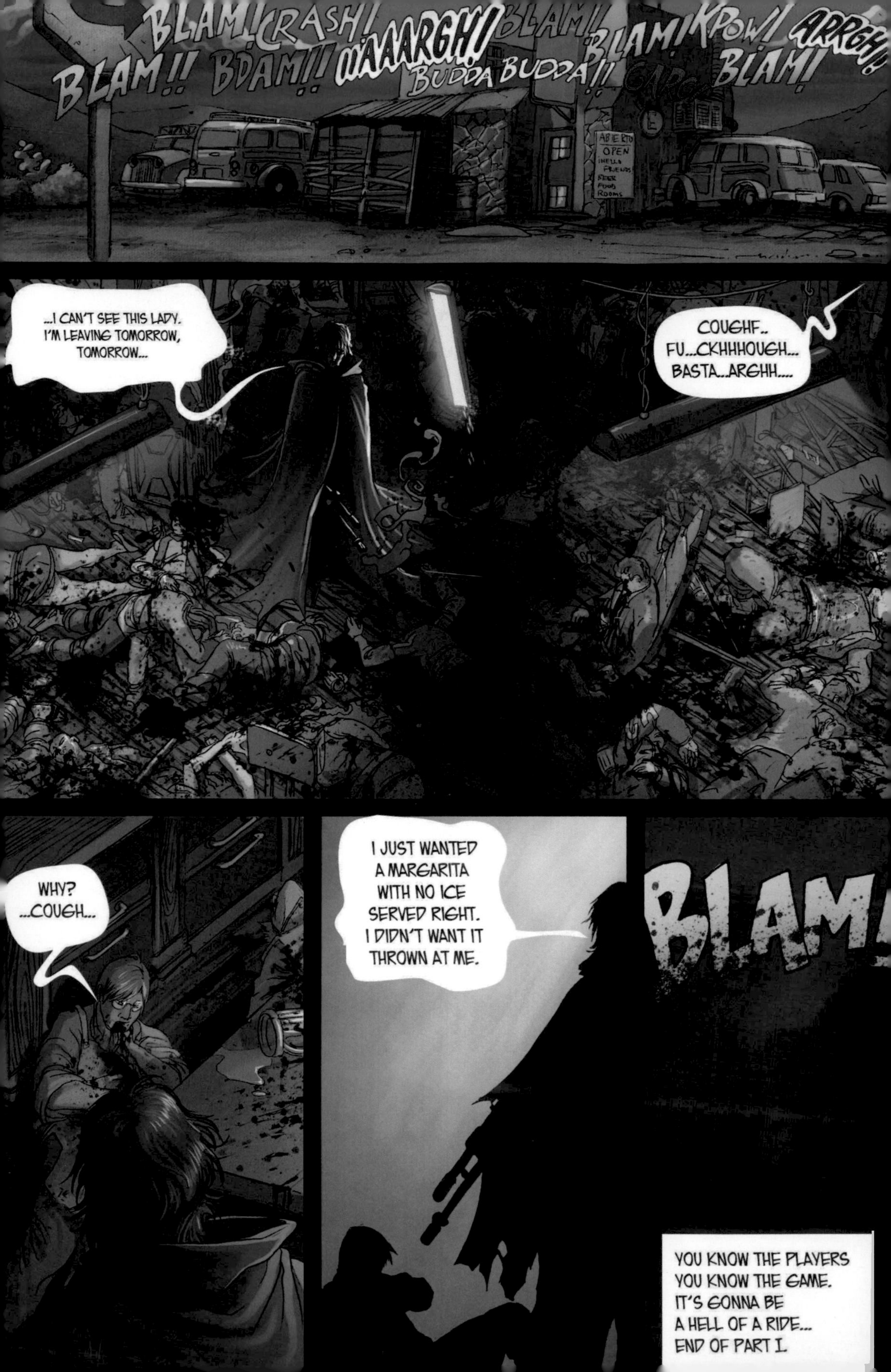
BLAM! CRASH!
BLAM!!
BDAM!!
AAAARGH!
BLAM!
BUDDA BUDDA!!
BLAM! KPOW!
ARRGH!!
BLAM!
ABIERTO
OPEN
...I CAN'T SEE THIS LADY. I'M LEAVING TOMORROW, TOMORROW...
COUGHF.. FU...CKHHHOUGH... BASTA...ARGHH....
WHY? ...COUGH...
I JUST WANTED A MARGARITA WITH NO ICE SERVED RIGHT. I DIDN'T WANT IT THROWN AT ME.
BLAM!
YOU KNOW THE PLAYERS YOU KNOW THE GAME. IT'S GONNA BE A HELL OF A RIDE... END OF PART I.

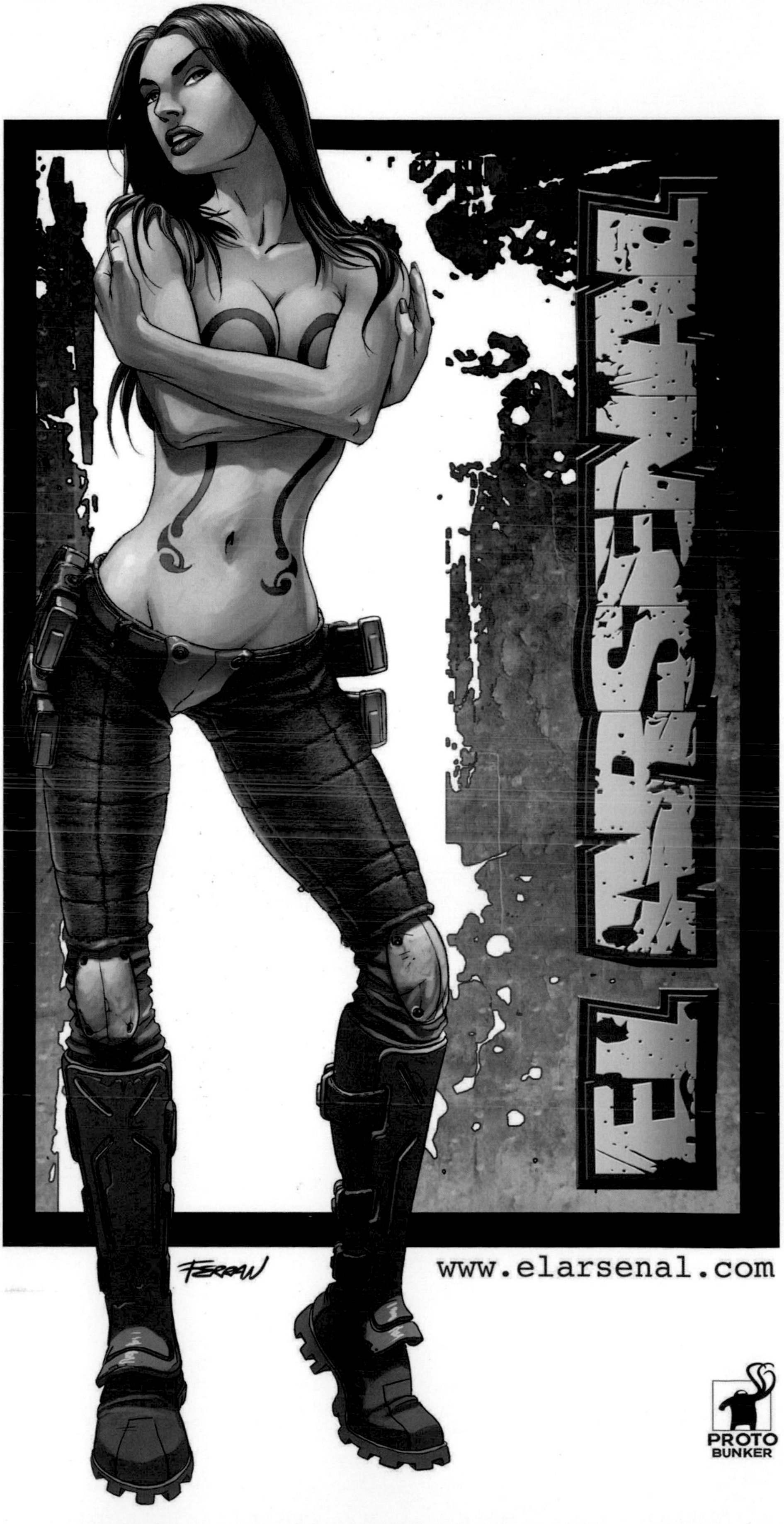
EL ARSENAL
FERRAN

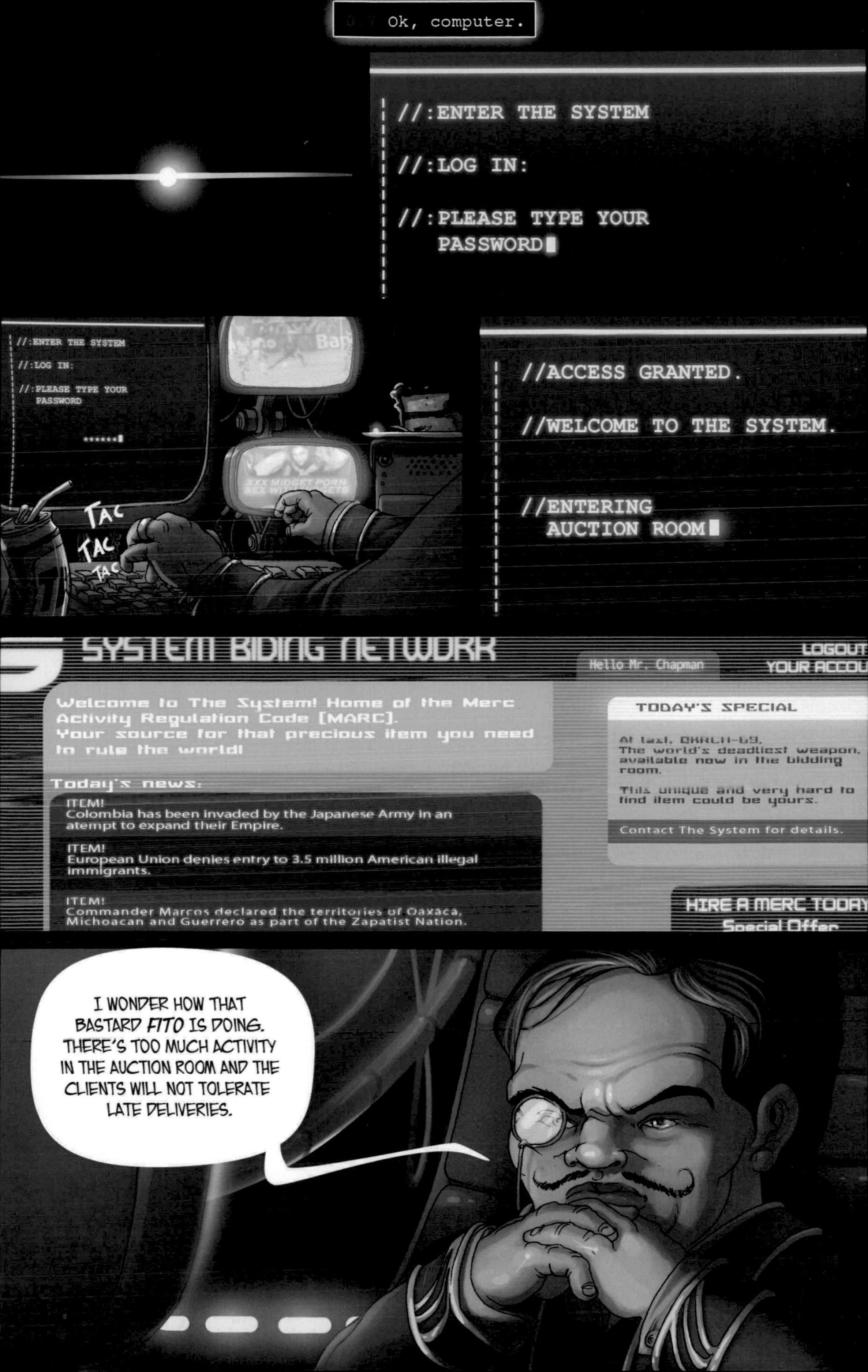

Ok, computer.
//:ENTER THE SYSTEM
//:LOG IN:
//:PLEASE TYPE YOUR PASSWORD
//:ENTER THE SYSTEM
//:LOG IN:
//:PLEASE TYPE YOUR PASSWORD
******
TAC
TAC
TAC
//ACCESS GRANTED.
//WELCOME TO THE SYSTEM.
//ENTERING AUCTION ROOM
SYSTEM BIDING NETWORK
Hello Mr. Chapman
LOGOUT
YOUR ACCOU
Welcome to The System! Home of the Merc Activity Regulation Code [MARC]. Your source for that precious item you need to rule the world!
Today's news:
ITEM! Colombia has been invaded by the Japanese Army in an atempt to expand their Empire.
ITEM! European Union denies entry to 3.5 million American illegal immigrants.
ITEM! Commander Marcos declared the territories of Oaxaca, Michoacan and Guerrero as part of the Zapatist Nation.
TODAY'S SPECIAL
At last,
The world's deadliest weapon, available now in the bidding room.
This unique and very hard to find item could be yours.
Contact The System for details.
HIRE A MERC TODAY
Special Offer
I WONDER HOW THAT BASTARD FITO IS DOING. THERE'S TOO MUCH ACTIVITY IN THE AUCTION ROOM AND THE CLIENTS WILL NOT TOLERATE LATE DELIVERIES.

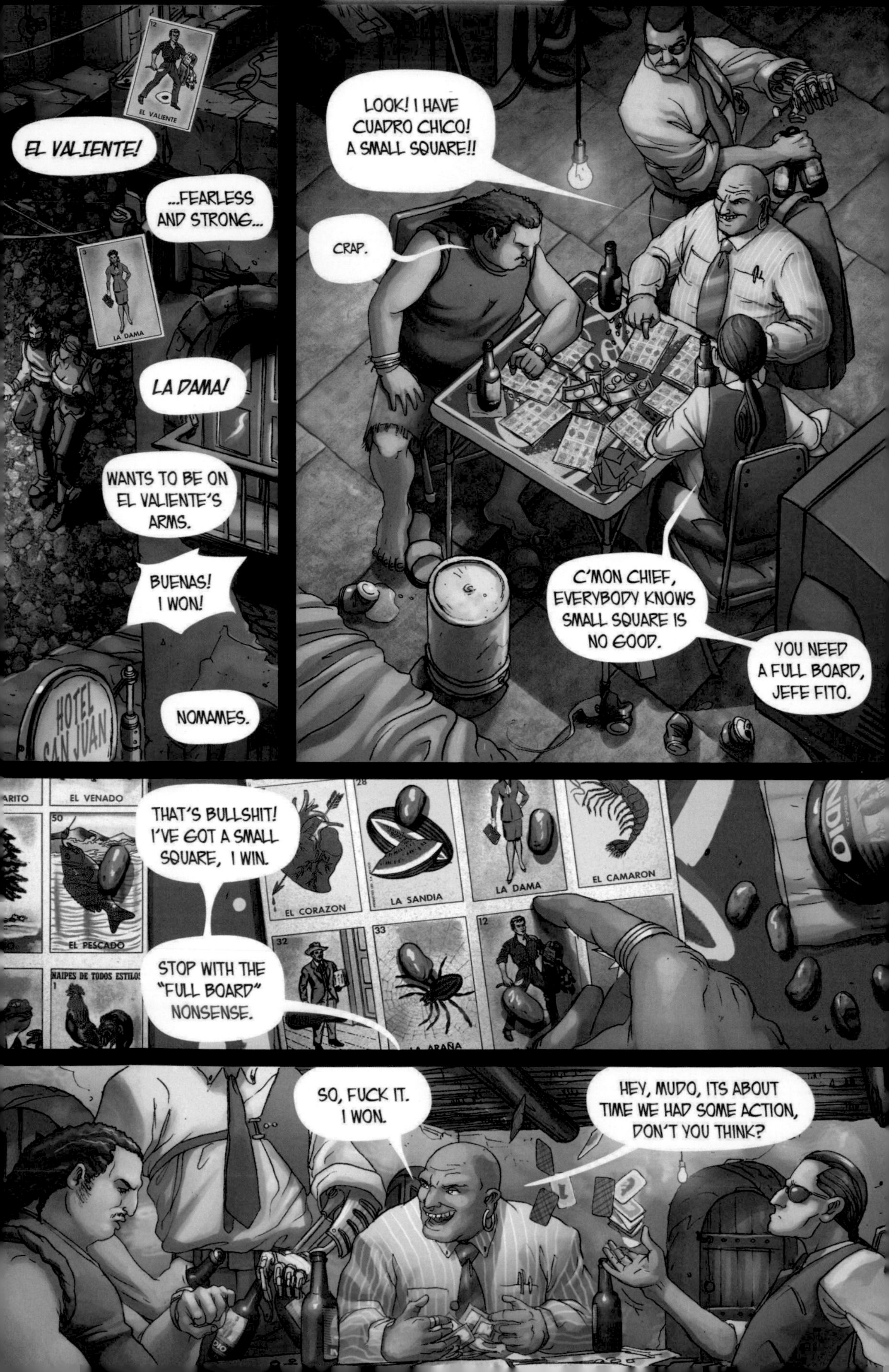

12
EL VALIENTE
EL VALIENTE!
...FEARLESS AND STRONG...
3
LA DAMA
LA DAMA!
WANTS TO BE ON EL VALIENTE'S ARMS.
BUENAS! I WON!
HOTEL SAN JUAN
NOMAMES.
LOOK! I HAVE CUADRO CHICO! A SMALL SQUARE!!
CRAP.
C'MON CHIEF, EVERYBODY KNOWS SMALL SQUARE IS NO GOOD.
YOU NEED A FULL BOARD, JEFE FITO.
EL VENADO
50
EL PESCADO
NAIPES DE TODOS ESTILOS
THAT'S BULLSHIT! I'VE GOT A SMALL SQUARE, I WIN.
STOP WITH THE "FULL BOARD" NONSENSE.
EL CORAZON
28
LA SANDIA
LA DAMA
EL CAMARON
32
33
12
LA ARAÑA
SO, FUCK IT. I WON.
HEY, MUDO, ITS ABOUT TIME WE HAD SOME ACTION, DON'T YOU THINK?

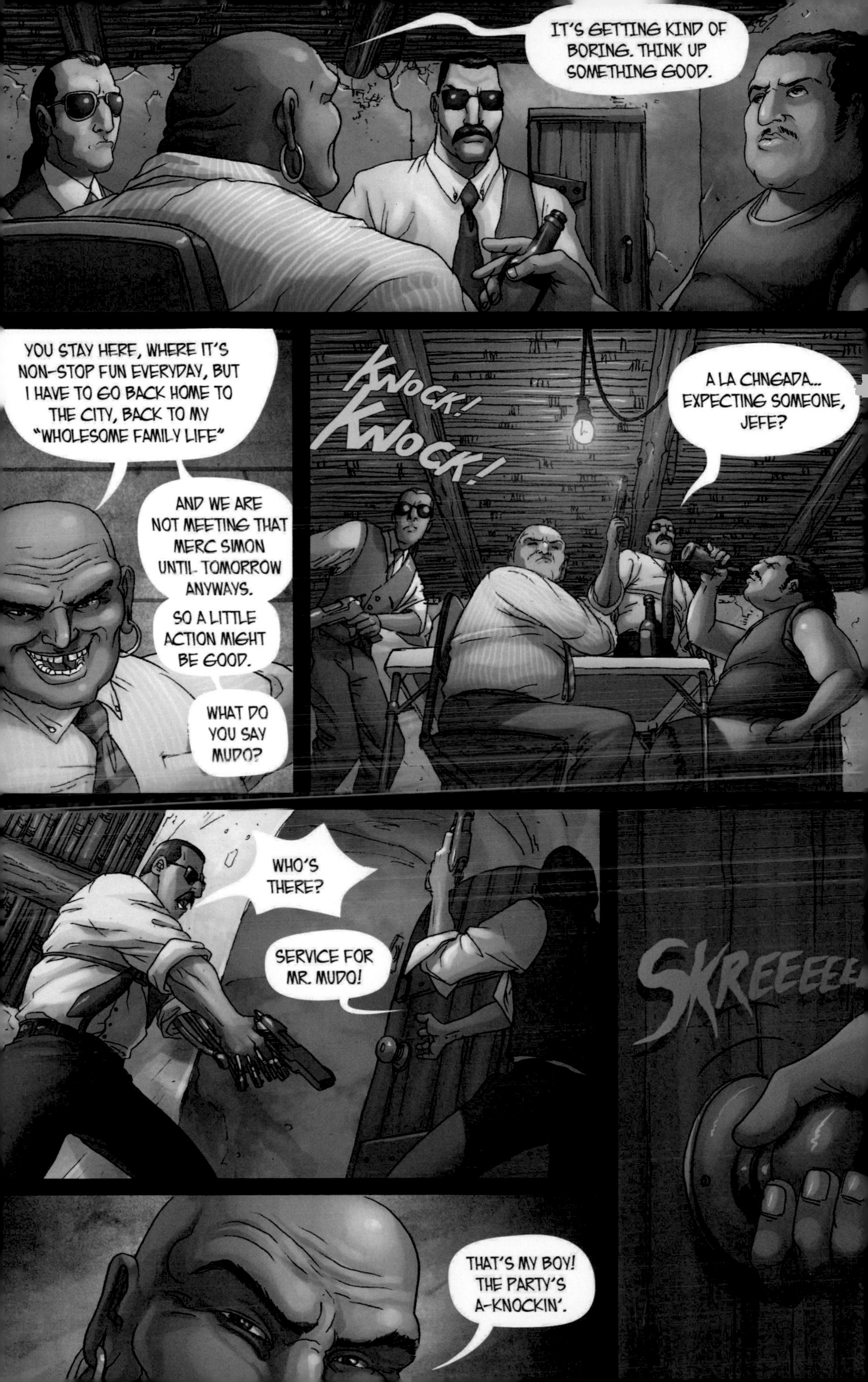
IT'S GETTING KIND OF BORING. THINK UP SOMETHING GOOD.
YOU STAY HERE, WHERE IT'S NON-STOP FUN EVERYDAY, BUT I HAVE TO GO BACK HOME TO THE CITY, BACK TO MY "WHOLESOME FAMILY LIFE"
AND WE ARE NOT MEETING THAT MERC SIMON UNTIL TOMORROW ANYWAYS.
SO A LITTLE ACTION MIGHT BE GOOD.
WHAT DO YOU SAY MUDO?
KNOCK! KNOCK!
A LA CHNGADA... EXPECTING SOMEONE, JEFE?
WHO'S THERE?
SERVICE FOR MR. MUDO!
SKREEEEE
THAT'S MY BOY! THE PARTY'S A-KNOCKIN'.

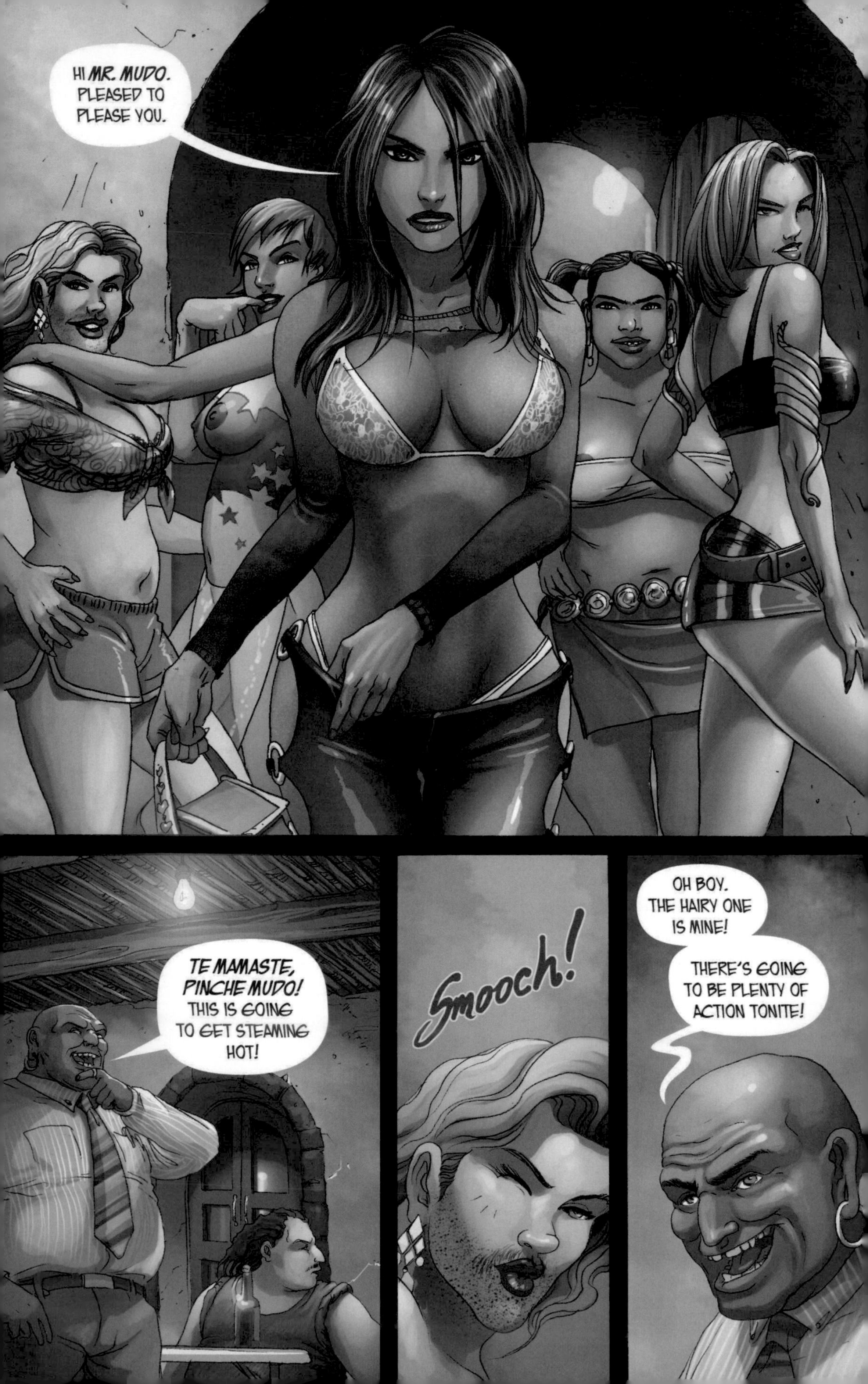
HI MR. MUDO. PLEASED TO PLEASE YOU.
TE MAMASTE, PINCHE MUDO! THIS IS GOING TO GET STEAMING HOT!
Smooch!
OH BOY. THE HAIRY ONE IS MINE!
THERE'S GOING TO BE PLENTY OF ACTION TONITE!

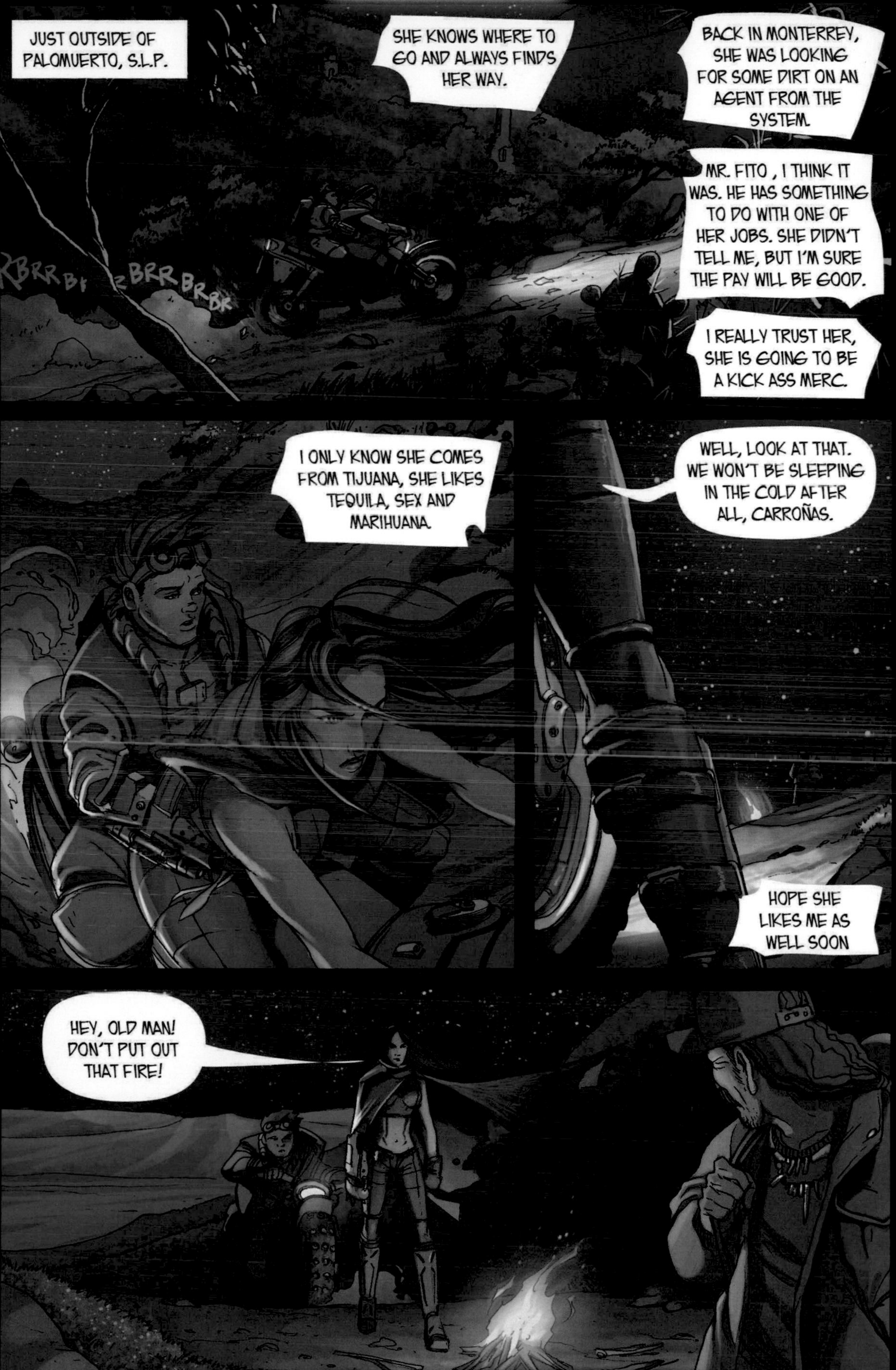
JUST OUTSIDE OF PALOMUERTO, S.L.P.
SHE KNOWS WHERE TO GO AND ALWAYS FINDS HER WAY.
BACK IN MONTERREY, SHE WAS LOOKING FOR SOME DIRT ON AN AGENT FROM THE SYSTEM.
MR. FITO , I THINK IT WAS. HE HAS SOMETHING TO DO WITH ONE OF HER JOBS. SHE DIDN'T TELL ME, BUT I'M SURE THE PAY WILL BE GOOD.
I REALLY TRUST HER, SHE IS GOING TO BE A KICK ASS MERC.
KBRRBR BRRBRBR
I ONLY KNOW SHE COMES FROM TIJUANA, SHE LIKES TEQUILA, SEX AND MARIHUANA.
WELL, LOOK AT THAT. WE WON'T BE SLEEPING IN THE COLD AFTER ALL, CARROÑAS.
HOPE SHE LIKES ME AS WELL SOON
HEY, OLD MAN! DON'T PUT OUT THAT FIRE!

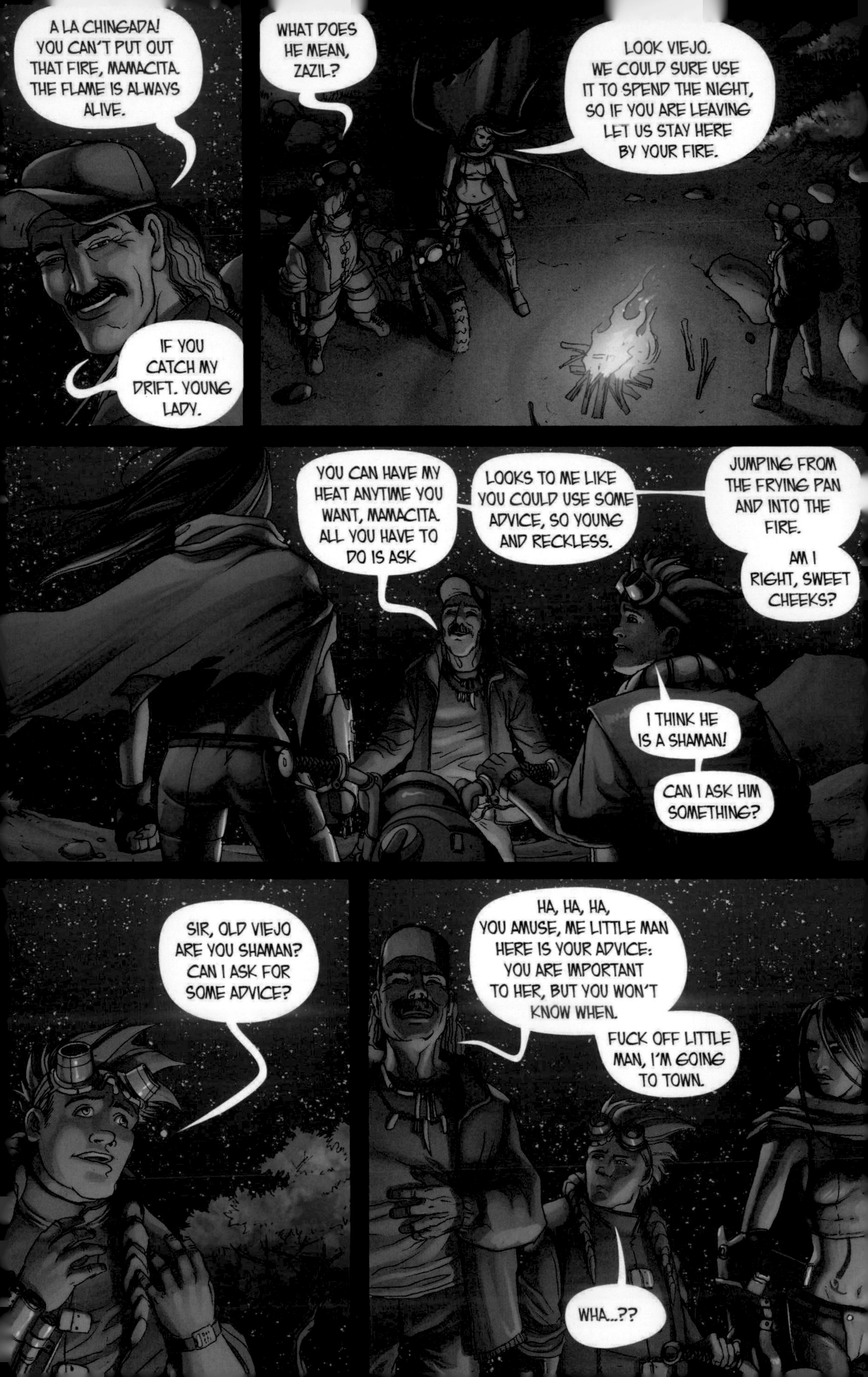
A LA CHINGADA! YOU CAN'T PUT OUT THAT FIRE, MAMACITA. THE FLAME IS ALWAYS ALIVE.
IF YOU CATCH MY DRIFT. YOUNG LADY.
WHAT DOES HE MEAN, ZAZIL?
LOOK VIEJO. WE COULD SURE USE IT TO SPEND THE NIGHT, SO IF YOU ARE LEAVING LET US STAY HERE BY YOUR FIRE.
YOU CAN HAVE MY HEAT ANYTIME YOU WANT, MAMACITA. ALL YOU HAVE TO DO IS ASK
LOOKS TO ME LIKE YOU COULD USE SOME ADVICE, SO YOUNG AND RECKLESS.
JUMPING FROM THE FRYING PAN AND INTO THE FIRE.
AM I RIGHT, SWEET CHEEKS?
I THINK HE IS A SHAMAN!
CAN I ASK HIM SOMETHING?
SIR, OLD VIEJO ARE YOU SHAMAN? CAN I ASK FOR SOME ADVICE?
HA, HA, HA, YOU AMUSE, ME LITTLE MAN HERE IS YOUR ADVICE: YOU ARE IMPORTANT TO HER, BUT YOU WON'T KNOW WHEN.
FUCK OFF LITTLE MAN, I'M GOING TO TOWN.
WHA...??

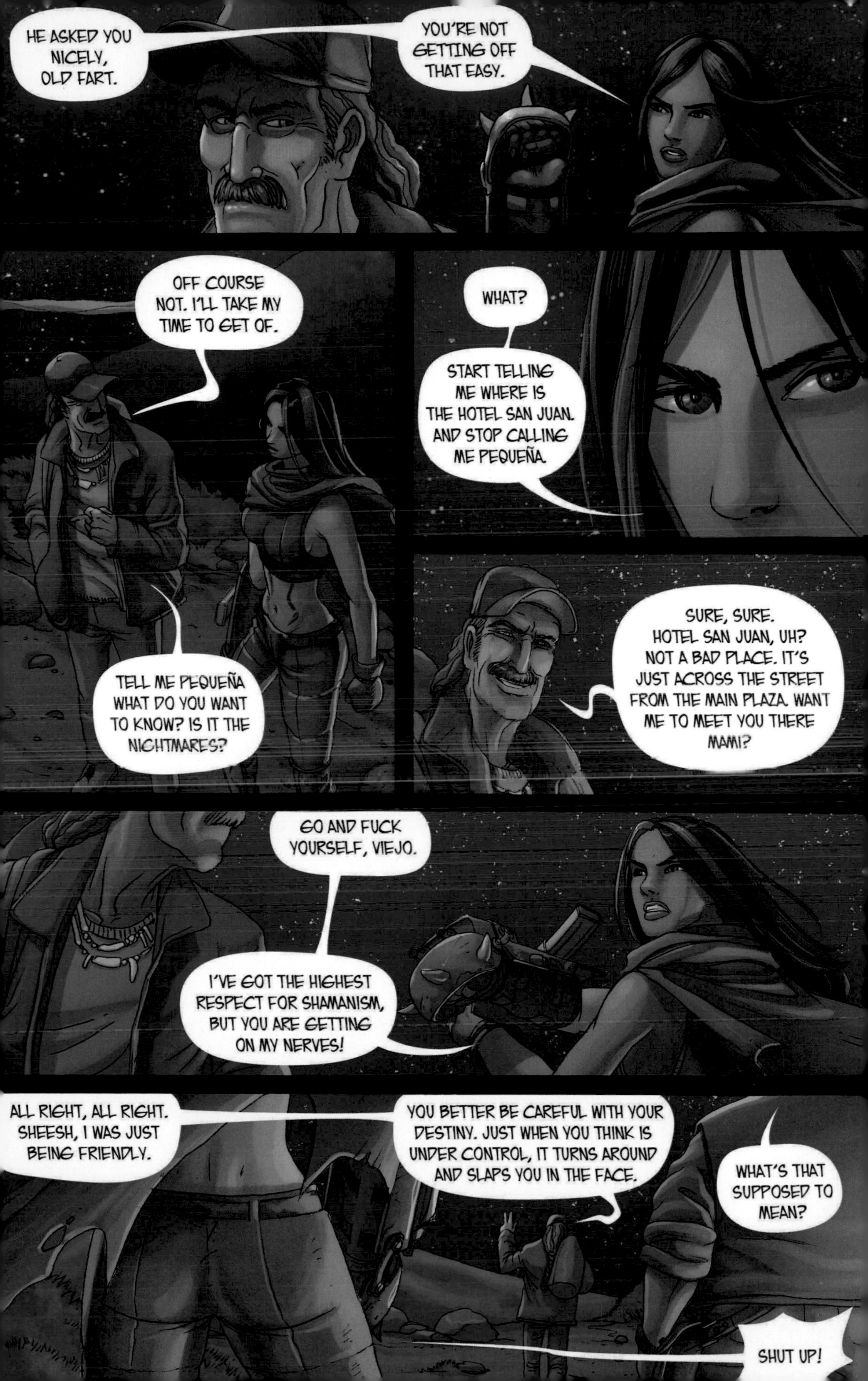

HE ASKED YOU NICELY, OLD FART.
YOU'RE NOT GETTING OFF THAT EASY.
OFF COURSE NOT. I'LL TAKE MY TIME TO GET OF.
TELL ME PEQUEÑA WHAT DO YOU WANT TO KNOW? IS IT THE NIGHTMARES?
WHAT?
START TELLING ME WHERE IS THE HOTEL SAN JUAN. AND STOP CALLING ME PEQUEÑA.
SURE, SURE. HOTEL SAN JUAN, UH? NOT A BAD PLACE. IT'S JUST ACROSS THE STREET FROM THE MAIN PLAZA. WANT ME TO MEET YOU THERE MAMI?
GO AND FUCK YOURSELF, VIEJO.
I'VE GOT THE HIGHEST RESPECT FOR SHAMANISM, BUT YOU ARE GETTING ON MY NERVES!
ALL RIGHT, ALL RIGHT. SHEESH, I WAS JUST BEING FRIENDLY.
YOU BETTER BE CAREFUL WITH YOUR DESTINY. JUST WHEN YOU THINK IS UNDER CONTROL, IT TURNS AROUND AND SLAPS YOU IN THE FACE.
WHAT'S THAT SUPPOSED TO MEAN?
SHUT UP!

Love me two times (part I)

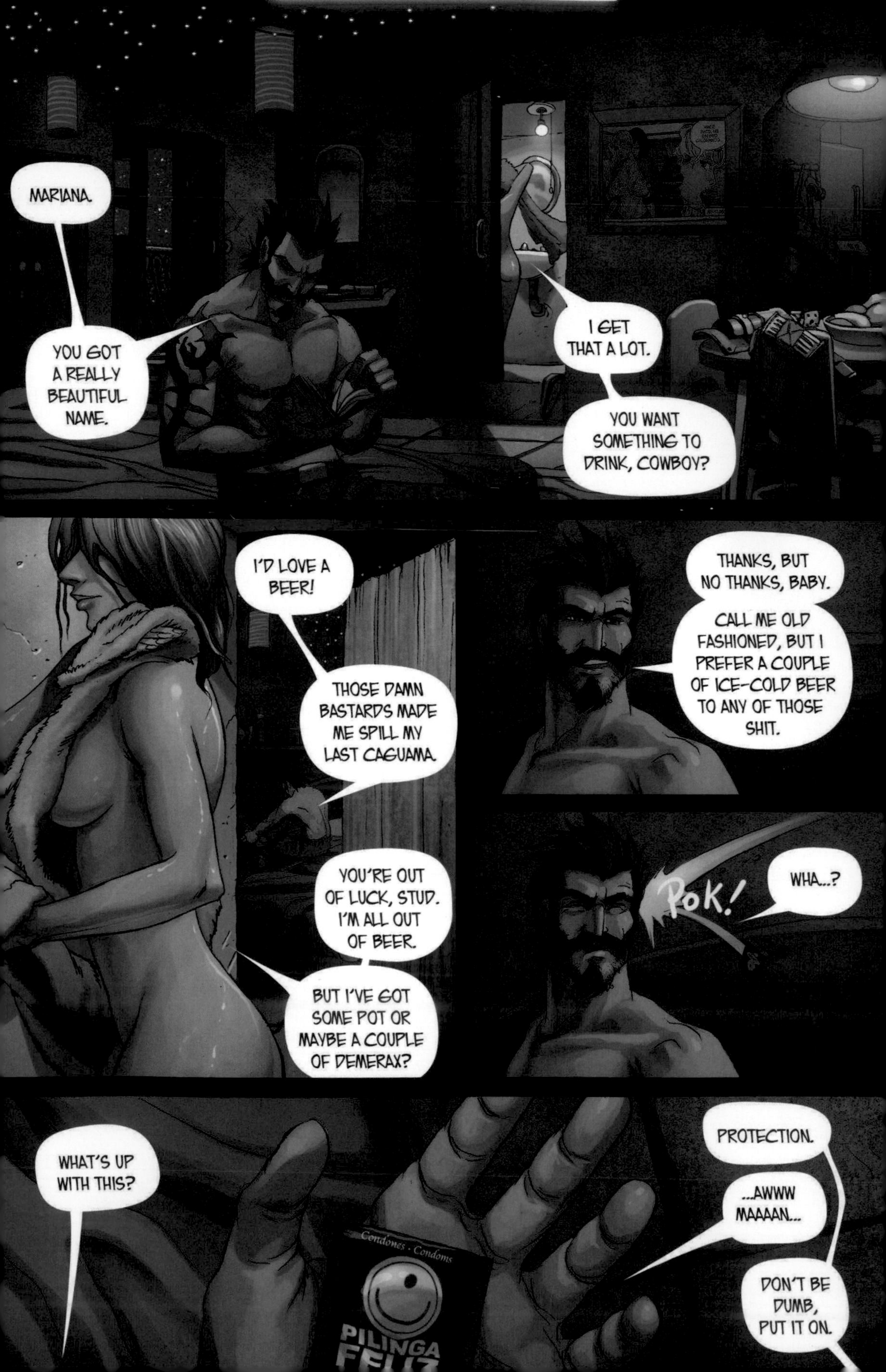

MARIANA.
YOU GOT A REALLY BEAUTIFUL NAME.
I GET THAT A LOT.
YOU WANT SOMETHING TO DRINK, COWBOY?
I'D LOVE A BEER!
THOSE DAMN BASTARDS MADE ME SPILL MY LAST CAGUAMA.
YOU'RE OUT OF LUCK, STUD. I'M ALL OUT OF BEER.
BUT I'VE GOT SOME POT OR MAYBE A COUPLE OF DEMERAX?
THANKS, BUT NO THANKS, BABY.
CALL ME OLD FASHIONED, BUT I PREFER A COUPLE OF ICE-COLD BEER TO ANY OF THOSE SHIT.
POK!
WHA...?
WHAT'S UP WITH THIS?
Condones · Condoms
PILINGA
PROTECTION.
...AWWW MAAAAN...
DON'T BE DUMB, PUT IT ON.

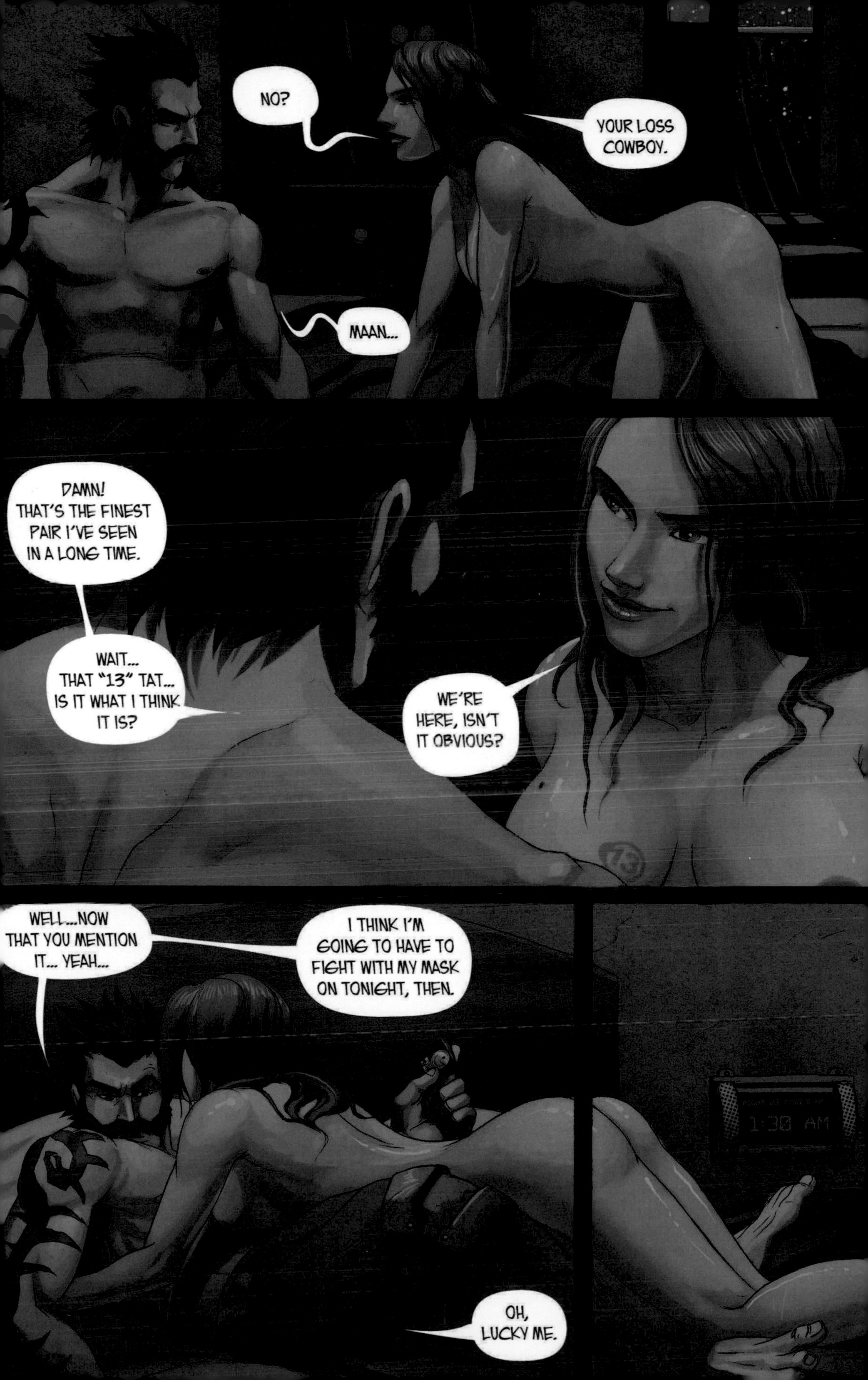

NO?
YOUR LOSS COWBOY.
MAAN...
DAMN! THAT'S THE FINEST PAIR I'VE SEEN IN A LONG TIME.
WAIT... THAT "13" TAT... IS IT WHAT I THINK IT IS?
WE'RE HERE, ISN'T IT OBVIOUS?
WELL...NOW THAT YOU MENTION IT... YEAH...
I THINK I'M GOING TO HAVE TO FIGHT WITH MY MASK ON TONIGHT, THEN.
1:30 AM
OH, LUCKY ME.

IT'S SO GOOD TO SEE YOU, ZAZIL.

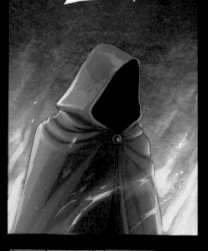

I'VE MISSED YOU SO MUCH.

I'M GLAD IT IS OVER.

AREN'T YOU?

PINCHE SHAMAN!

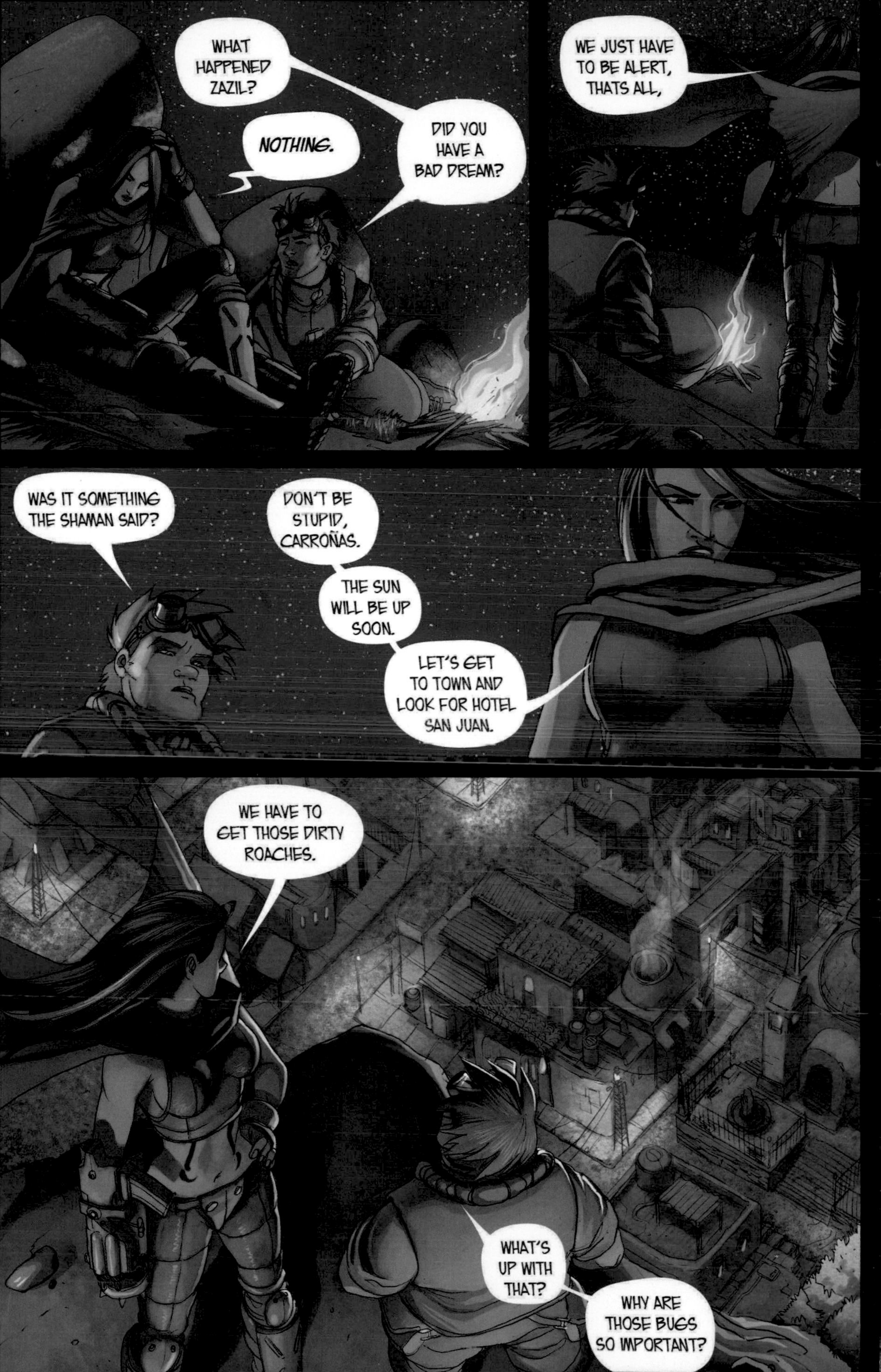
WHAT HAPPENED ZAZIL?
NOTHING.
DID YOU HAVE A BAD DREAM?
WE JUST HAVE TO BE ALERT, THATS ALL,
WAS IT SOMETHING THE SHAMAN SAID?
DON'T BE STUPID, CARROÑAS.
THE SUN WILL BE UP SOON.
LET'S GET TO TOWN AND LOOK FOR HOTEL SAN JUAN.
WE HAVE TO GET THOSE DIRTY ROACHES.
WHAT'S UP WITH THAT?
WHY ARE THOSE BUGS SO IMPORTANT?

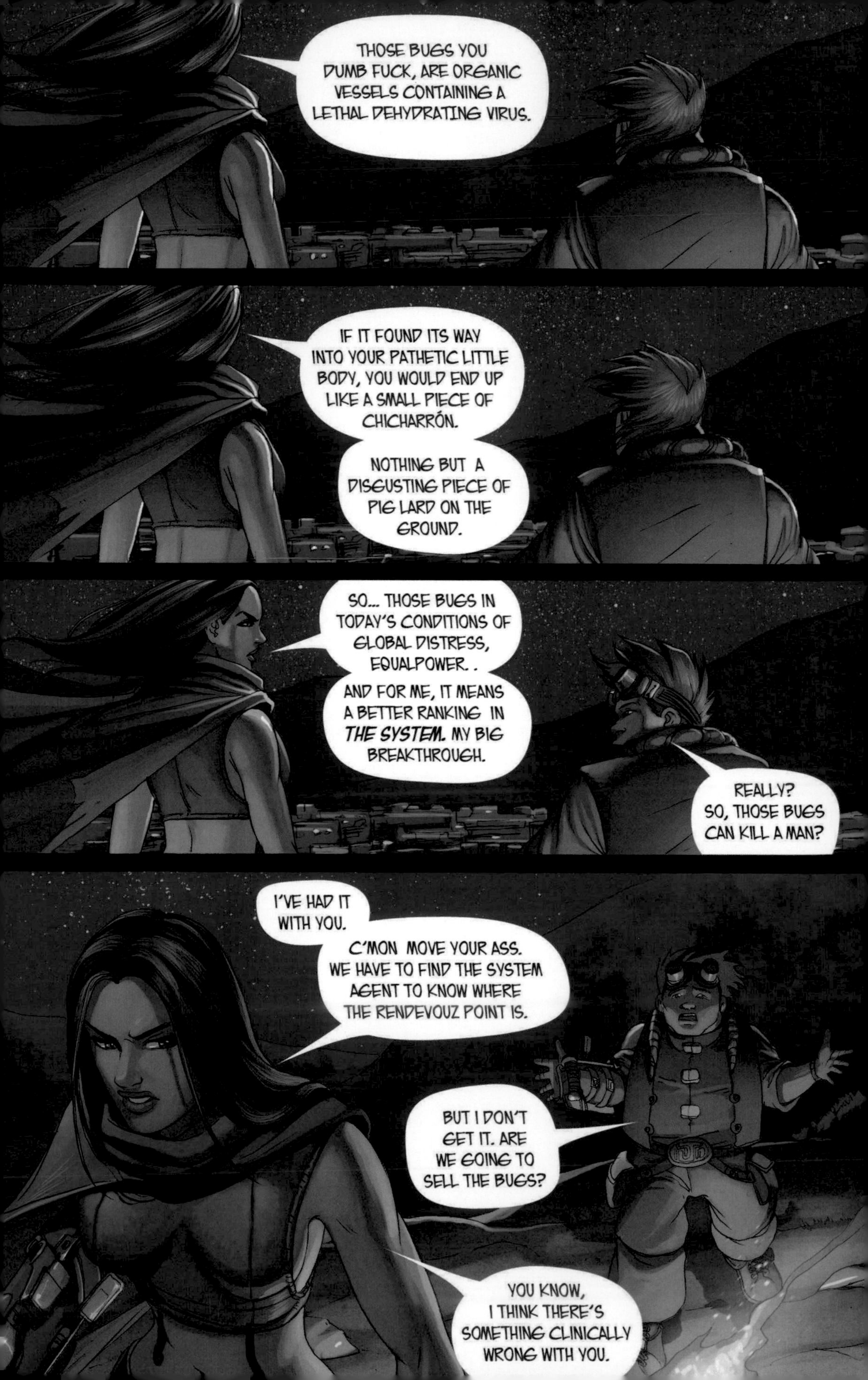
THOSE BUGS YOU DUMB FUCK, ARE ORGANIC VESSELS CONTAINING A LETHAL DEHYDRATING VIRUS.
IF IT FOUND ITS WAY INTO YOUR PATHETIC LITTLE BODY, YOU WOULD END UP LIKE A SMALL PIECE OF CHICHARRÓN.
NOTHING BUT A DISGUSTING PIECE OF PIG LARD ON THE GROUND.
SO... THOSE BUGS IN TODAY'S CONDITIONS OF GLOBAL DISTRESS, EQUALPOWER. .
AND FOR ME, IT MEANS A BETTER RANKING IN *THE SYSTEM.* MY BIG BREAKTHROUGH.
REALLY? SO, THOSE BUGS CAN KILL A MAN?
I'VE HAD IT WITH YOU.
C'MON MOVE YOUR ASS. WE HAVE TO FIND THE SYSTEM AGENT TO KNOW WHERE THE RENDEVOUZ POINT IS.
BUT I DON'T GET IT. ARE WE GOING TO SELL THE BUGS?
YOU KNOW, I THINK THERE'S SOMETHING CLINICALLY WRONG WITH YOU.

Money for nothing.

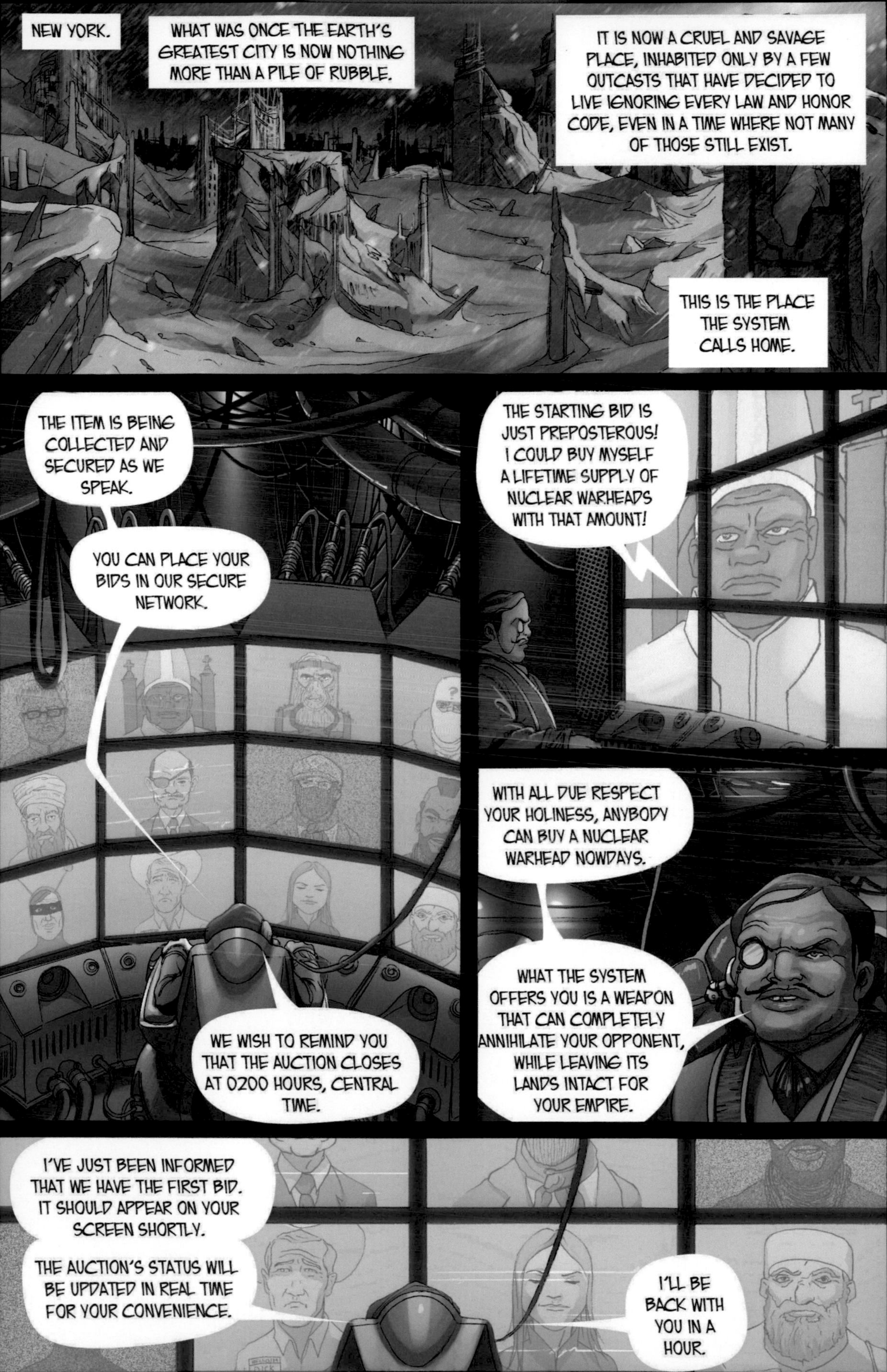

NEW YORK.
WHAT WAS ONCE THE EARTH'S GREATEST CITY IS NOW NOTHING MORE THAN A PILE OF RUBBLE.
IT IS NOW A CRUEL AND SAVAGE PLACE, INHABITED ONLY BY A FEW OUTCASTS THAT HAVE DECIDED TO LIVE IGNORING EVERY LAW AND HONOR CODE, EVEN IN A TIME WHERE NOT MANY OF THOSE STILL EXIST.
THIS IS THE PLACE THE SYSTEM CALLS HOME.
THE ITEM IS BEING COLLECTED AND SECURED AS WE SPEAK.
YOU CAN PLACE YOUR BIDS IN OUR SECURE NETWORK.
WE WISH TO REMIND YOU THAT THE AUCTION CLOSES AT 0200 HOURS, CENTRAL TIME.
THE STARTING BID IS JUST PREPOSTEROUS! I COULD BUY MYSELF A LIFETIME SUPPLY OF NUCLEAR WARHEADS WITH THAT AMOUNT!
WITH ALL DUE RESPECT YOUR HOLINESS, ANYBODY CAN BUY A NUCLEAR WARHEAD NOWDAYS.
WHAT THE SYSTEM OFFERS YOU IS A WEAPON THAT CAN COMPLETELY ANNIHILATE YOUR OPPONENT, WHILE LEAVING ITS LANDS INTACT FOR YOUR EMPIRE.
I'VE JUST BEEN INFORMED THAT WE HAVE THE FIRST BID. IT SHOULD APPEAR ON YOUR SCREEN SHORTLY.
THE AUCTION'S STATUS WILL BE UPDATED IN REAL TIME FOR YOUR CONVENIENCE.
I'LL BE BACK WITH YOU IN A HOUR.

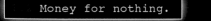

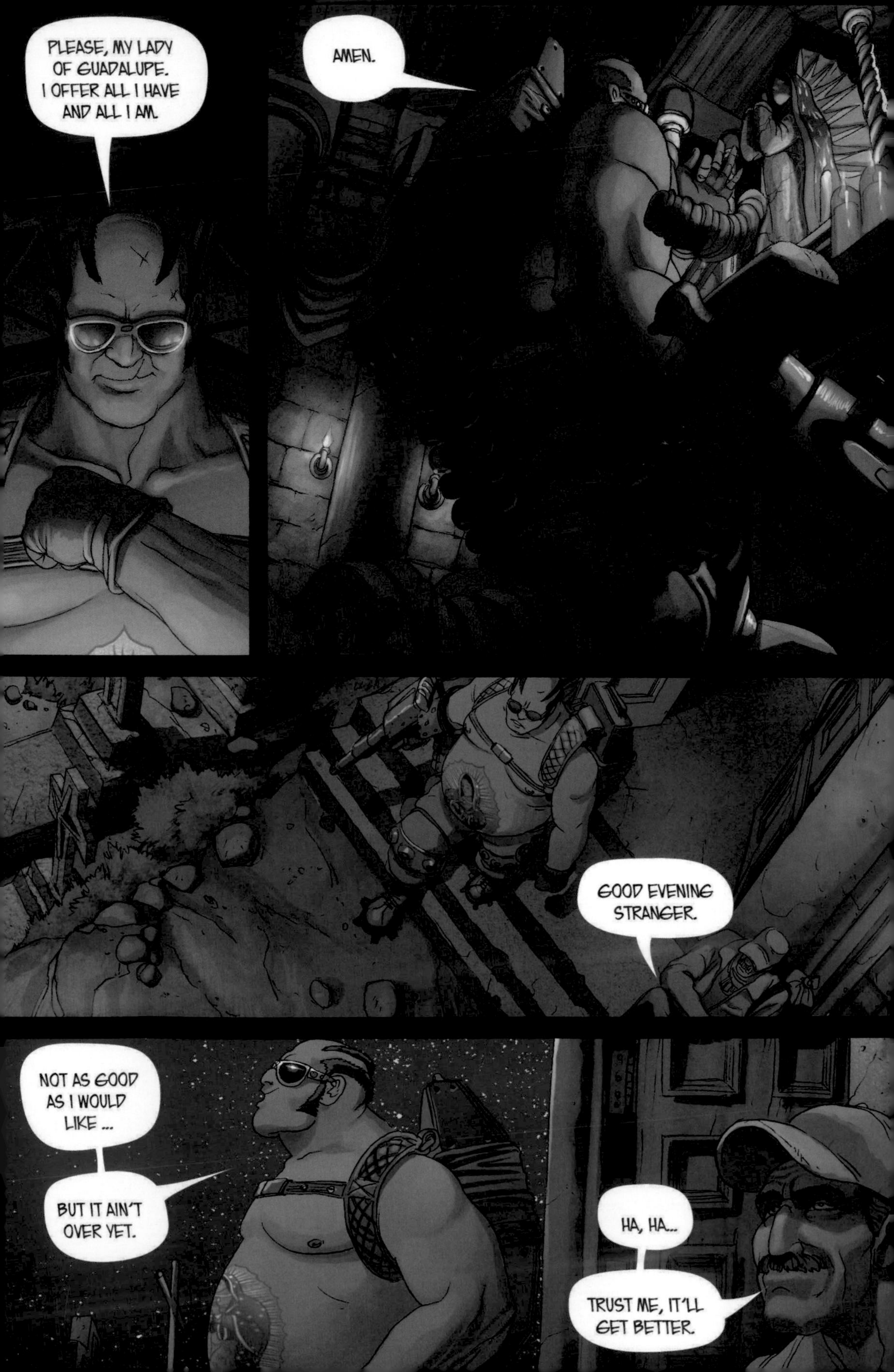
PLEASE, MY LADY OF GUADALUPE. I OFFER ALL I HAVE AND ALL I AM.
AMEN.
GOOD EVENING STRANGER.
NOT AS GOOD AS I WOULD LIKE ...
BUT IT AIN'T OVER YET.
HA, HA...
TRUST ME, IT'LL GET BETTER.

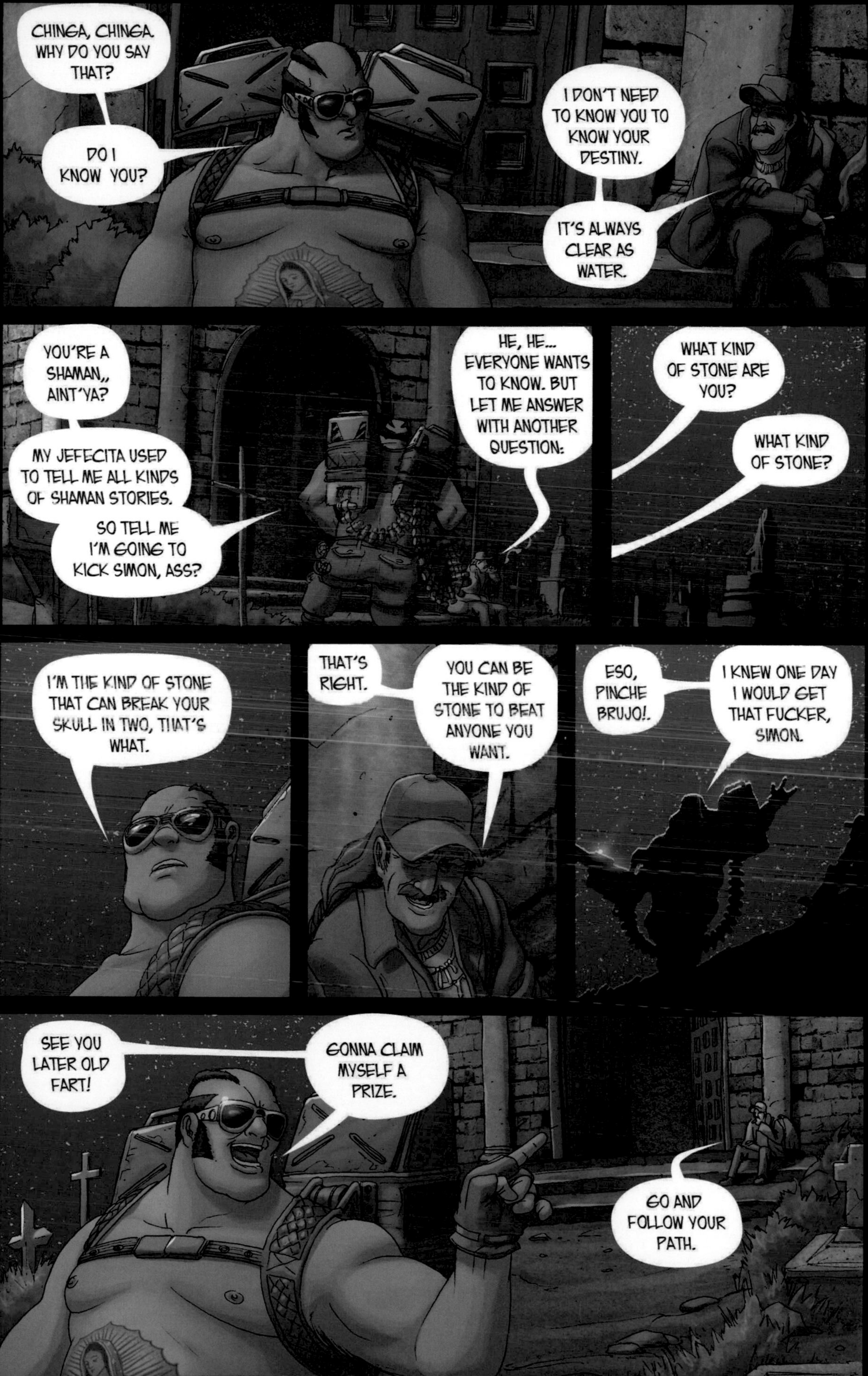
CHINGA, CHINGA. WHY DO YOU SAY THAT?
DO I KNOW YOU?
I DON'T NEED TO KNOW YOU TO KNOW YOUR DESTINY.
IT'S ALWAYS CLEAR AS WATER.
YOU'RE A SHAMAN,, AINT'YA?
MY JEFECITA USED TO TELL ME ALL KINDS OF SHAMAN STORIES.
SO TELL ME I'M GOING TO KICK SIMON, ASS?
HE, HE... EVERYONE WANTS TO KNOW. BUT LET ME ANSWER WITH ANOTHER QUESTION:
WHAT KIND OF STONE ARE YOU?
WHAT KIND OF STONE?
I'M THE KIND OF STONE THAT CAN BREAK YOUR SKULL IN TWO, THAT'S WHAT.
THAT'S RIGHT.
YOU CAN BE THE KIND OF STONE TO BEAT ANYONE YOU WANT.
ESO, PINCHE BRUJO!.
I KNEW ONE DAY I WOULD GET THAT FUCKER, SIMON.
SEE YOU LATER OLD FART!
GONNA CLAIM MYSELF A PRIZE.
GO AND FOLLOW YOUR PATH.

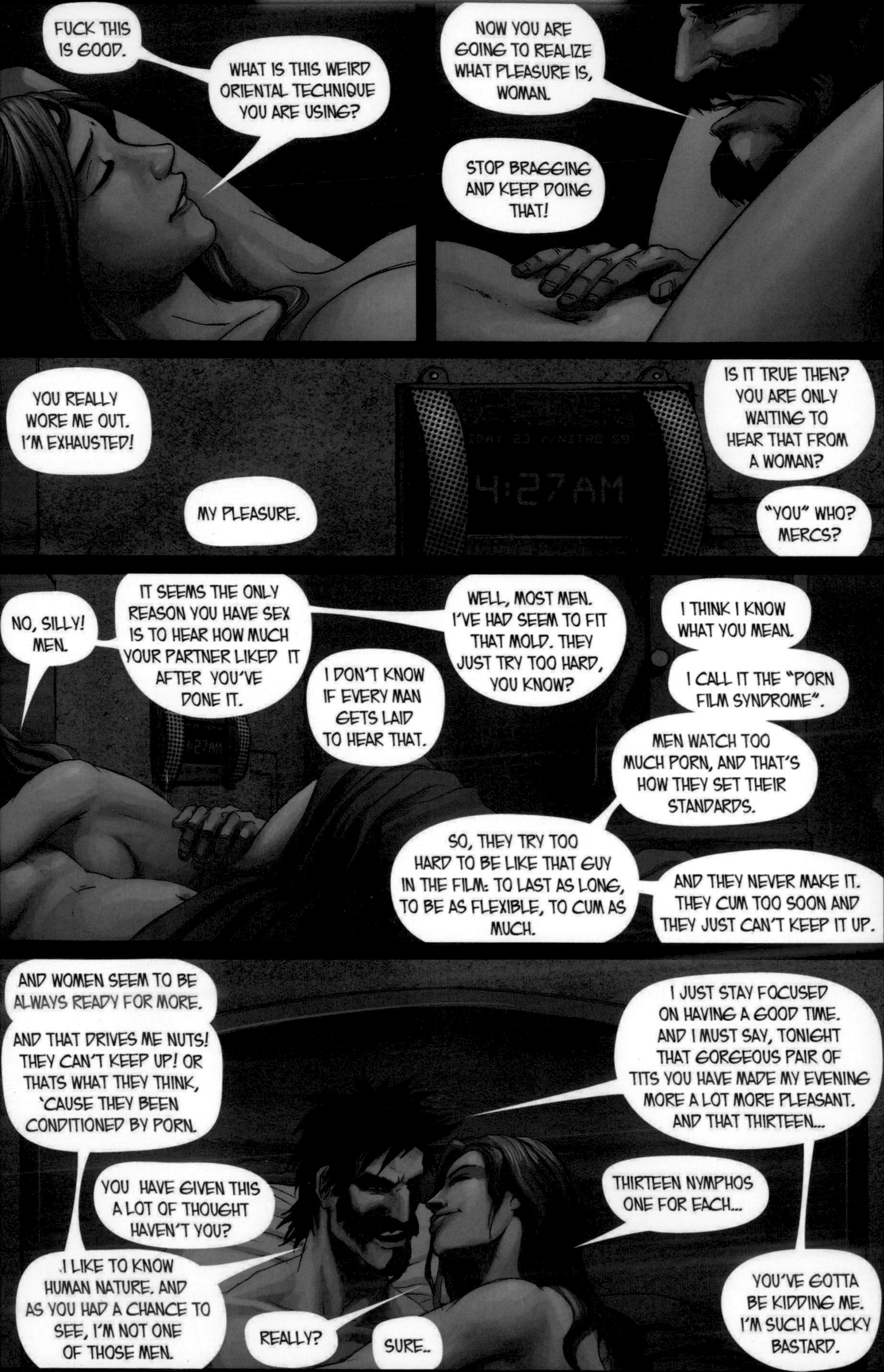
FUCK THIS IS GOOD.
WHAT IS THIS WEIRD ORIENTAL TECHNIQUE YOU ARE USING?
NOW YOU ARE GOING TO REALIZE WHAT PLEASURE IS, WOMAN.
STOP BRAGGING AND KEEP DOING THAT!
YOU REALLY WORE ME OUT. I'M EXHAUSTED!
MY PLEASURE.
4:27AM
IS IT TRUE THEN? YOU ARE ONLY WAITING TO HEAR THAT FROM A WOMAN?
"YOU" WHO? MERCS?
NO, SILLY! MEN.
IT SEEMS THE ONLY REASON YOU HAVE SEX IS TO HEAR HOW MUCH YOUR PARTNER LIKED IT AFTER YOU'VE DONE IT.
I DON'T KNOW IF EVERY MAN GETS LAID TO HEAR THAT.
WELL, MOST MEN. I'VE HAD SEEM TO FIT THAT MOLD. THEY JUST TRY TOO HARD, YOU KNOW?
I THINK I KNOW WHAT YOU MEAN.
I CALL IT THE "PORN FILM SYNDROME".
MEN WATCH TOO MUCH PORN, AND THAT'S HOW THEY SET THEIR STANDARDS.
SO, THEY TRY TOO HARD TO BE LIKE THAT GUY IN THE FILM: TO LAST AS LONG, TO BE AS FLEXIBLE, TO CUM AS MUCH.
AND THEY NEVER MAKE IT. THEY CUM TOO SOON AND THEY JUST CAN'T KEEP IT UP.
AND WOMEN SEEM TO BE ALWAYS READY FOR MORE.
AND THAT DRIVES ME NUTS! THEY CAN'T KEEP UP! OR THATS WHAT THEY THINK, 'CAUSE THEY BEEN CONDITIONED BY PORN.
YOU HAVE GIVEN THIS A LOT OF THOUGHT HAVEN'T YOU?
I LIKE TO KNOW HUMAN NATURE. AND AS YOU HAD A CHANCE TO SEE, I'M NOT ONE OF THOSE MEN.
REALLY?
SURE..
I JUST STAY FOCUSED ON HAVING A GOOD TIME. AND I MUST SAY, TONIGHT THAT GORGEOUS PAIR OF TITS YOU HAVE MADE MY EVENING MORE A LOT MORE PLEASANT. AND THAT THIRTEEN...
THIRTEEN NYMPHOS ONE FOR EACH...
YOU'VE GOTTA BE KIDDING ME. I'M SUCH A LUCKY BASTARD.

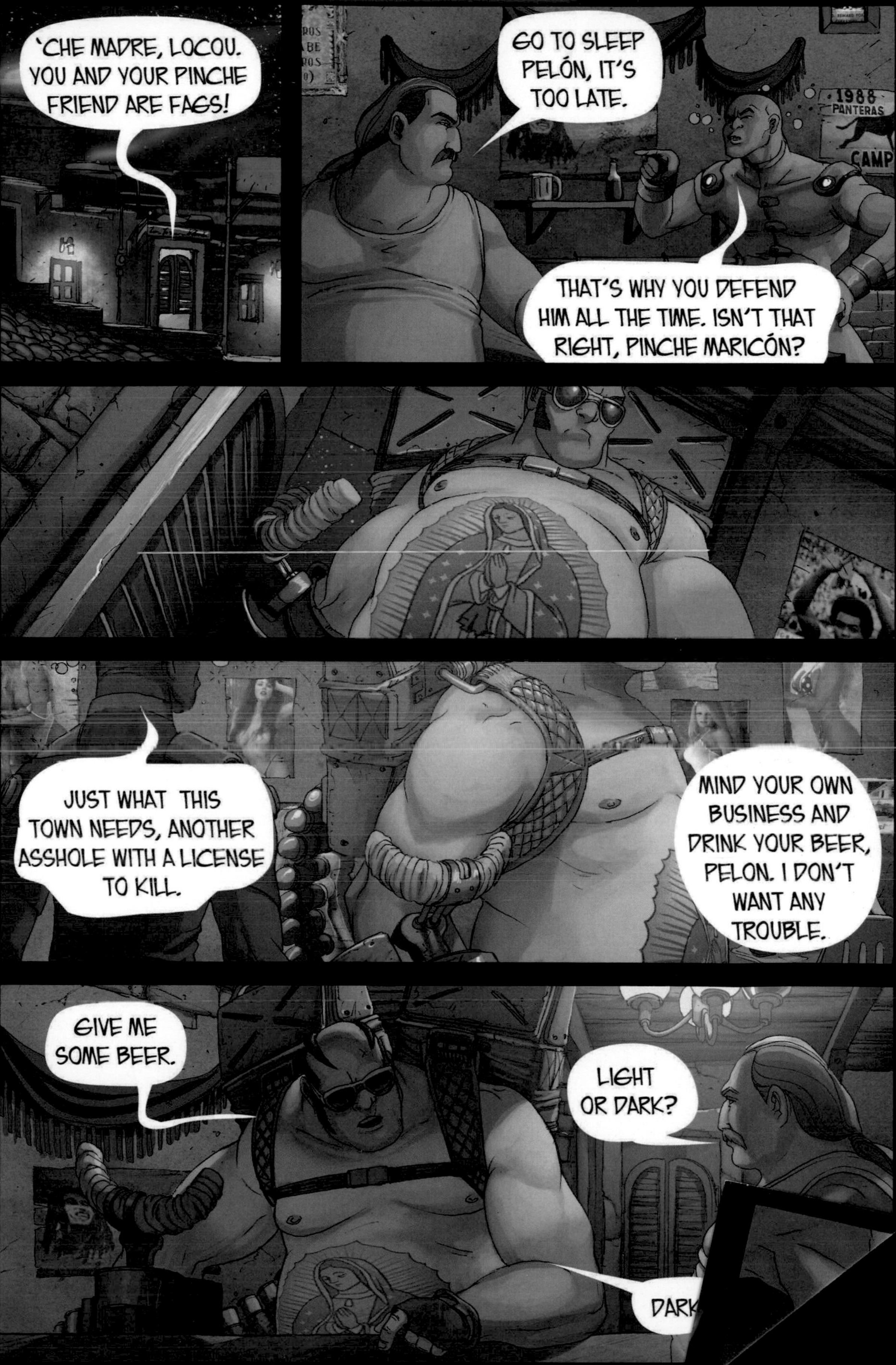
'CHE MADRE, LOCOU. YOU AND YOUR PINCHE FRIEND ARE FAGS!
GO TO SLEEP PELÓN, IT'S TOO LATE.
THAT'S WHY YOU DEFEND HIM ALL THE TIME. ISN'T THAT RIGHT, PINCHE MARICÓN?
1988 PANTERAS
CAMP
JUST WHAT THIS TOWN NEEDS, ANOTHER ASSHOLE WITH A LICENSE TO KILL.
MIND YOUR OWN BUSINESS AND DRINK YOUR BEER, PELON. I DON'T WANT ANY TROUBLE.
GIVE ME SOME BEER.
LIGHT OR DARK?
DARK

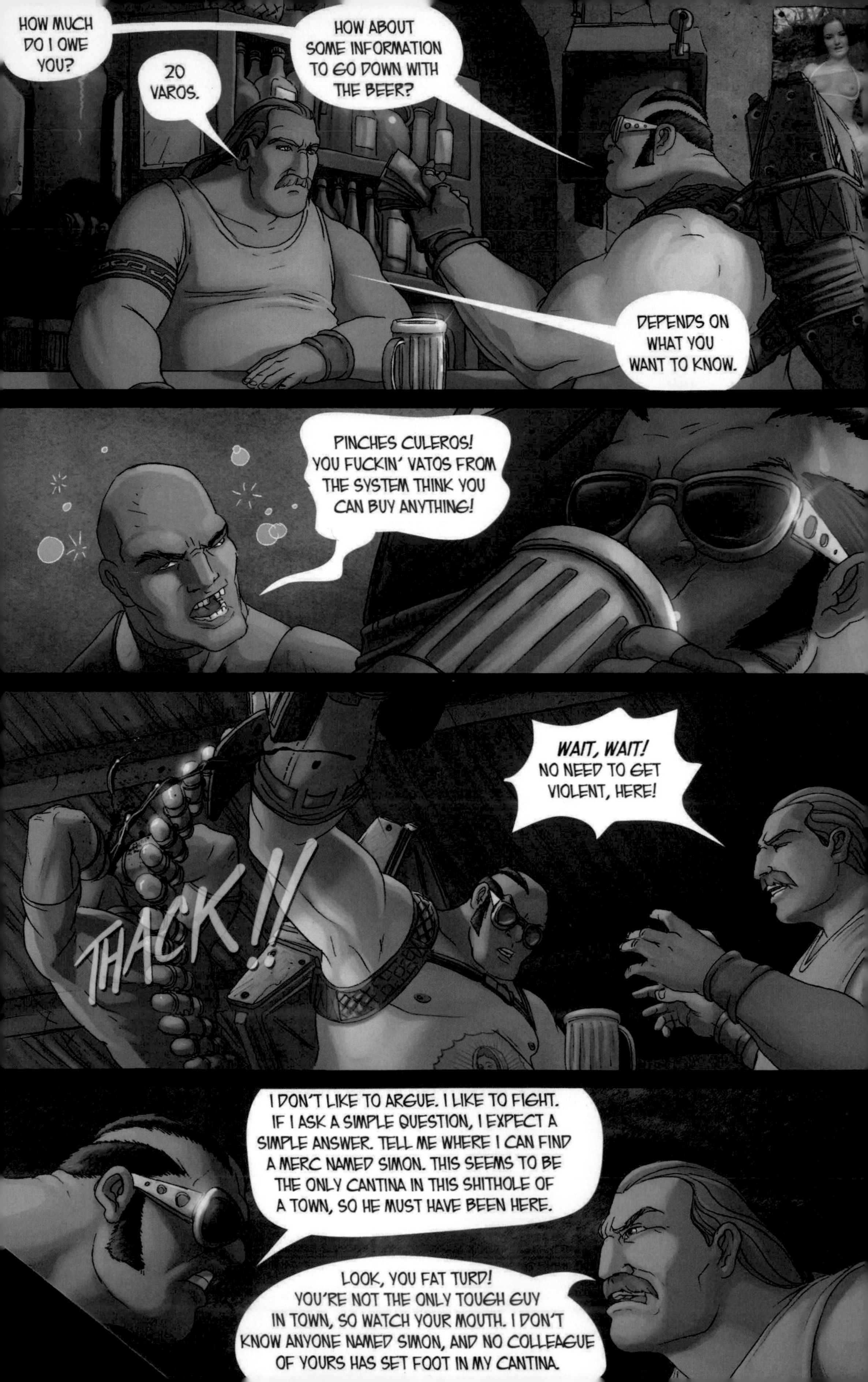

HOW MUCH DO I OWE YOU?
20 VAROS.
HOW ABOUT SOME INFORMATION TO GO DOWN WITH THE BEER?
DEPENDS ON WHAT YOU WANT TO KNOW.
PINCHES CULEROS! YOU FUCKIN' VATOS FROM THE SYSTEM THINK YOU CAN BUY ANYTHING!
THACK!!
WAIT, WAIT! NO NEED TO GET VIOLENT, HERE!
I DON'T LIKE TO ARGUE. I LIKE TO FIGHT. IF I ASK A SIMPLE QUESTION, I EXPECT A SIMPLE ANSWER. TELL ME WHERE I CAN FIND A MERC NAMED SIMON. THIS SEEMS TO BE THE ONLY CANTINA IN THIS SHITHOLE OF A TOWN, SO HE MUST HAVE BEEN HERE.
LOOK, YOU FAT TURD! YOU'RE NOT THE ONLY TOUGH GUY IN TOWN, SO WATCH YOUR MOUTH. I DON'T KNOW ANYONE NAMED SIMON, AND NO COLLEAGUE OF YOURS HAS SET FOOT IN MY CANTINA.

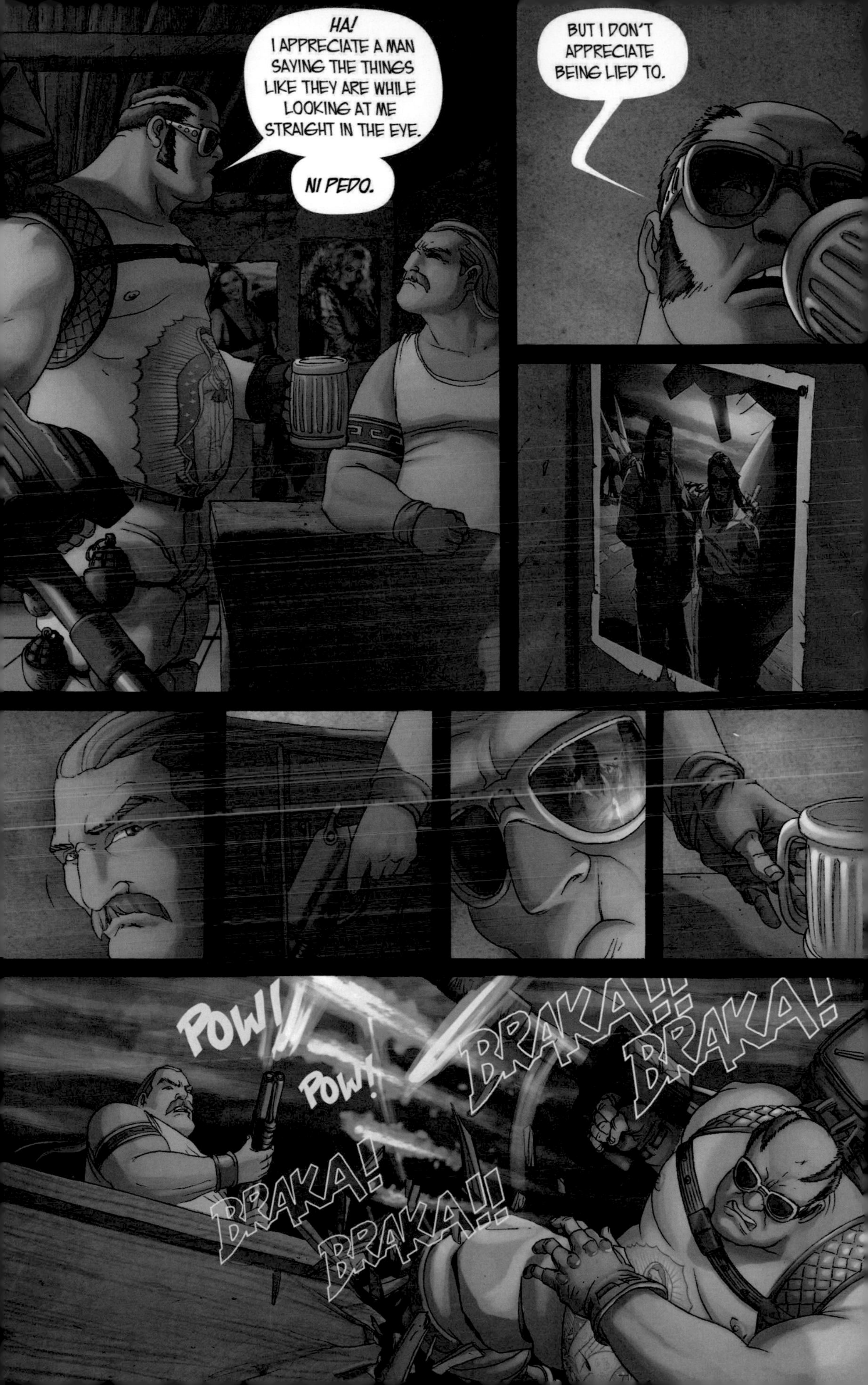
HA! I APPRECIATE A MAN SAYING THE THINGS LIKE THEY ARE WHILE LOOKING AT ME STRAIGHT IN THE EYE.
NI PEDO.
BUT I DON'T APPRECIATE BEING LIED TO.
POW!
POW!
BRAKA!!
BRAKA!
BRAKA!
BRAKA!!

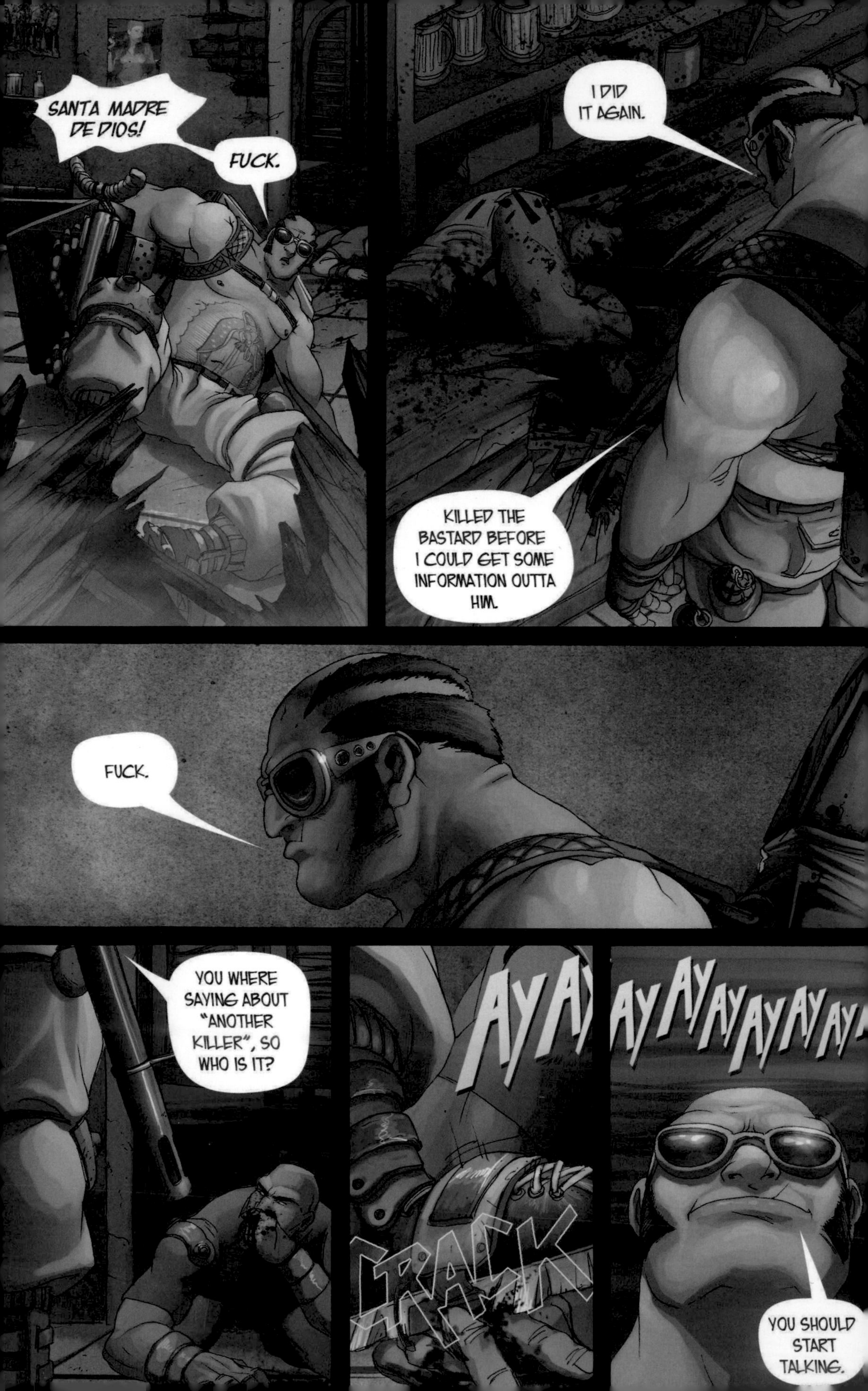
SANTA MADRE DE DIOS!
FUCK.
I DID IT AGAIN.
KILLED THE BASTARD BEFORE I COULD GET SOME INFORMATION OUTTA HIM.
FUCK.
YOU WHERE SAYING ABOUT "ANOTHER KILLER", SO WHO IS IT?
TRACK
AY AY AY AY AY AY AY AY AY
YOU SHOULD START TALKING.

Kinky sex makes the world go 'round (part I).

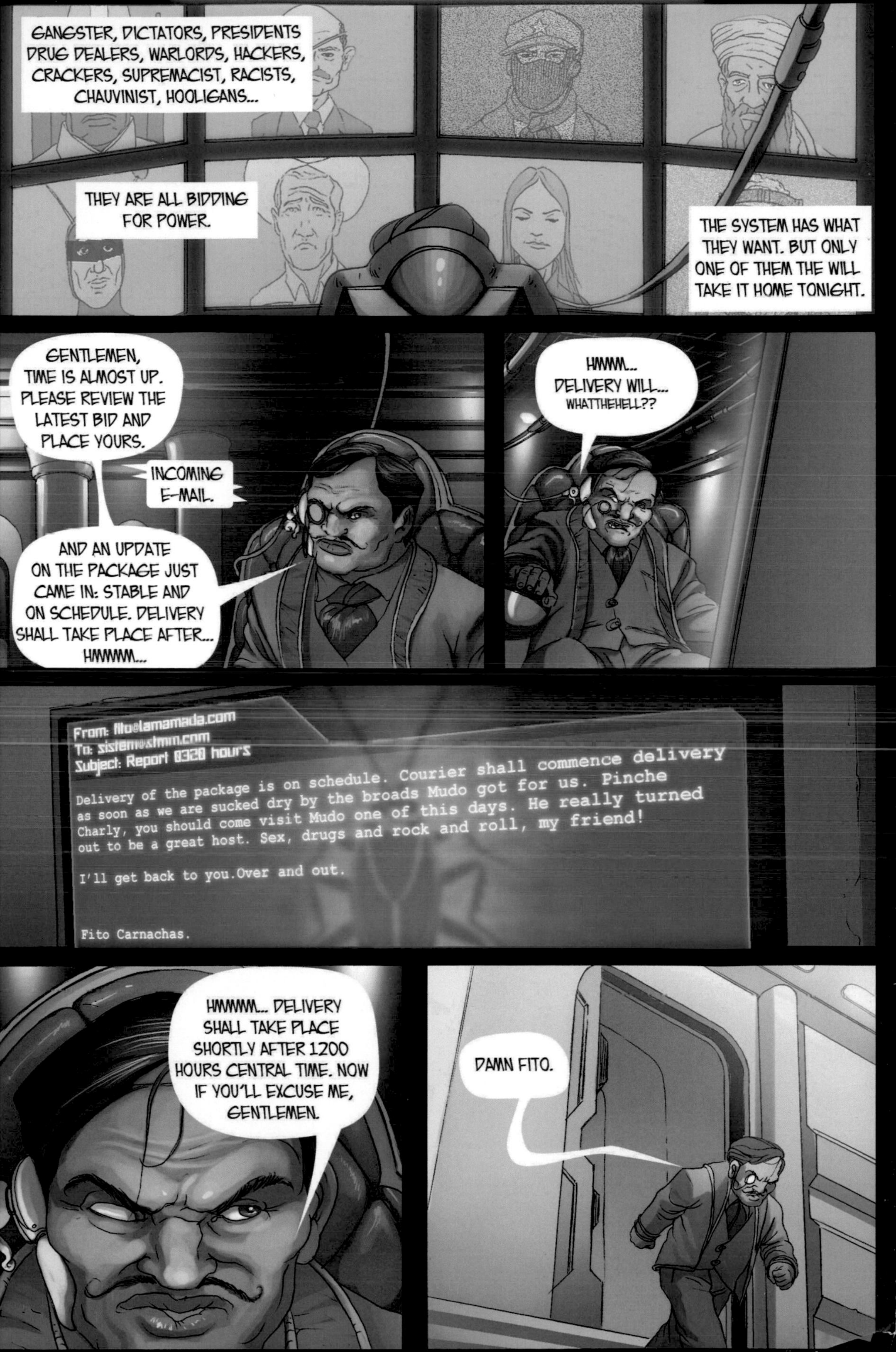
GANGSTER, DICTATORS, PRESIDENTS DRUG DEALERS, WARLORDS, HACKERS, CRACKERS, SUPREMACIST, RACISTS, CHAUVINIST, HOOLIGANS...
THEY ARE ALL BIDDING FOR POWER.
THE SYSTEM HAS WHAT THEY WANT. BUT ONLY ONE OF THEM THE WILL TAKE IT HOME TONIGHT.
GENTLEMEN, TIME IS ALMOST UP. PLEASE REVIEW THE LATEST BID AND PLACE YOURS.
INCOMING E-MAIL.
AND AN UPDATE ON THE PACKAGE JUST CAME IN: STABLE AND ON SCHEDULE. DELIVERY SHALL TAKE PLACE AFTER... HMMMM...
HMMM... DELIVERY WILL... WHATTHEHELL??
From: fito@lamamada.com
To: sistem@xtmm.com
Subject: Report 0320 hours
Delivery of the package is on schedule. Courier shall commence delivery as soon as we are sucked dry by the broads Mudo got for us. Pinche Charly, you should come visit Mudo one of this days. He really turned out to be a great host. Sex, drugs and rock and roll, my friend!
I'll get back to you.Over and out.
Fito Carnachas.
HMMMM... DELIVERY SHALL TAKE PLACE SHORTLY AFTER 1200 HOURS CENTRAL TIME. NOW IF YOU'LL EXCUSE ME, GENTLEMEN.
DAMN FITO.

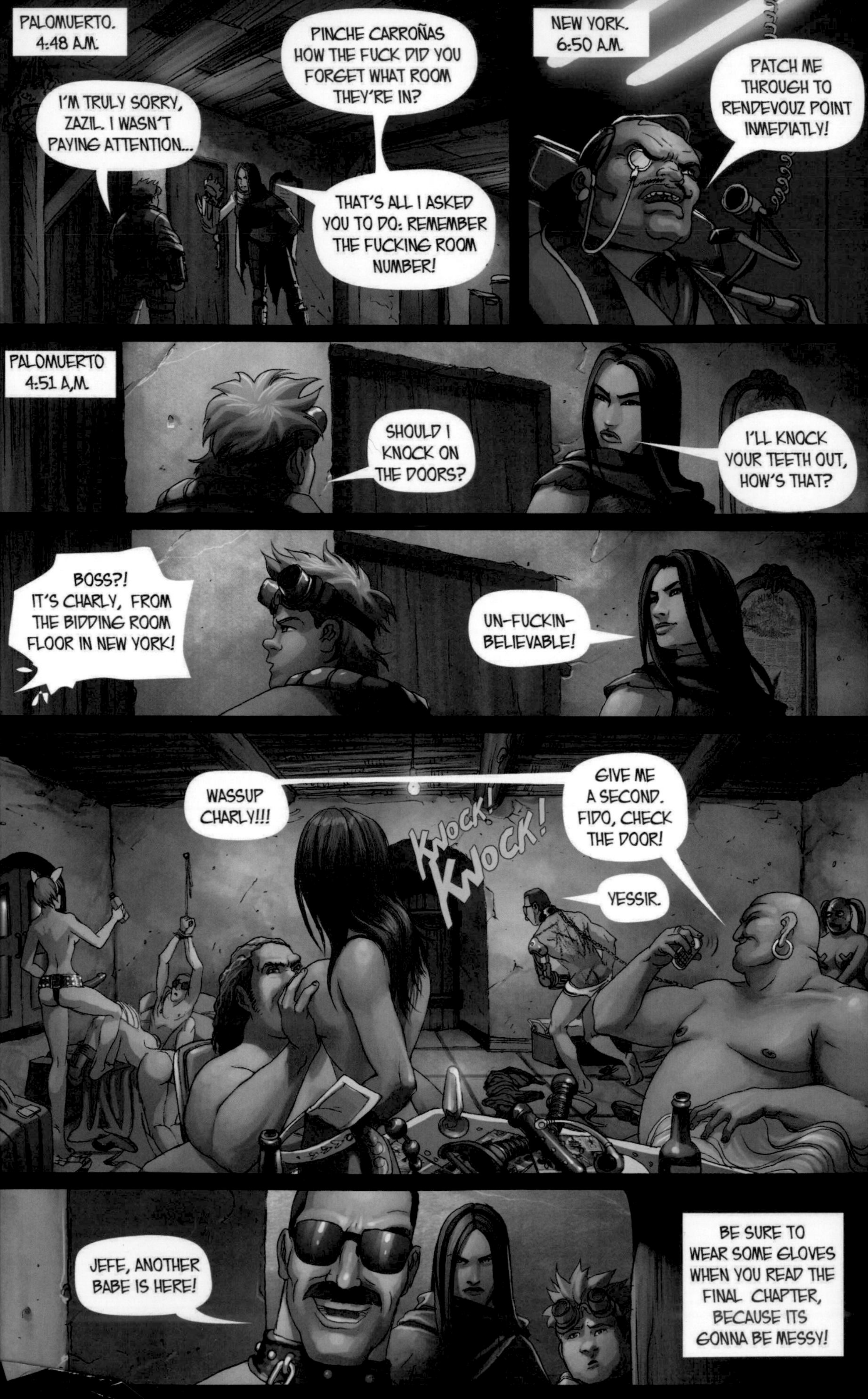
PALOMUERTO. 4:48 A.M.
I'M TRULY SORRY, ZAZIL. I WASN'T PAYING ATTENTION...
PINCHE CARROÑAS HOW THE FUCK DID YOU FORGET WHAT ROOM THEY'RE IN?
THAT'S ALL I ASKED YOU TO DO: REMEMBER THE FUCKING ROOM NUMBER!
NEW YORK. 6:50 A.M.
PATCH ME THROUGH TO RENDEVOUZ POINT INMEDIATLY!
PALOMUERTO 4:51 A.M.
SHOULD I KNOCK ON THE DOORS?
I'LL KNOCK YOUR TEETH OUT, HOW'S THAT?
BOSS?! IT'S CHARLY, FROM THE BIDDING ROOM FLOOR IN NEW YORK!
UN-FUCKIN-BELIEVABLE!
WASSUP CHARLY!!!
GIVE ME A SECOND. FIDO, CHECK THE DOOR!
KNOCK! KNOCK!
YESSIR.
JEFE, ANOTHER BABE IS HERE!
BE SURE TO WEAR SOME GLOVES WHEN YOU READ THE FINAL CHAPTER, BECAUSE ITS GONNA BE MESSY!

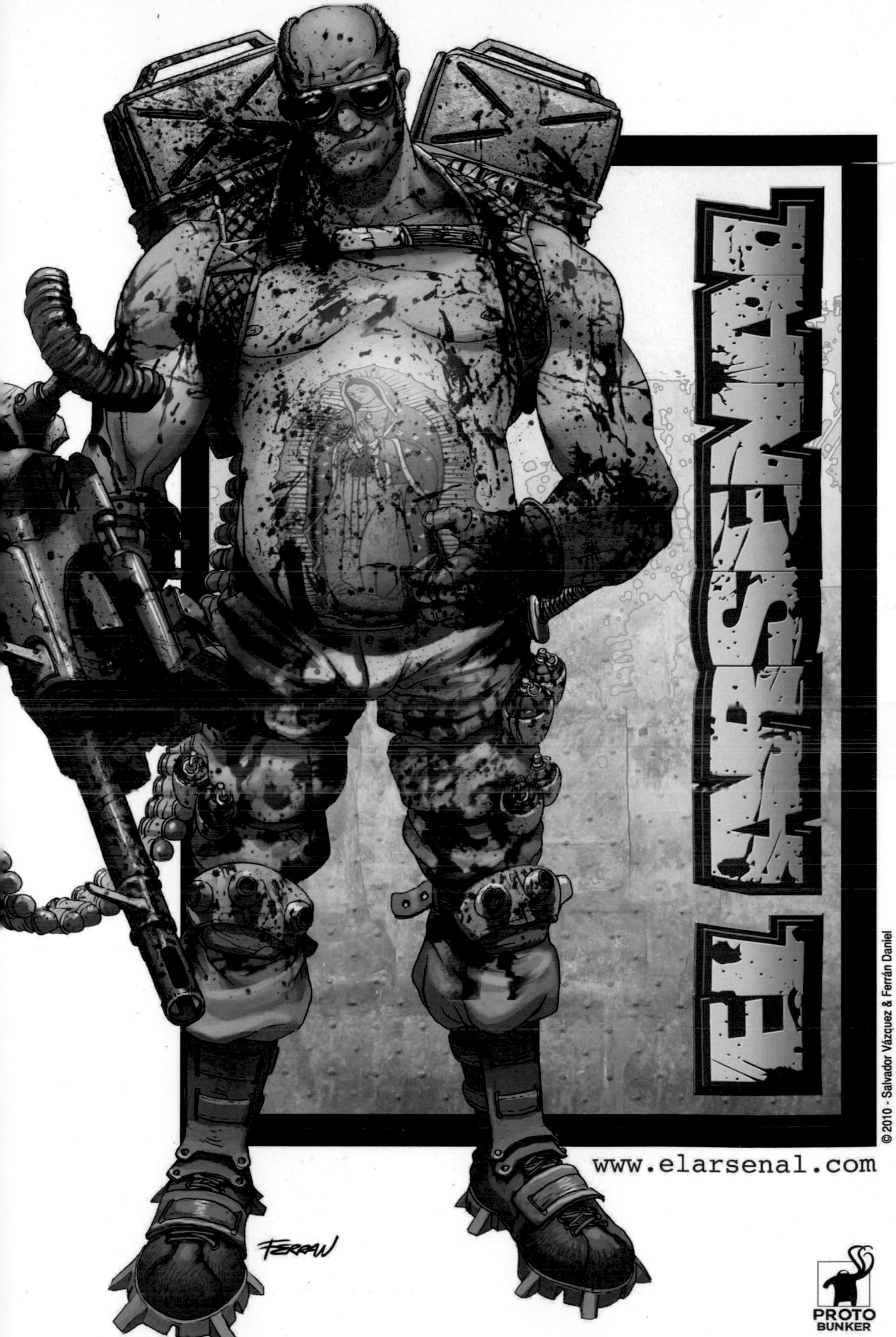
EL ARSENAL
© 2010 - Salvador Vázquez & Ferrán Daniel
www.elarsenal.com
FERRAN
PROTO BUNKER

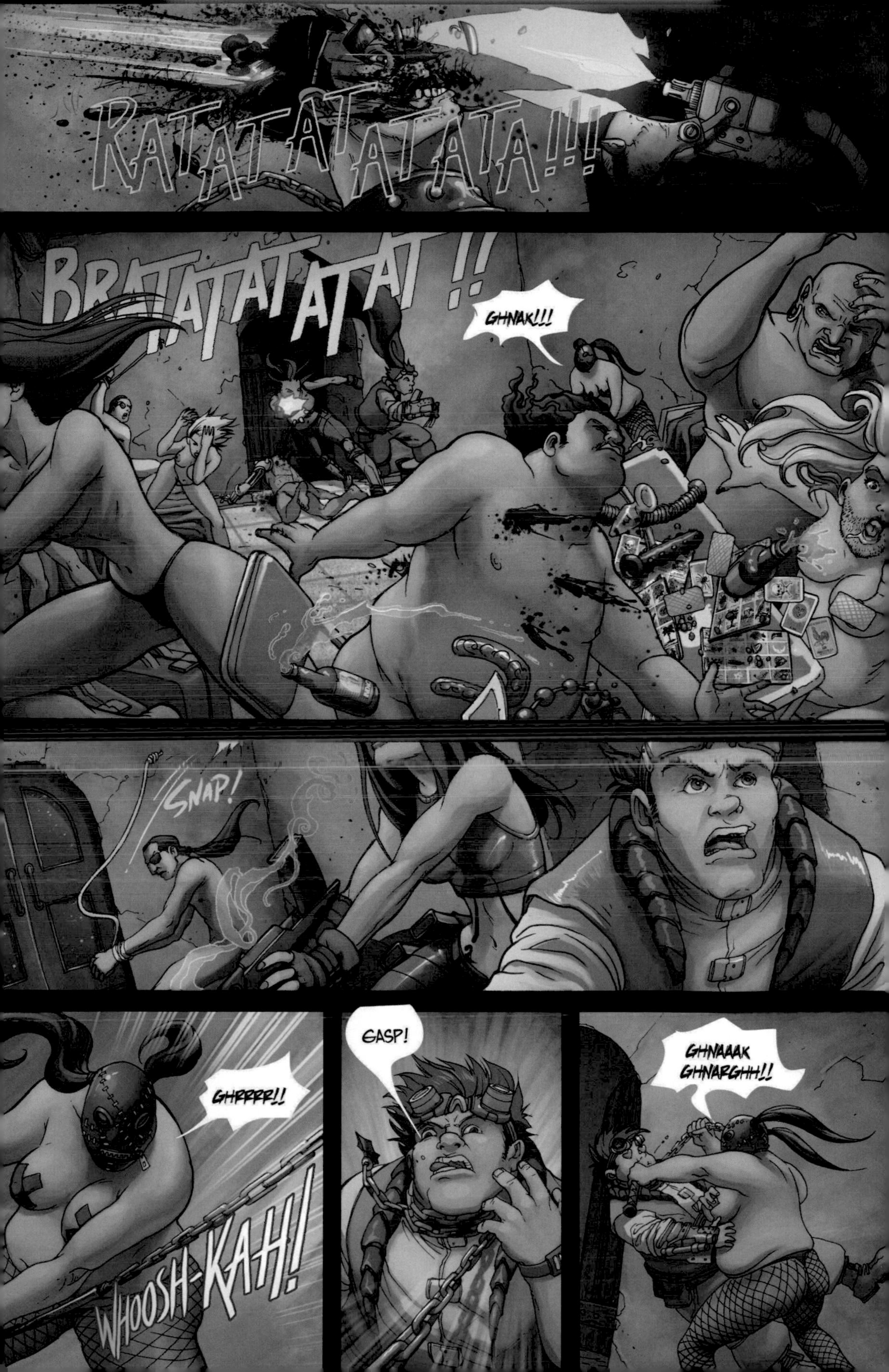
RATATATATATA!!!
BRATATATATAT!!
GHNAK!!!
SNAP!
GHRRRR!!
WHOOSH-KAH!
GASP!
GHNAAAK
GHNARGHH!!

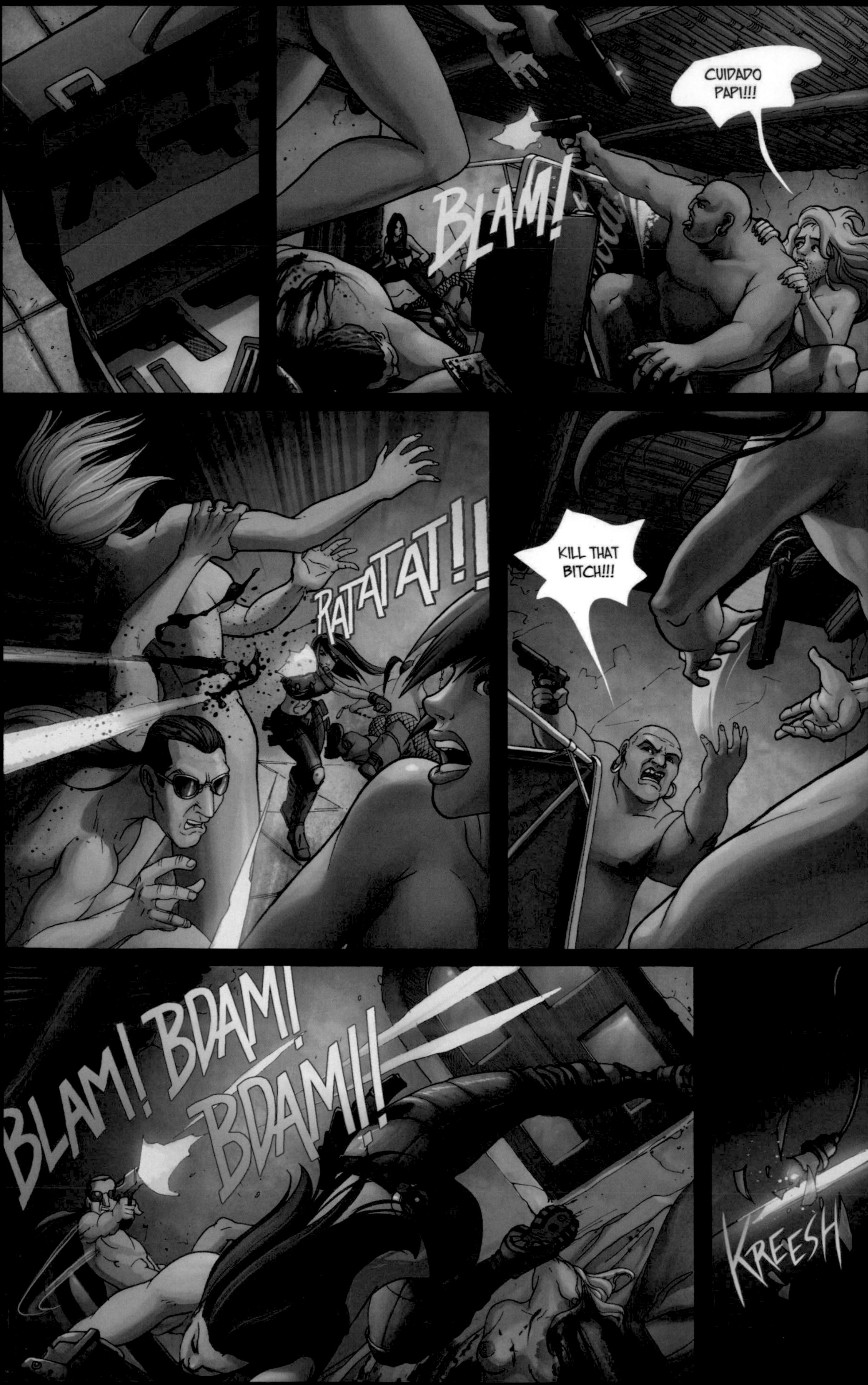

CUIDADO PAPI!!!
BLAM!
RATATAT!!
KILL THAT BITCH!!!
BLAM! BDAM!
BDAM!!
KREESH

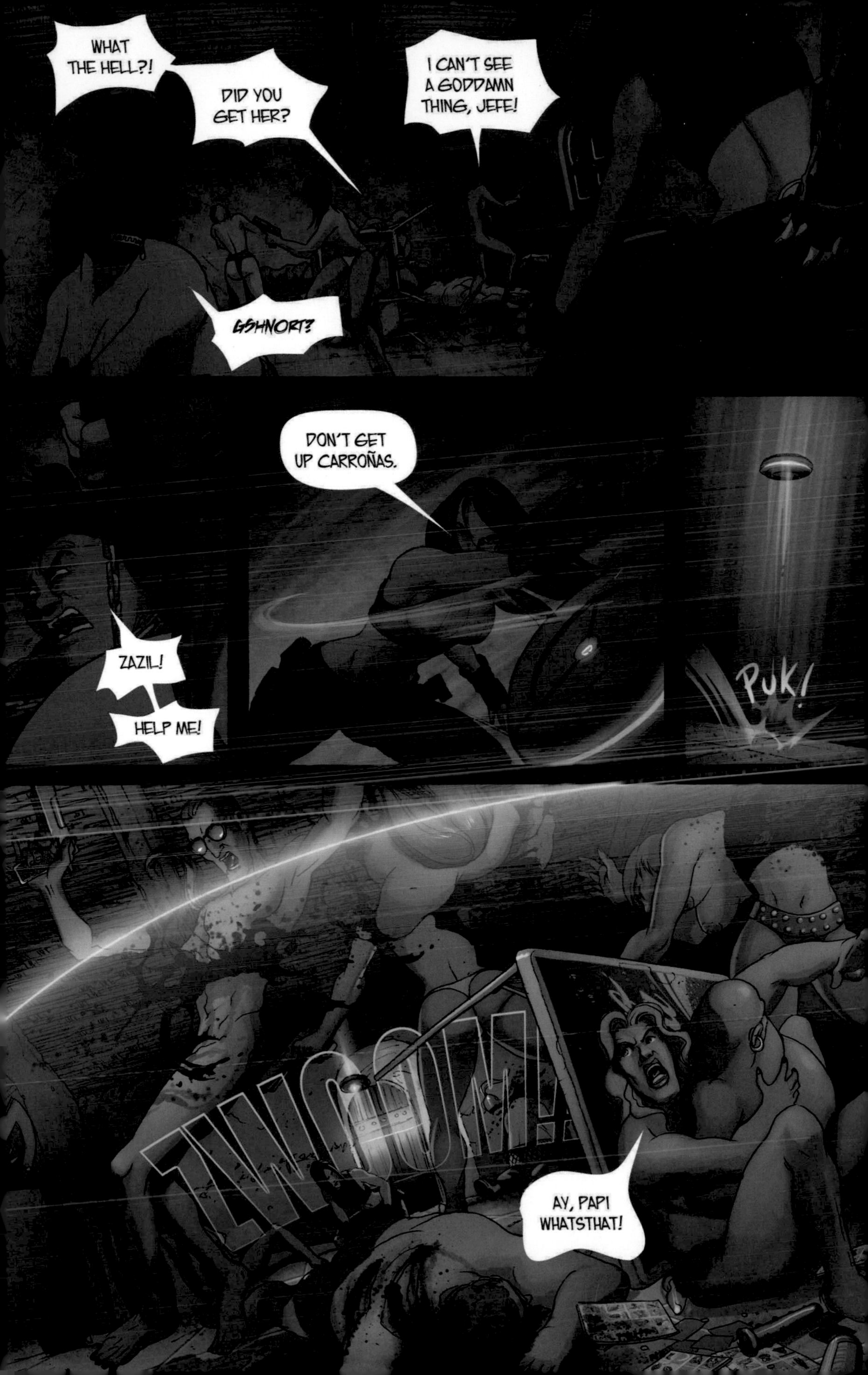
WHAT THE HELL?!
DID YOU GET HER?
I CAN'T SEE A GODDAMN THING, JEFE!
GSHNORT?
DON'T GET UP CARROÑAS.
ZAZIL!
HELP ME!
PUK!
TWOOOM!
AY, PAPI WHATSTHAT!

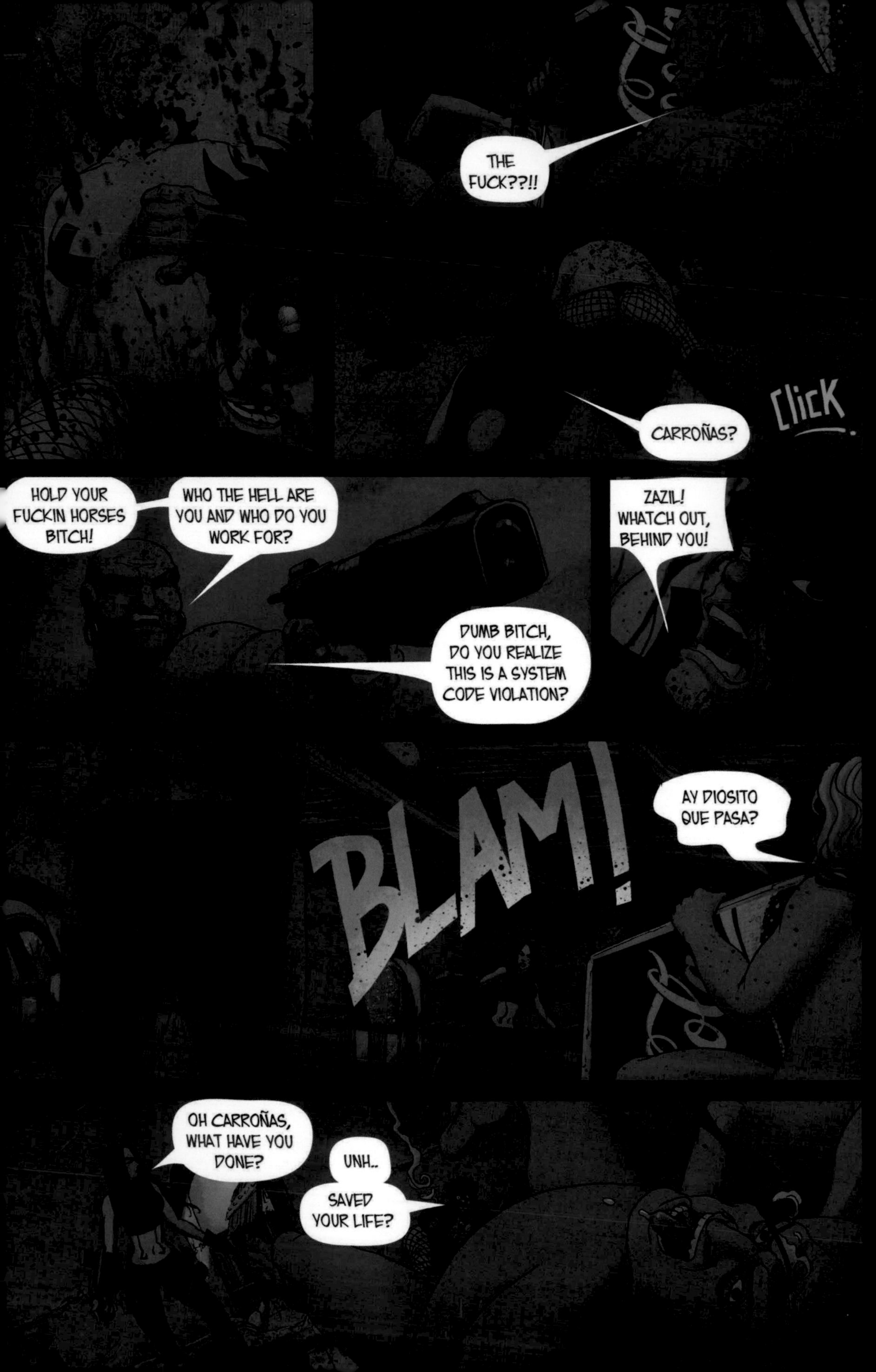
THE FUCK??!!
CARROÑAS?
ClicK
HOLD YOUR FUCKIN HORSES BITCH!
WHO THE HELL ARE YOU AND WHO DO YOU WORK FOR?
DUMB BITCH, DO YOU REALIZE THIS IS A SYSTEM CODE VIOLATION?
ZAZIL! WHATCH OUT, BEHIND YOU!
BLAM!
AY DIOSITO QUE PASA?
OH CARROÑAS, WHAT HAVE YOU DONE?
UNH..
SAVED YOUR LIFE?

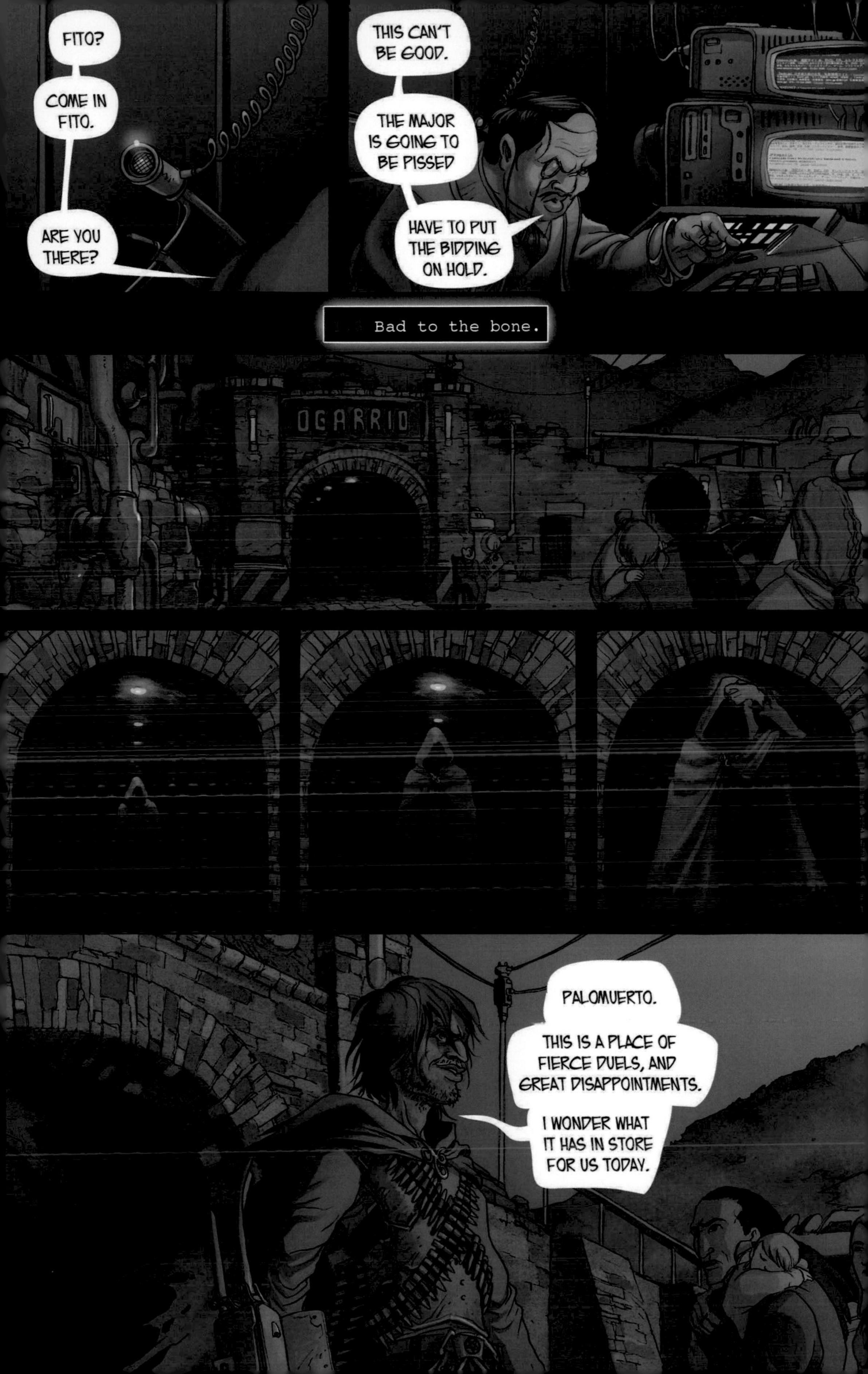
FITO?
COME IN FITO.
ARE YOU THERE?
THIS CAN'T BE GOOD.
THE MAJOR IS GOING TO BE PISSED
HAVE TO PUT THE BIDDING ON HOLD.
Bad to the bone.
OGARRIO
PALOMUERTO.
THIS IS A PLACE OF FIERCE DUELS, AND GREAT DISAPPOINTMENTS.
I WONDER WHAT IT HAS IN STORE FOR US TODAY.

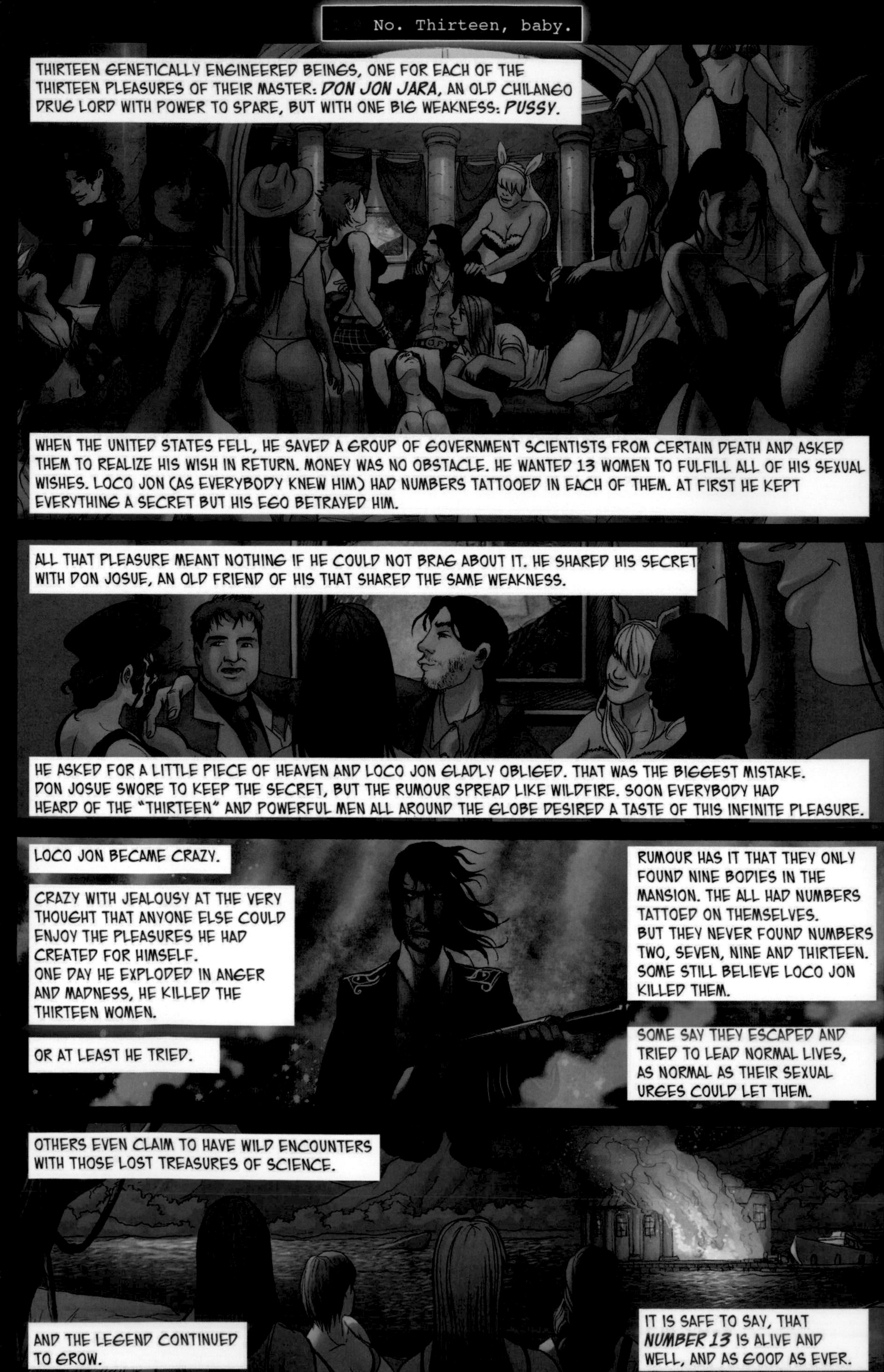
No. Thirteen, baby.
THIRTEEN GENETICALLY ENGINEERED BEINGS, ONE FOR EACH OF THE THIRTEEN PLEASURES OF THEIR MASTER: DON JON JARA, AN OLD CHILANGO DRUG LORD WITH POWER TO SPARE, BUT WITH ONE BIG WEAKNESS: PUSSY.
WHEN THE UNITED STATES FELL, HE SAVED A GROUP OF GOVERNMENT SCIENTISTS FROM CERTAIN DEATH AND ASKED THEM TO REALIZE HIS WISH IN RETURN. MONEY WAS NO OBSTACLE. HE WANTED 13 WOMEN TO FULFILL ALL OF HIS SEXUAL WISHES. LOCO JON (AS EVERYBODY KNEW HIM) HAD NUMBERS TATTOOED IN EACH OF THEM. AT FIRST HE KEPT EVERYTHING A SECRET BUT HIS EGO BETRAYED HIM.
ALL THAT PLEASURE MEANT NOTHING IF HE COULD NOT BRAG ABOUT IT. HE SHARED HIS SECRET WITH DON JOSUE, AN OLD FRIEND OF HIS THAT SHARED THE SAME WEAKNESS.
HE ASKED FOR A LITTLE PIECE OF HEAVEN AND LOCO JON GLADLY OBLIGED. THAT WAS THE BIGGEST MISTAKE. DON JOSUE SWORE TO KEEP THE SECRET, BUT THE RUMOUR SPREAD LIKE WILDFIRE. SOON EVERYBODY HAD HEARD OF THE "THIRTEEN" AND POWERFUL MEN ALL AROUND THE GLOBE DESIRED A TASTE OF THIS INFINITE PLEASURE.
LOCO JON BECAME CRAZY.
CRAZY WITH JEALOUSY AT THE VERY THOUGHT THAT ANYONE ELSE COULD ENJOY THE PLEASURES HE HAD CREATED FOR HIMSELF. ONE DAY HE EXPLODED IN ANGER AND MADNESS, HE KILLED THE THIRTEEN WOMEN.
OR AT LEAST HE TRIED.
RUMOUR HAS IT THAT THEY ONLY FOUND NINE BODIES IN THE MANSION. THE ALL HAD NUMBERS TATTOOED ON THEMSELVES. BUT THEY NEVER FOUND NUMBERS TWO, SEVEN, NINE AND THIRTEEN. SOME STILL BELIEVE LOCO JON KILLED THEM.
SOME SAY THEY ESCAPED AND TRIED TO LEAD NORMAL LIVES, AS NORMAL AS THEIR SEXUAL URGES COULD LET THEM.
OTHERS EVEN CLAIM TO HAVE WILD ENCOUNTERS WITH THOSE LOST TREASURES OF SCIENCE.
AND THE LEGEND CONTINUED TO GROW.
IT IS SAFE TO SAY, THAT NUMBER 13 IS ALIVE AND WELL, AND AS GOOD AS EVER.

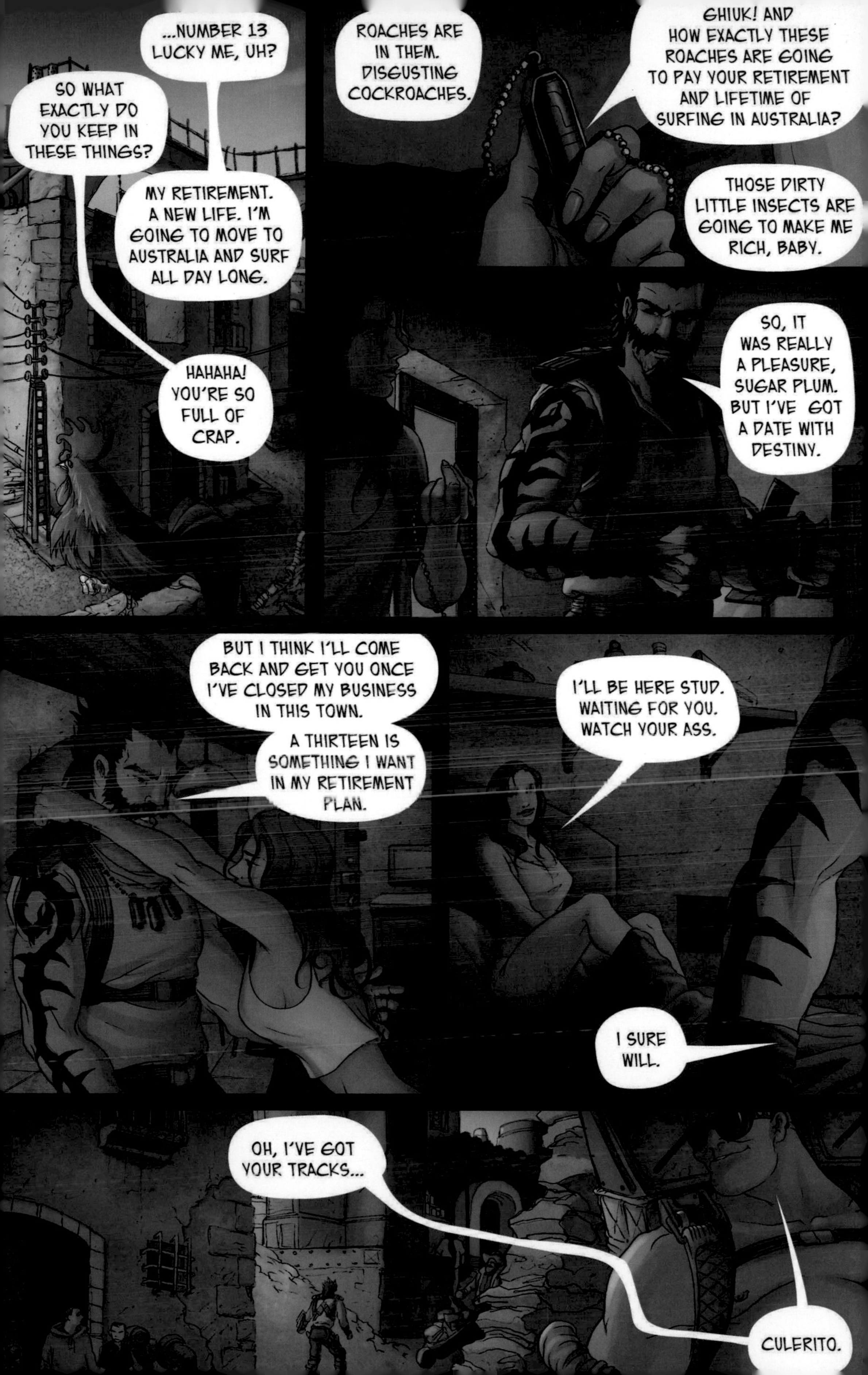
SO WHAT EXACTLY DO YOU KEEP IN THESE THINGS?
...NUMBER 13 LUCKY ME, UH?
MY RETIREMENT. A NEW LIFE. I'M GOING TO MOVE TO AUSTRALIA AND SURF ALL DAY LONG.
HAHAHA! YOU'RE SO FULL OF CRAP.
ROACHES ARE IN THEM. DISGUSTING COCKROACHES.
GHIUK! AND HOW EXACTLY THESE ROACHES ARE GOING TO PAY YOUR RETIREMENT AND LIFETIME OF SURFING IN AUSTRALIA?
THOSE DIRTY LITTLE INSECTS ARE GOING TO MAKE ME RICH, BABY.
SO, IT WAS REALLY A PLEASURE, SUGAR PLUM. BUT I'VE GOT A DATE WITH DESTINY.
BUT I THINK I'LL COME BACK AND GET YOU ONCE I'VE CLOSED MY BUSINESS IN THIS TOWN.
A THIRTEEN IS SOMETHING I WANT IN MY RETIREMENT PLAN.
I'LL BE HERE STUD. WAITING FOR YOU. WATCH YOUR ASS.
I SURE WILL.
OH, I'VE GOT YOUR TRACKS...
CULERITO.

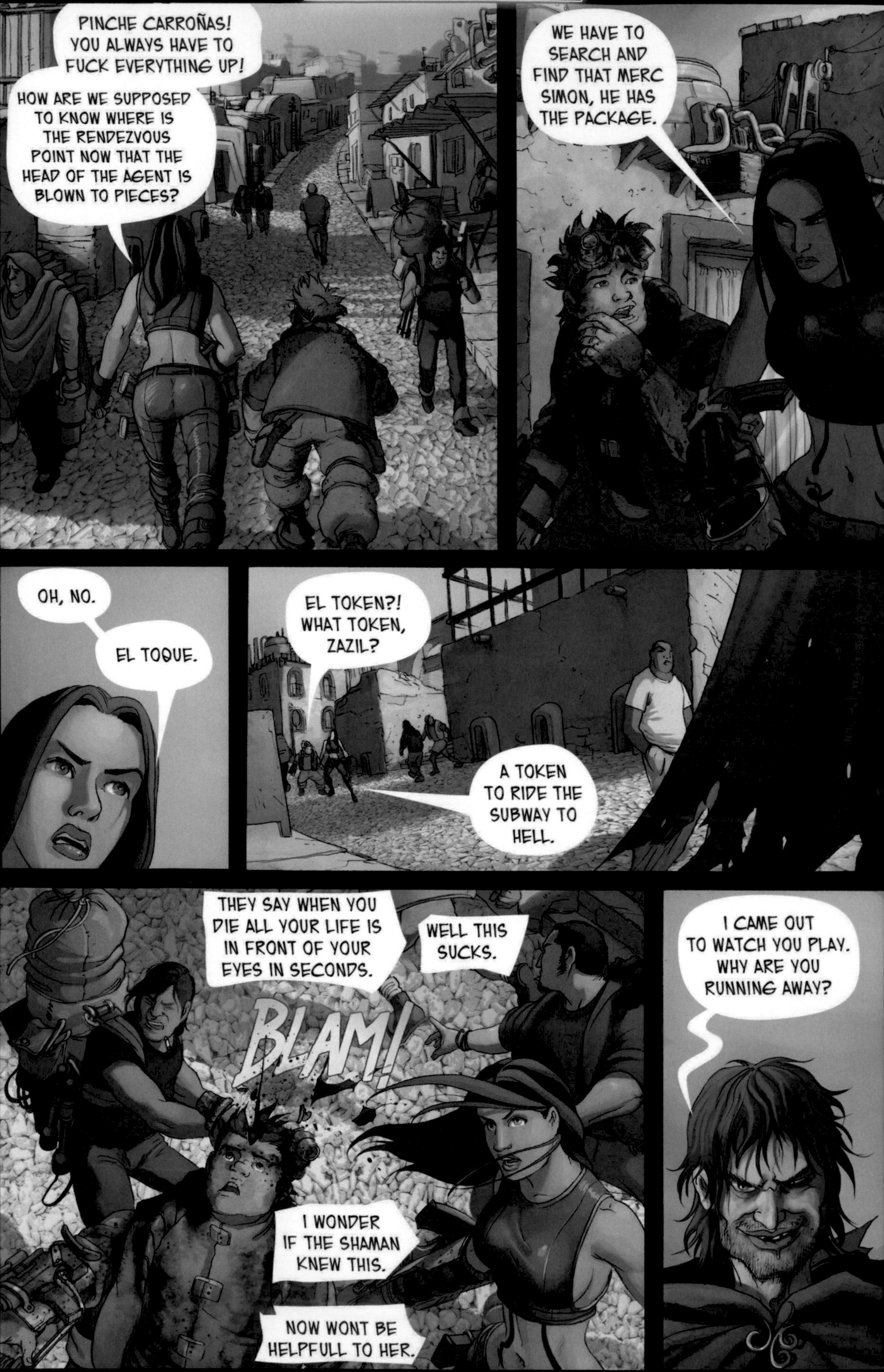
PINCHE CARROÑAS! YOU ALWAYS HAVE TO FUCK EVERYTHING UP!
HOW ARE WE SUPPOSED TO KNOW WHERE IS THE RENDEZVOUS POINT NOW THAT THE HEAD OF THE AGENT IS BLOWN TO PIECES?
WE HAVE TO SEARCH AND FIND THAT MERC SIMON, HE HAS THE PACKAGE.
OH, NO.
EL TOQUE.
EL TOKEN?! WHAT TOKEN, ZAZIL?
A TOKEN TO RIDE THE SUBWAY TO HELL.
THEY SAY WHEN YOU DIE ALL YOUR LIFE IS IN FRONT OF YOUR EYES IN SECONDS.
WELL THIS SUCKS.
BLAM!
I WONDER IF THE SHAMAN KNEW THIS.
NOW WONT BE HELPFULL TO HER.
I CAME OUT TO WATCH YOU PLAY. WHY ARE YOU RUNNING AWAY?

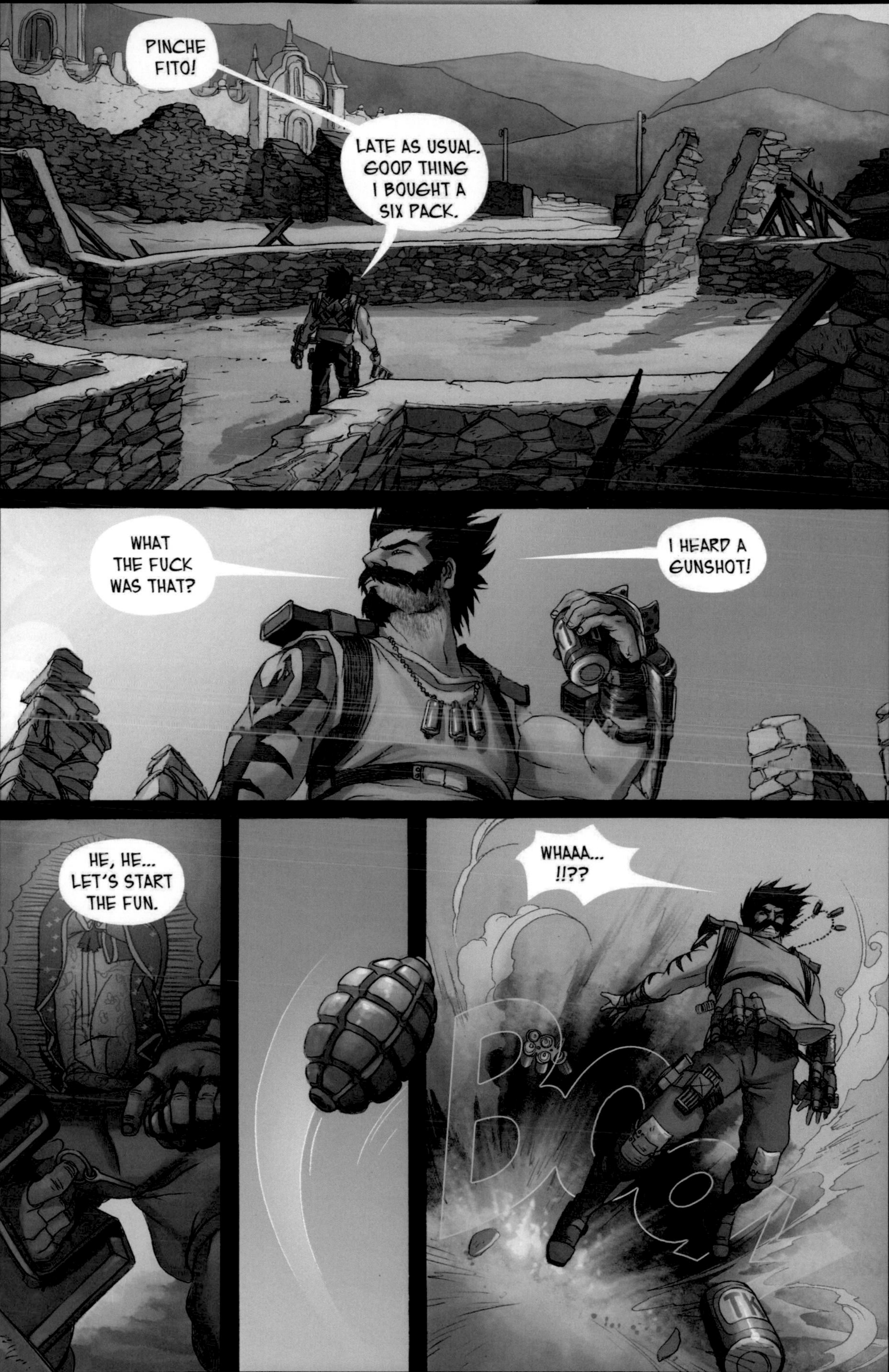
PINCHE FITO!
LATE AS USUAL. GOOD THING I BOUGHT A SIX PACK.
WHAT THE FUCK WAS THAT?
I HEARD A GUNSHOT!
HE, HE... LET'S START THE FUN.
WHAAA... !!??

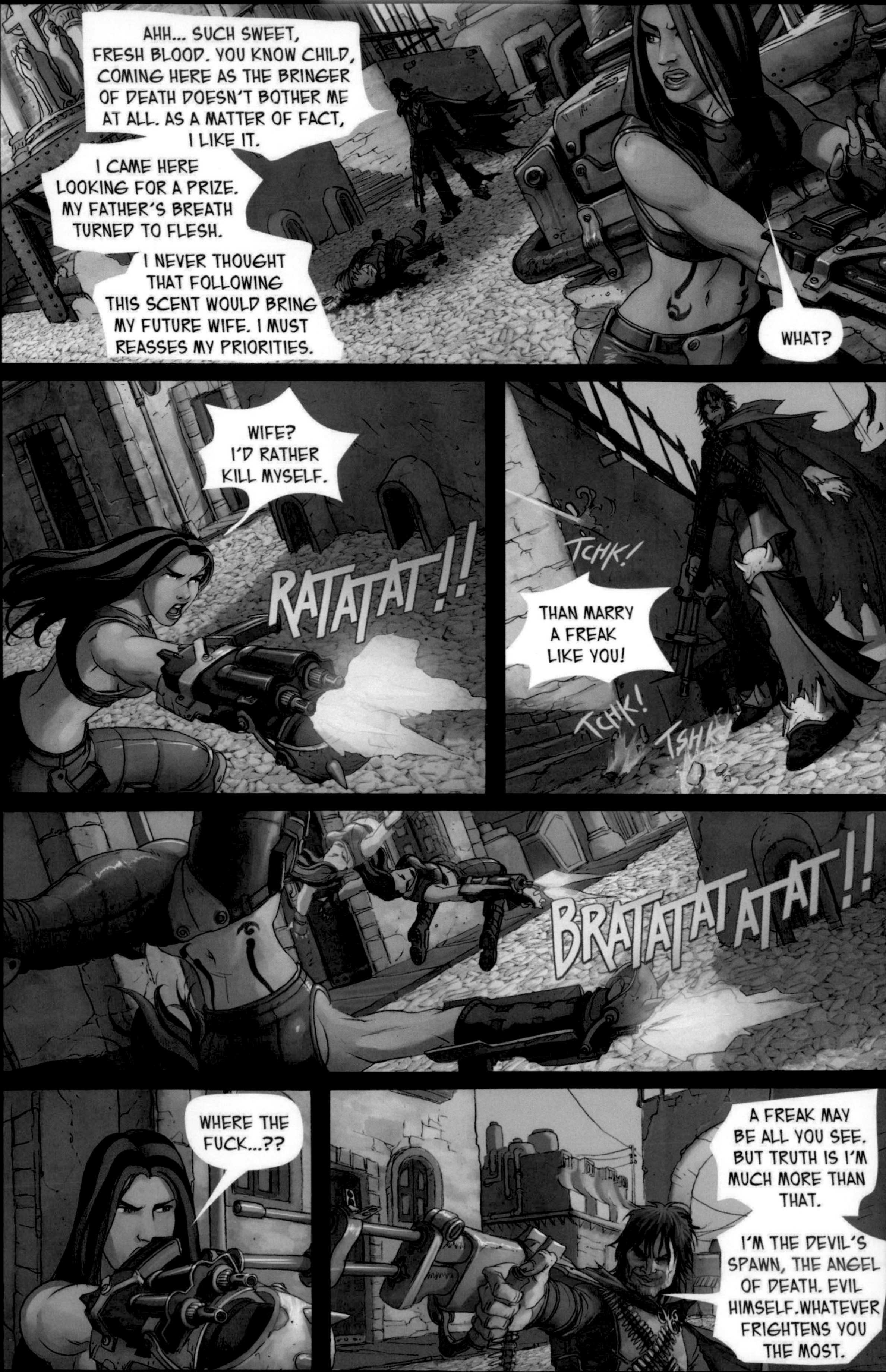
AHH... SUCH SWEET, FRESH BLOOD. YOU KNOW CHILD, COMING HERE AS THE BRINGER OF DEATH DOESN'T BOTHER ME AT ALL. AS A MATTER OF FACT, I LIKE IT.
I CAME HERE LOOKING FOR A PRIZE. MY FATHER'S BREATH TURNED TO FLESH.
I NEVER THOUGHT THAT FOLLOWING THIS SCENT WOULD BRING MY FUTURE WIFE. I MUST REASSES MY PRIORITIES.
WHAT?
WIFE? I'D RATHER KILL MYSELF.
RATATAT!!
TCHK!
THAN MARRY A FREAK LIKE YOU!
TCHK!
TSHK!
BRATATATATAT!!
WHERE THE FUCK...??
A FREAK MAY BE ALL YOU SEE. BUT TRUTH IS I'M MUCH MORE THAN THAT.
I'M THE DEVIL'S SPAWN, THE ANGEL OF DEATH. EVIL HIMSELF.WHATEVER FRIGHTENS YOU THE MOST.

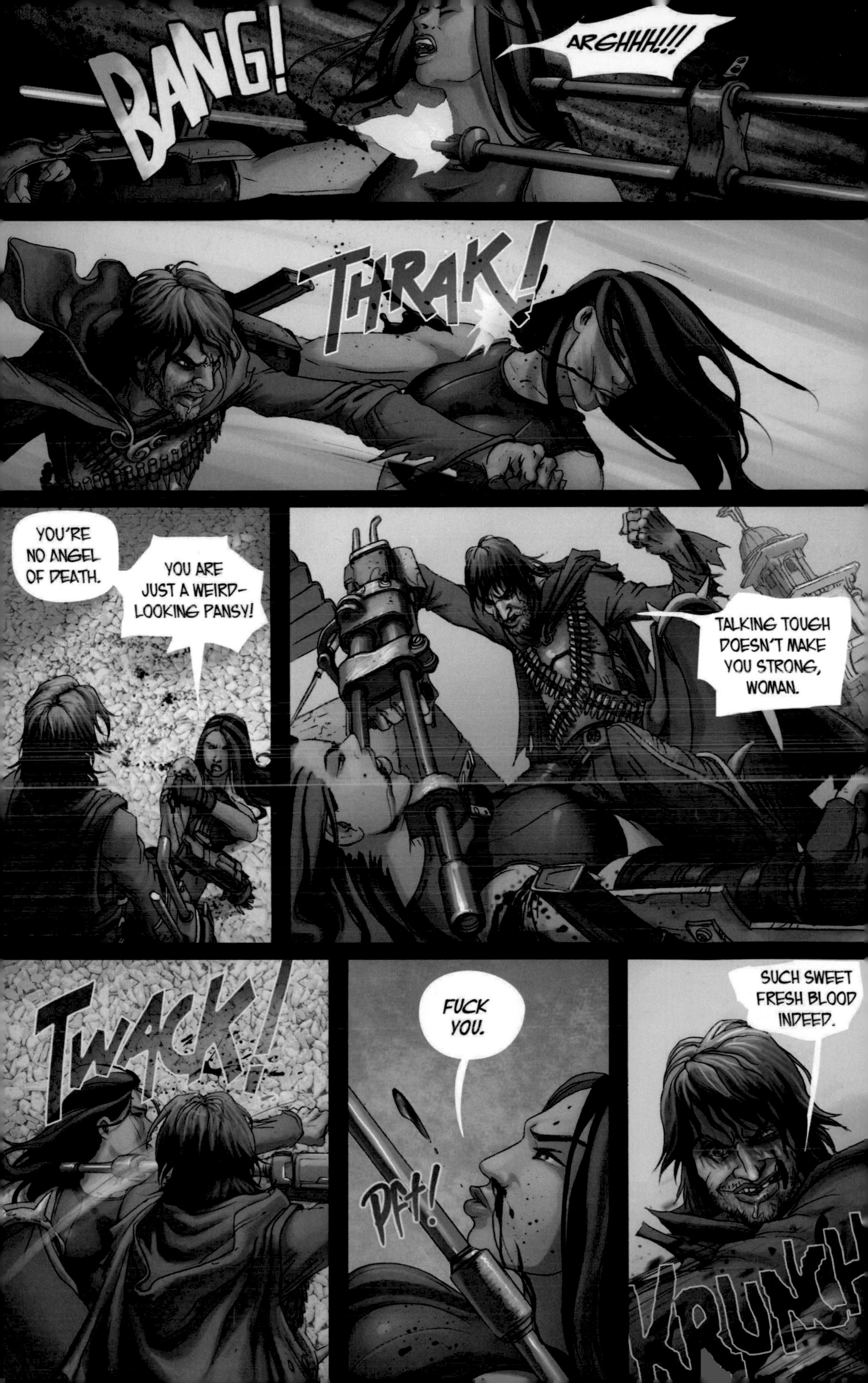
BANG!
ARGHHH!!!
THRAK!
YOU'RE NO ANGEL OF DEATH.
YOU ARE JUST A WEIRD-LOOKING PANSY!
TALKING TOUGH DOESN'T MAKE YOU STRONG, WOMAN.
TWACK!
FUCK YOU.
PFT!
SUCH SWEET FRESH BLOOD INDEED.
KRUNK!

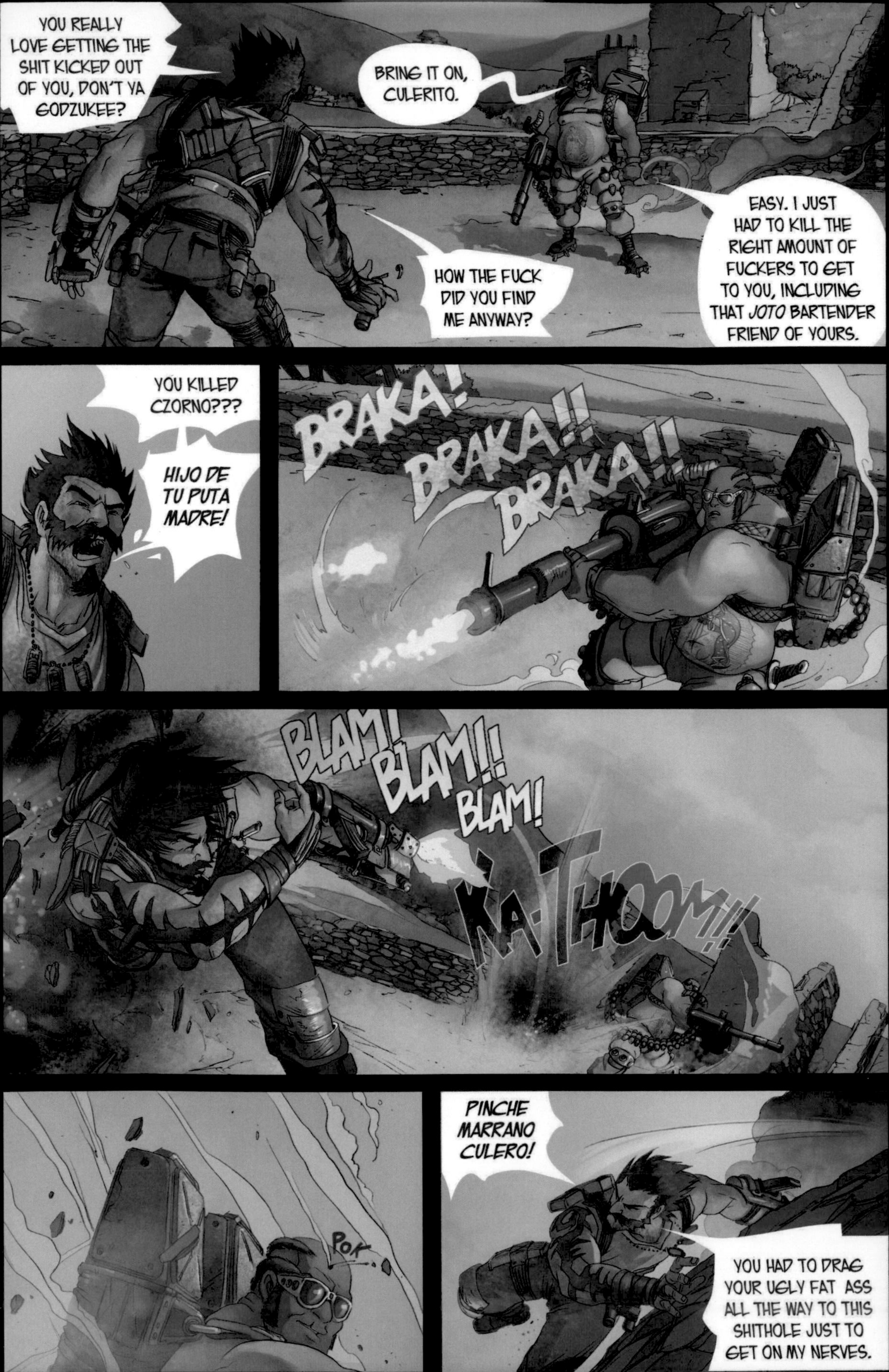

YOU REALLY LOVE GETTING THE SHIT KICKED OUT OF YOU, DON'T YA GODZUKEE?
BRING IT ON, CULERITO.
HOW THE FUCK DID YOU FIND ME ANYWAY?
EASY. I JUST HAD TO KILL THE RIGHT AMOUNT OF FUCKERS TO GET TO YOU, INCLUDING THAT *JOTO* BARTENDER FRIEND OF YOURS.
YOU KILLED CZORNO???
HIJO DE TU PUTA MADRE!
BRAKA! BRAKA!! BRAKA!!
BLAM! BLAM!! BLAM!
KA-THOOM!!!
POK
PINCHE MARRANO CULERO!
YOU HAD TO DRAG YOUR UGLY FAT ASS ALL THE WAY TO THIS SHITHOLE JUST TO GET ON MY NERVES.

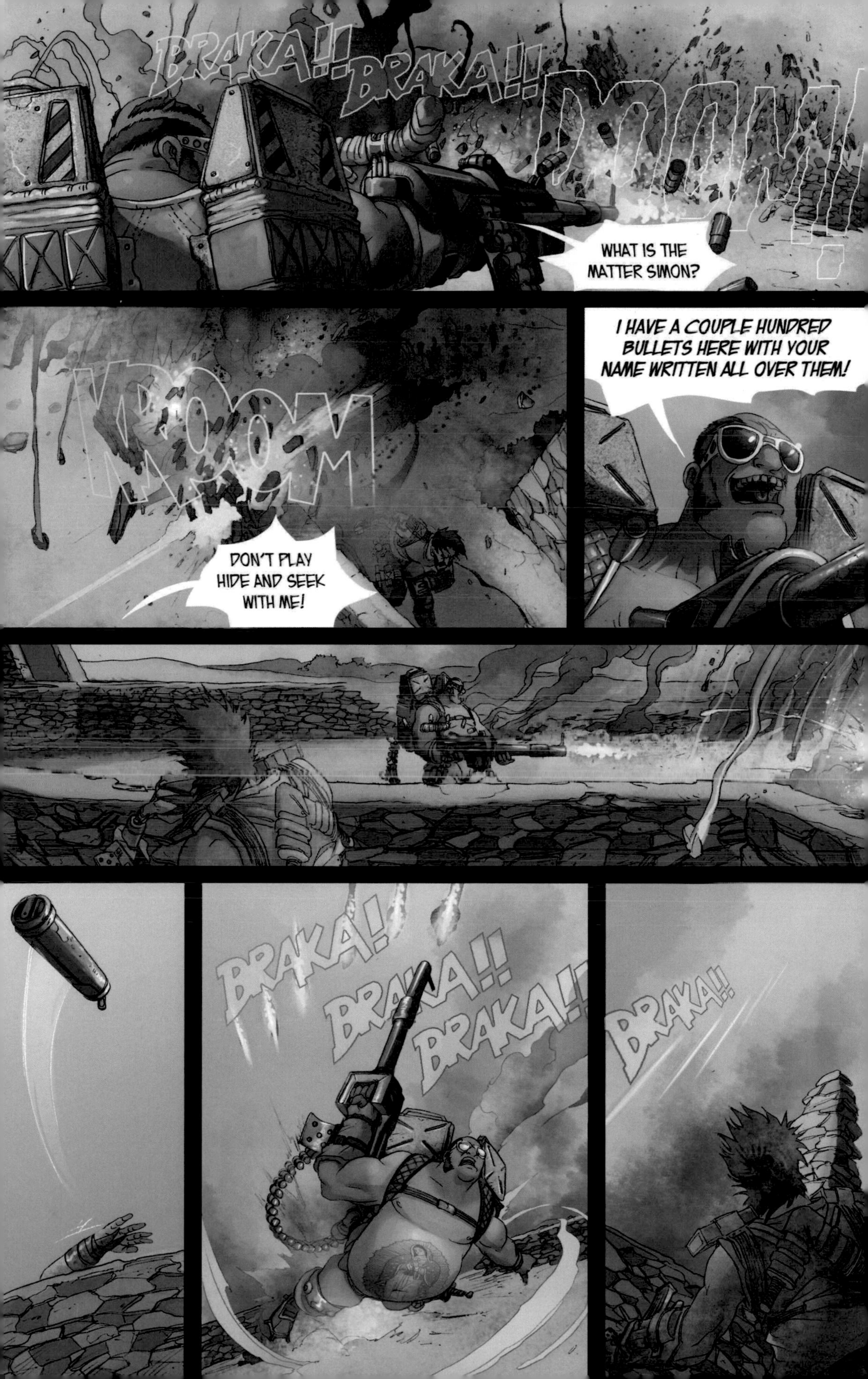
BRAKA!!
BRAKA!!
DOOM!!
WHAT IS THE MATTER SIMON?
KROOM
DON'T PLAY HIDE AND SEEK WITH ME!
I HAVE A COUPLE HUNDRED BULLETS HERE WITH YOUR NAME WRITTEN ALL OVER THEM!
BRAKA!!
BRAKA!!
BRAKA!!
BRAKA!!

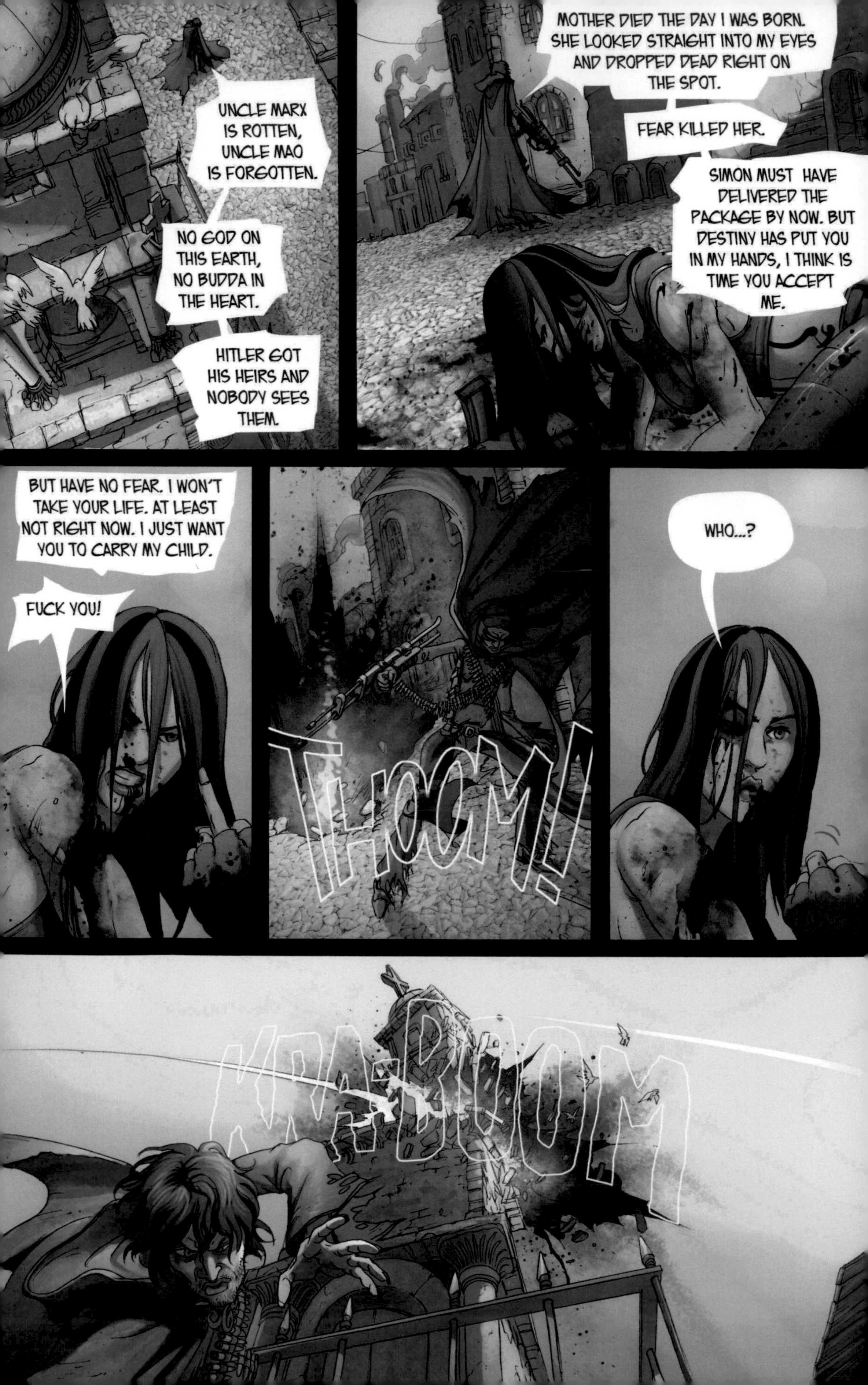

UNCLE MARX IS ROTTEN, UNCLE MAO IS FORGOTTEN.
NO GOD ON THIS EARTH, NO BUDDA IN THE HEART.
HITLER GOT HIS HEIRS AND NOBODY SEES THEM.
MOTHER DIED THE DAY I WAS BORN. SHE LOOKED STRAIGHT INTO MY EYES AND DROPPED DEAD RIGHT ON THE SPOT.
FEAR KILLED HER.
SIMON MUST HAVE DELIVERED THE PACKAGE BY NOW. BUT DESTINY HAS PUT YOU IN MY HANDS, I THINK IS TIME YOU ACCEPT ME.
BUT HAVE NO FEAR. I WON'T TAKE YOUR LIFE. AT LEAST NOT RIGHT NOW. I JUST WANT YOU TO CARRY MY CHILD.
FUCK YOU!
THOOM!
WHO...?
KRA-BOOM

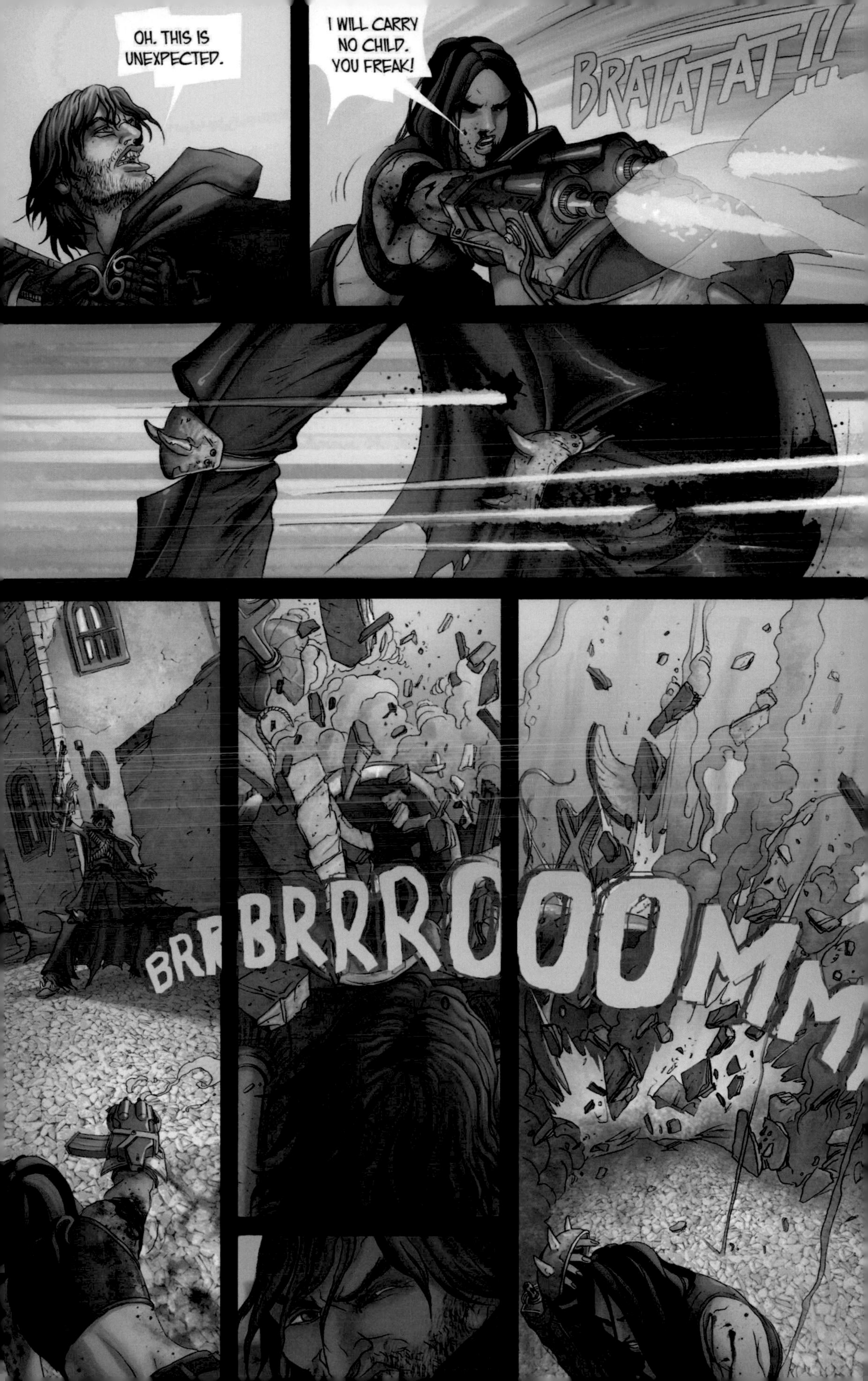
OH. THIS IS UNEXPECTED.
I WILL CARRY NO CHILD. YOU FREAK!
BRATATAT!!
BRRBRRRROOOMM

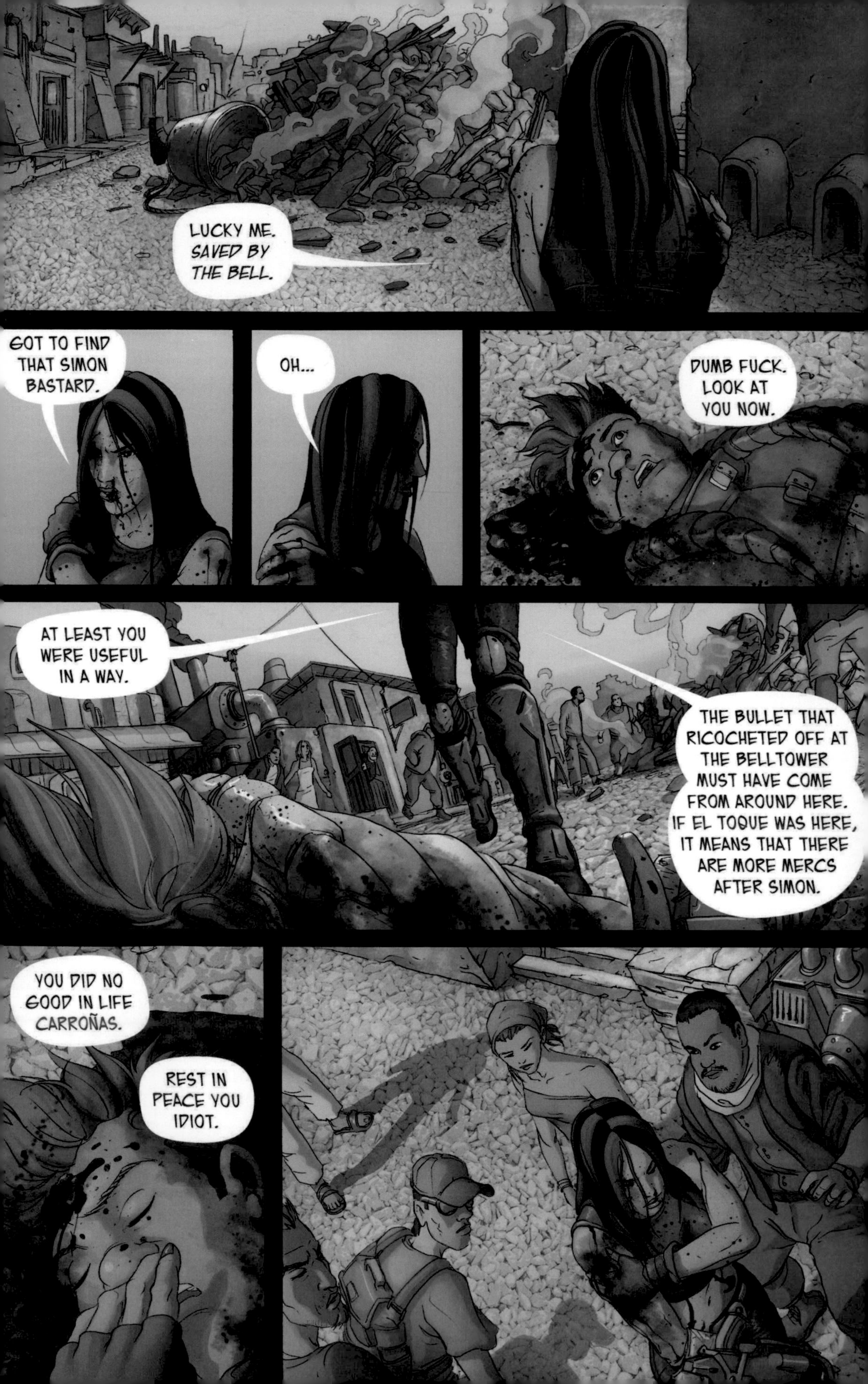
LUCKY ME. SAVED BY THE BELL.
GOT TO FIND THAT SIMON BASTARD.
OH...
DUMB FUCK. LOOK AT YOU NOW.
AT LEAST YOU WERE USEFUL IN A WAY.
THE BULLET THAT RICOCHETED OFF AT THE BELLTOWER MUST HAVE COME FROM AROUND HERE. IF EL TOQUE WAS HERE, IT MEANS THAT THERE ARE MORE MERCS AFTER SIMON.
YOU DID NO GOOD IN LIFE CARROÑAS.
REST IN PEACE YOU IDIOT.

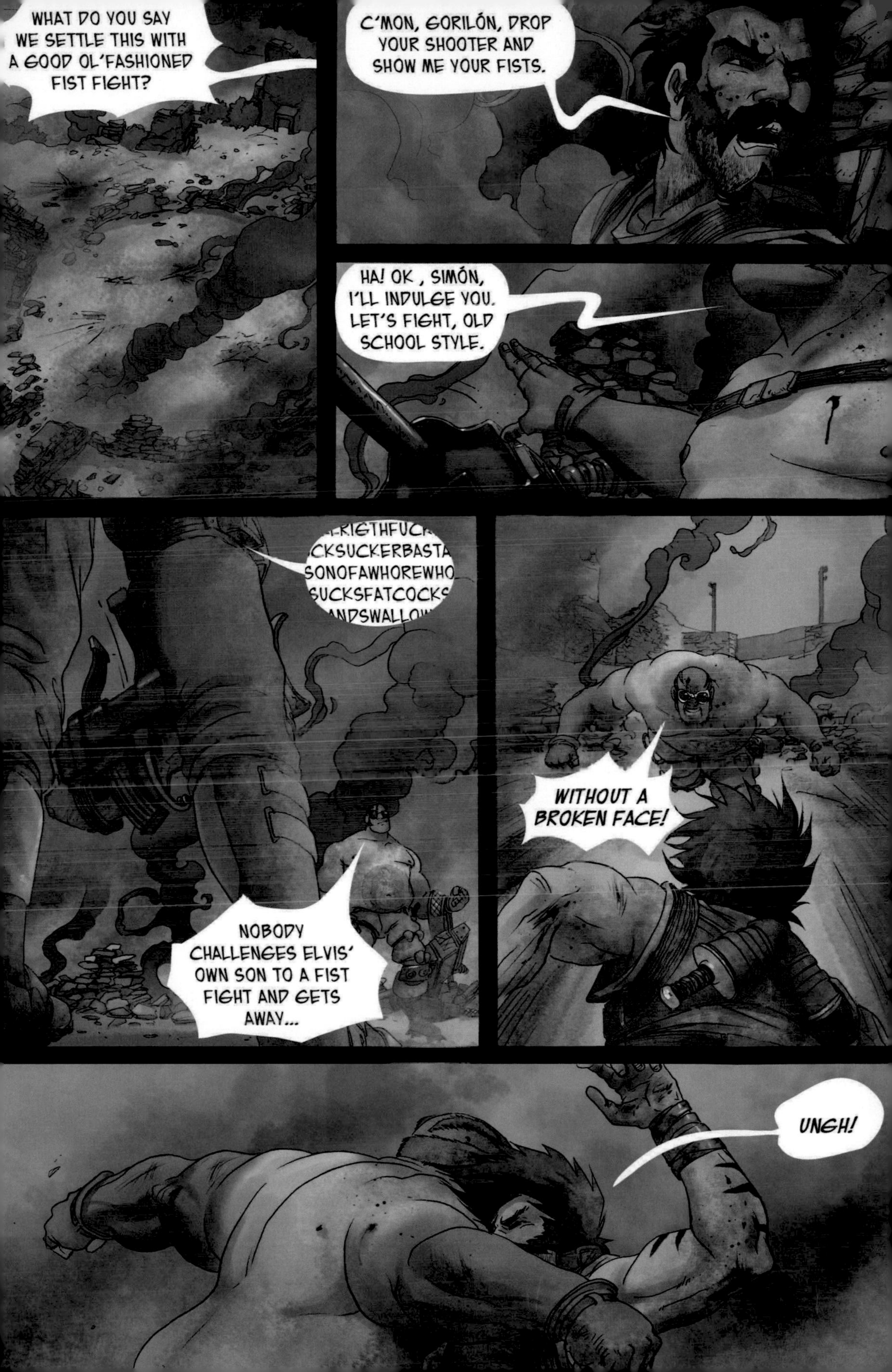
WHAT DO YOU SAY WE SETTLE THIS WITH A GOOD OL'FASHIONED FIST FIGHT?
C'MON, GORILÓN, DROP YOUR SHOOTER AND SHOW ME YOUR FISTS.
HA! OK , SIMÓN, I'LL INDULGE YOU. LET'S FIGHT, OLD SCHOOL STYLE.
RIGTHFUCK
CKSUCKERBASTA
SONOFAWHOREWHO
SUCKSFATCOCKS
ANDSWALLOW
NOBODY CHALLENGES ELVIS' OWN SON TO A FIST FIGHT AND GETS AWAY...
WITHOUT A BROKEN FACE!
UNGH!

Falling to pieces.

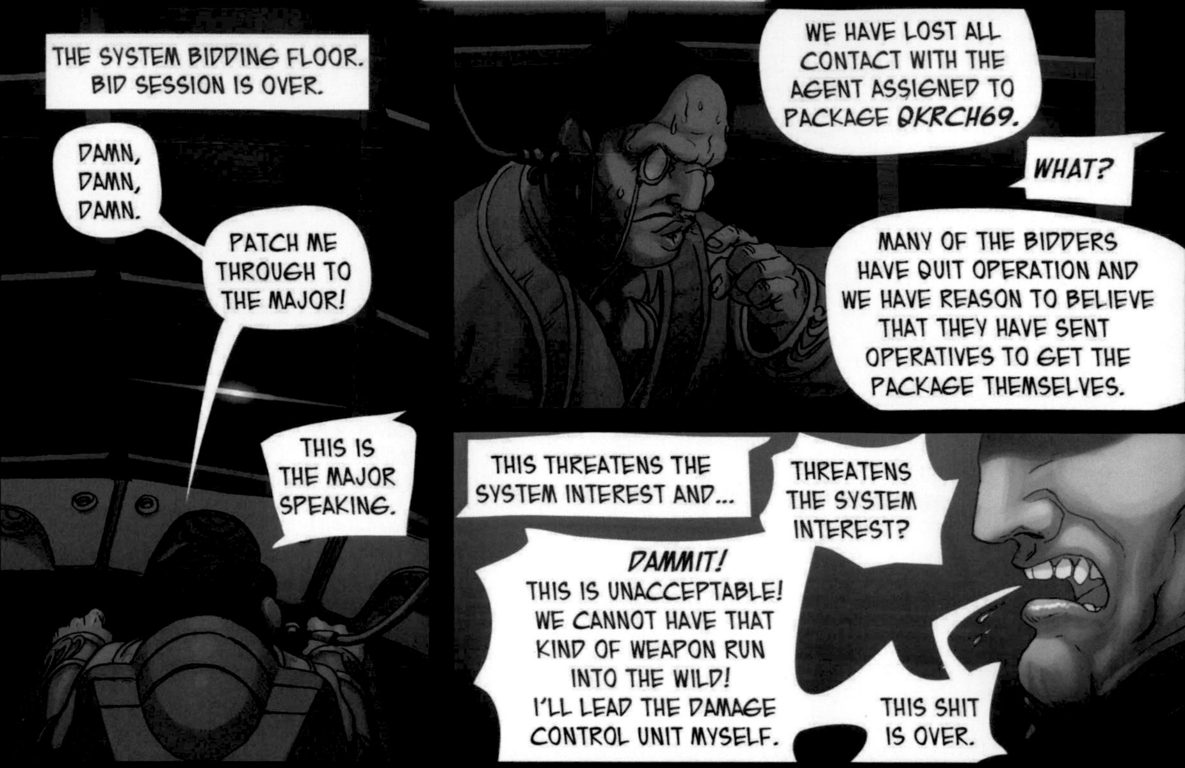
THE SYSTEM BIDDING FLOOR. BID SESSION IS OVER.
DAMN, DAMN, DAMN.
PATCH ME THROUGH TO THE MAJOR!
WE HAVE LOST ALL CONTACT WITH THE AGENT ASSIGNED TO PACKAGE QKRCH69.
WHAT?
MANY OF THE BIDDERS HAVE QUIT OPERATION AND WE HAVE REASON TO BELIEVE THAT THEY HAVE SENT OPERATIVES TO GET THE PACKAGE THEMSELVES.
THIS IS THE MAJOR SPEAKING.
THIS THREATENS THE SYSTEM INTEREST AND...
THREATENS THE SYSTEM INTEREST?
DAMMIT! THIS IS UNACCEPTABLE! WE CANNOT HAVE THAT KIND OF WEAPON RUN INTO THE WILD! I'LL LEAD THE DAMAGE CONTROL UNIT MYSELF.
THIS SHIT IS OVER.

Broken face.

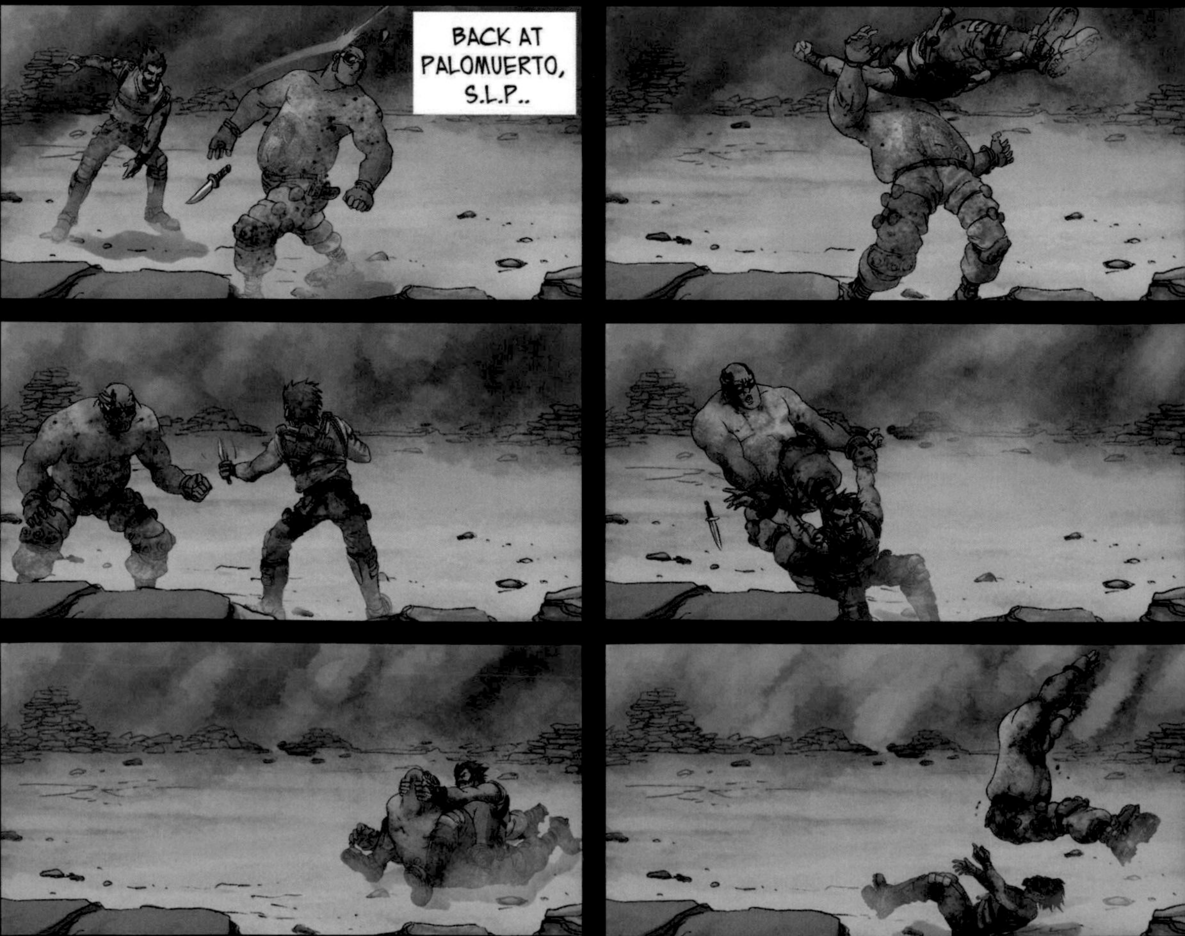
BACK AT PALOMUERTO, S.L.P..

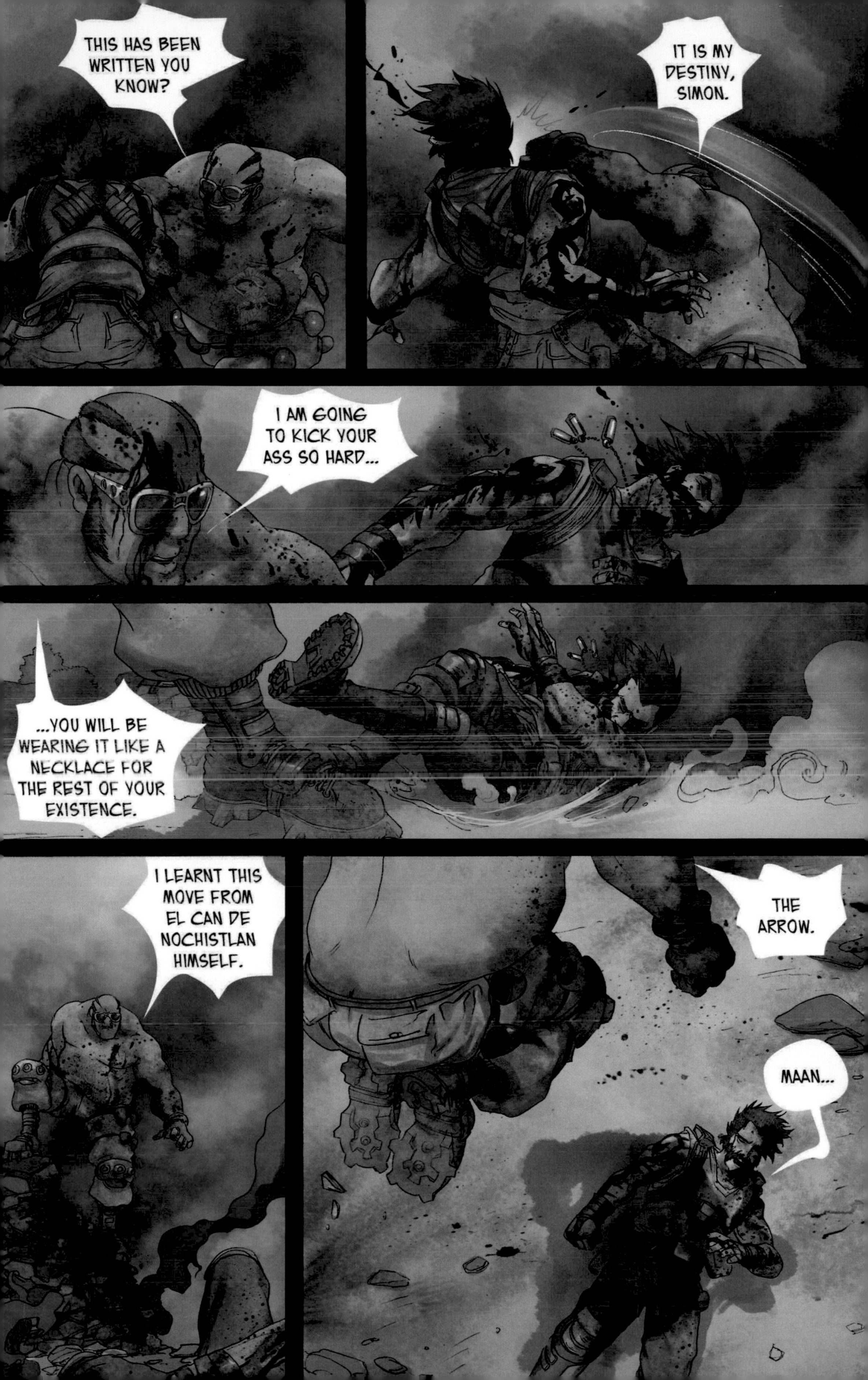
THIS HAS BEEN WRITTEN YOU KNOW?
IT IS MY DESTINY, SIMON.
I AM GOING TO KICK YOUR ASS SO HARD...
...YOU WILL BE WEARING IT LIKE A NECKLACE FOR THE REST OF YOUR EXISTENCE.
I LEARNT THIS MOVE FROM EL CAN DE NOCHISTLAN HIMSELF.
THE ARROW.
MAAN...

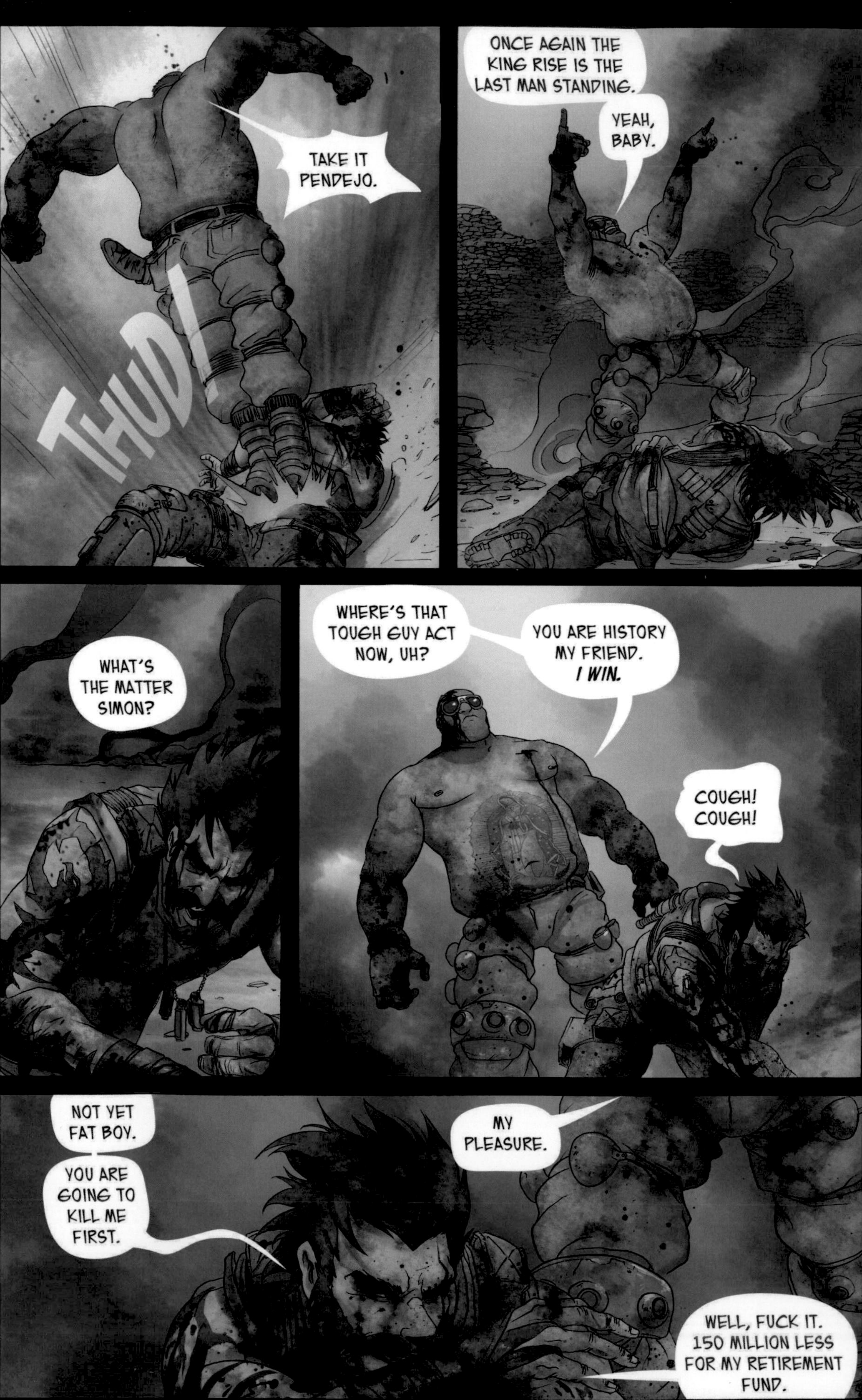
TAKE IT PENDEJO.
THUD!
ONCE AGAIN THE KING RISE IS THE LAST MAN STANDING.
YEAH, BABY.
WHAT'S THE MATTER SIMON?
WHERE'S THAT TOUGH GUY ACT NOW, UH?
YOU ARE HISTORY MY FRIEND. *I WIN.*
COUGH! COUGH!
NOT YET FAT BOY.
YOU ARE GOING TO KILL ME FIRST.
MY PLEASURE.
WELL, FUCK IT. 150 MILLION LESS FOR MY RETIREMENT FUND.

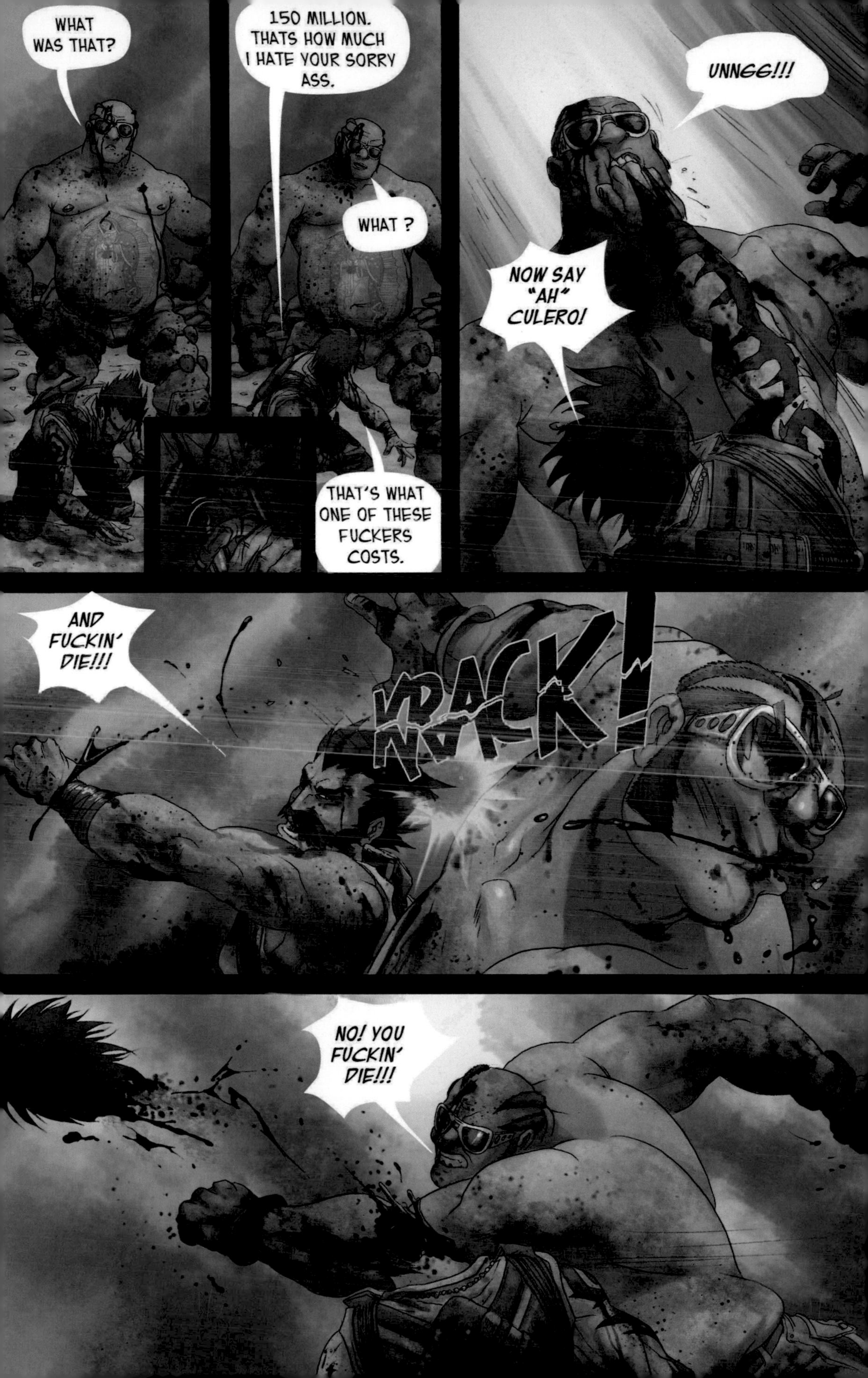
WHAT WAS THAT?
150 MILLION. THATS HOW MUCH I HATE YOUR SORRY ASS.
WHAT ?
THAT'S WHAT ONE OF THESE FUCKERS COSTS.
UNNGG!!!
NOW SAY "AH" CULERO!
AND FUCKIN' DIE!!!
KRACK!
NO! YOU FUCKIN' DIE!!!

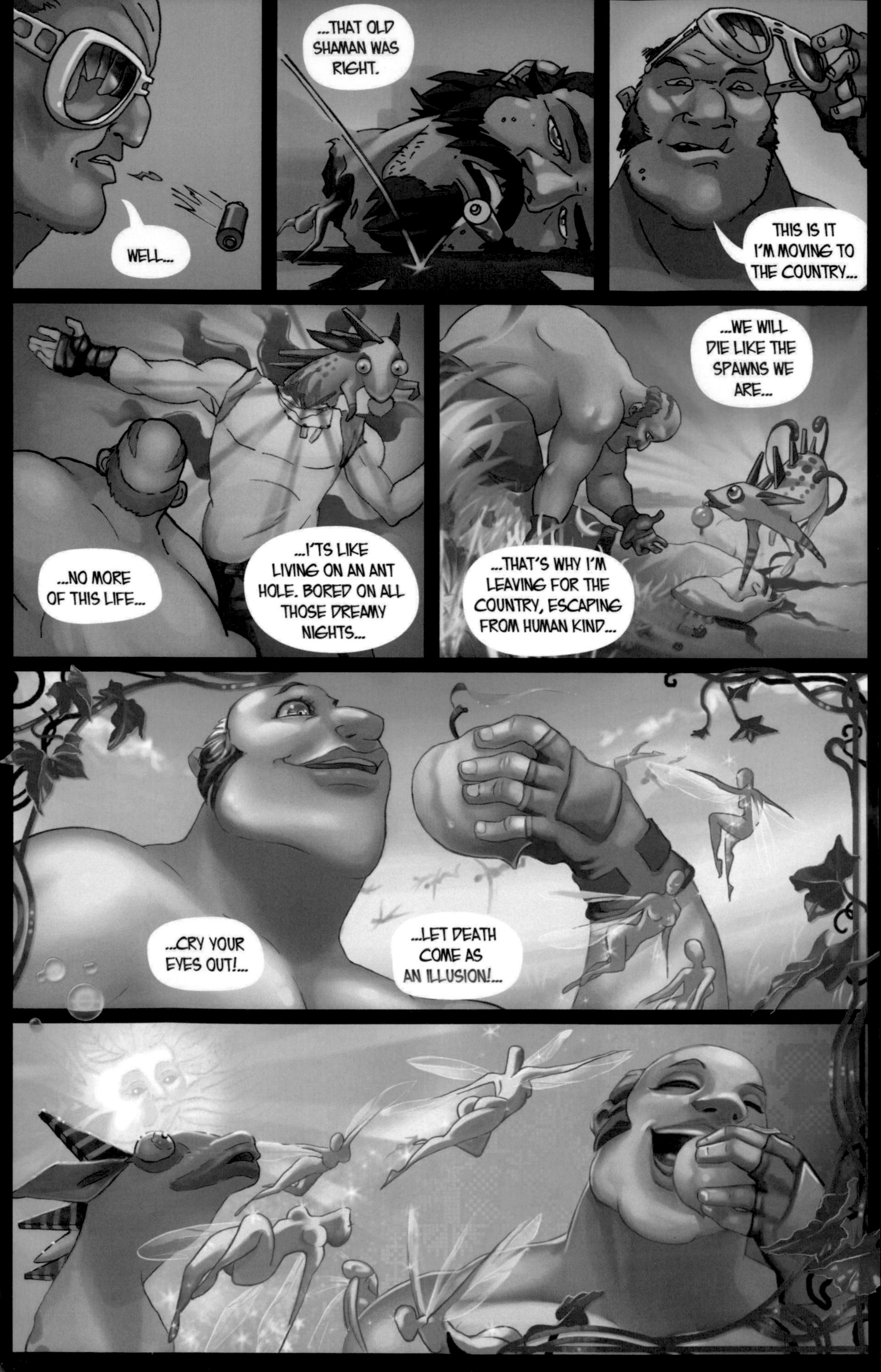
WELL...
...THAT OLD SHAMAN WAS RIGHT.
THIS IS IT I'M MOVING TO THE COUNTRY...
...NO MORE OF THIS LIFE...
...IT'S LIKE LIVING ON AN ANT HOLE. BORED ON ALL THOSE DREAMY NIGHTS...
...WE WILL DIE LIKE THE SPAWNS WE ARE...
...THAT'S WHY I'M LEAVING FOR THE COUNTRY, ESCAPING FROM HUMAN KIND...
...CRY YOUR EYES OUT!...
...LET DEATH COME AS AN ILLUSION!...

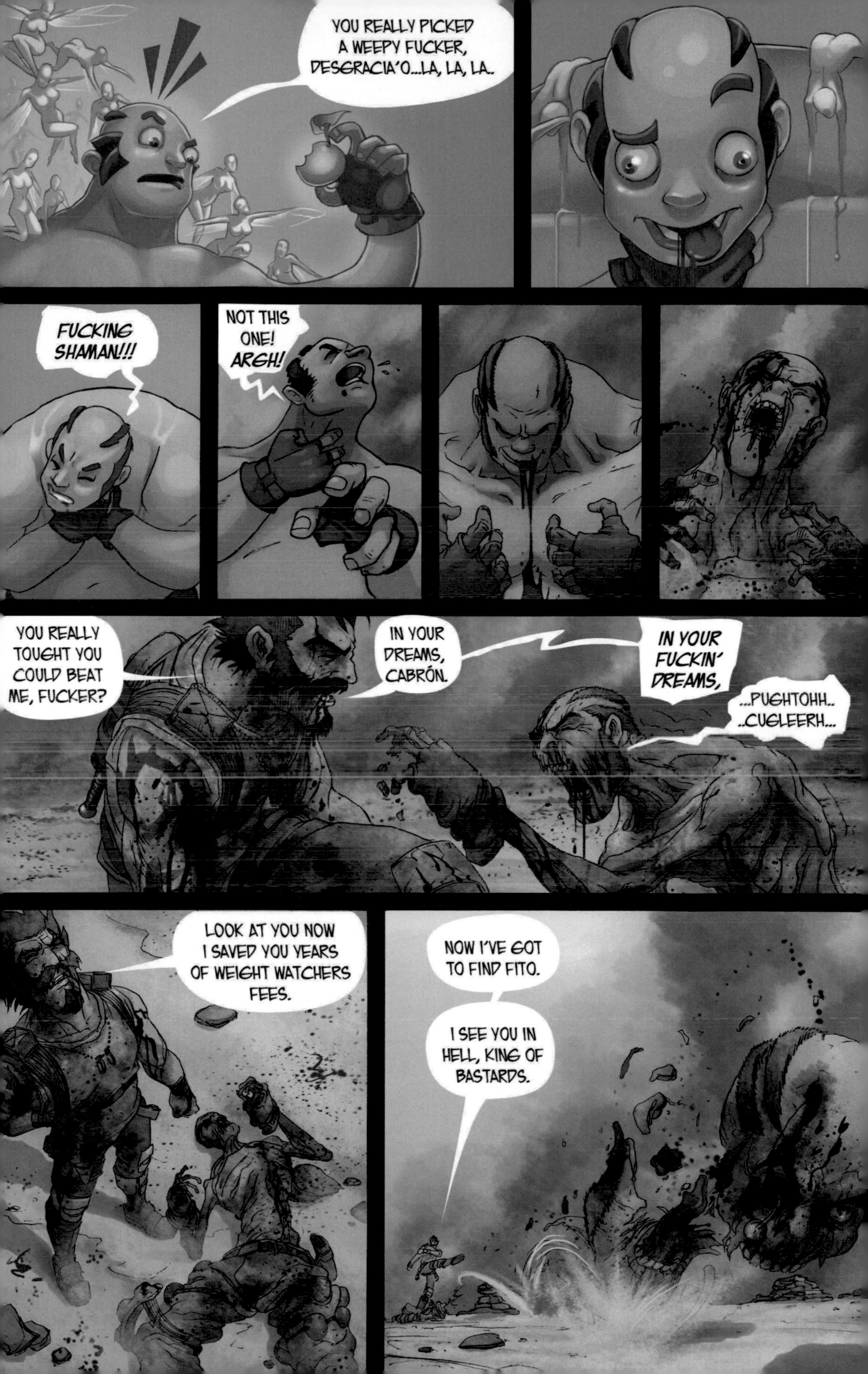
YOU REALLY PICKED A WEEPY FUCKER, DESGRACIA'O...LA, LA, LA..
FUCKING SHAMAN!!!
NOT THIS ONE! ARGH!
YOU REALLY TOUGHT YOU COULD BEAT ME, FUCKER?
IN YOUR DREAMS, CABRÓN.
IN YOUR FUCKIN' DREAMS,
...PUGHTOHH.. ..CUGLEERH...
LOOK AT YOU NOW I SAVED YOU YEARS OF WEIGHT WATCHERS FEES.
NOW I'VE GOT TO FIND FITO.
I SEE YOU IN HELL, KING OF BASTARDS.

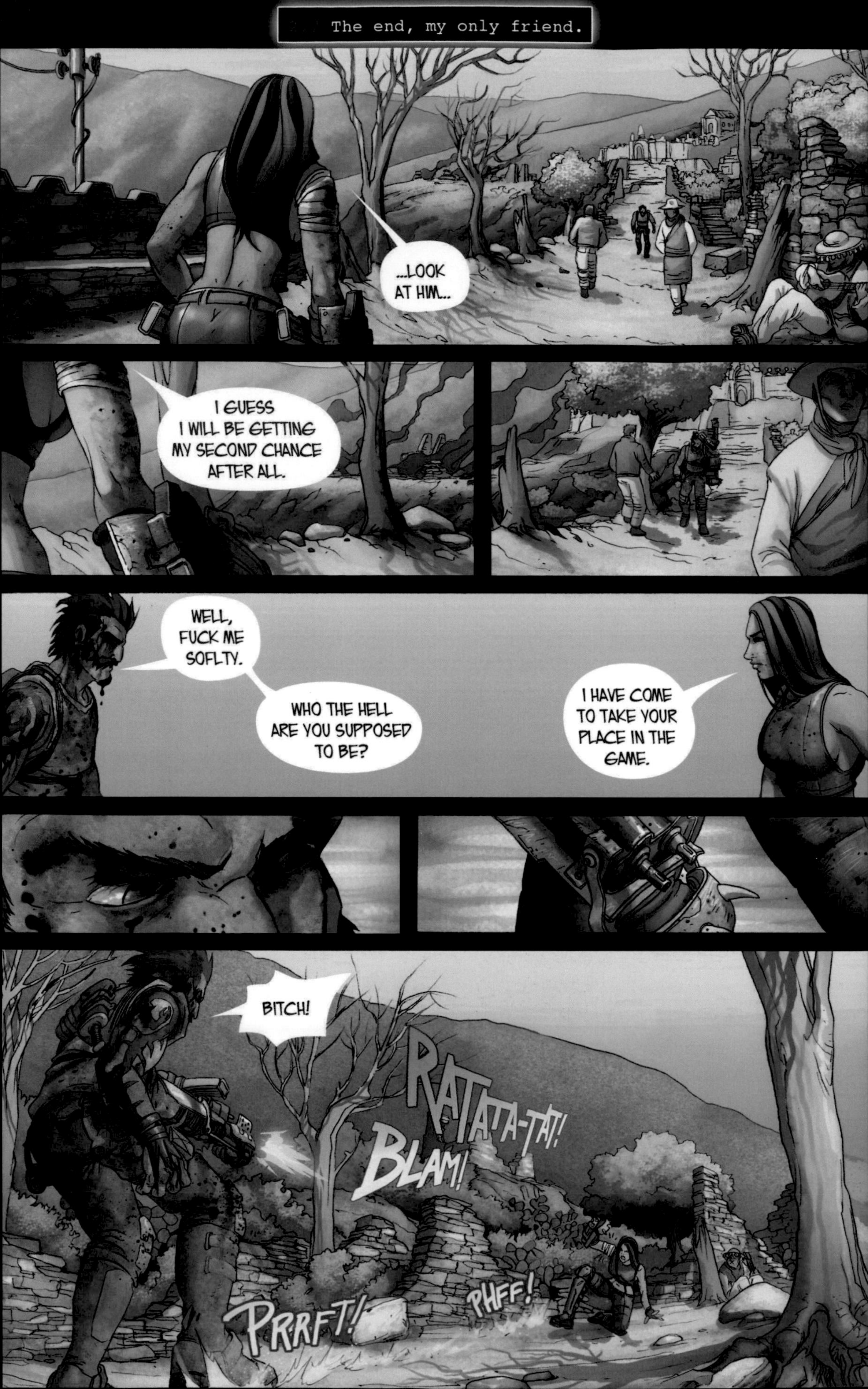

The end, my only friend.
...LOOK AT HIM...
I GUESS I WILL BE GETTING MY SECOND CHANCE AFTER ALL.
WELL, FUCK ME SOFLTY.
WHO THE HELL ARE YOU SUPPOSED TO BE?
I HAVE COME TO TAKE YOUR PLACE IN THE GAME.
BITCH!
RATATATA-TAT!
BLAM!
PRRFT!
PHFF!

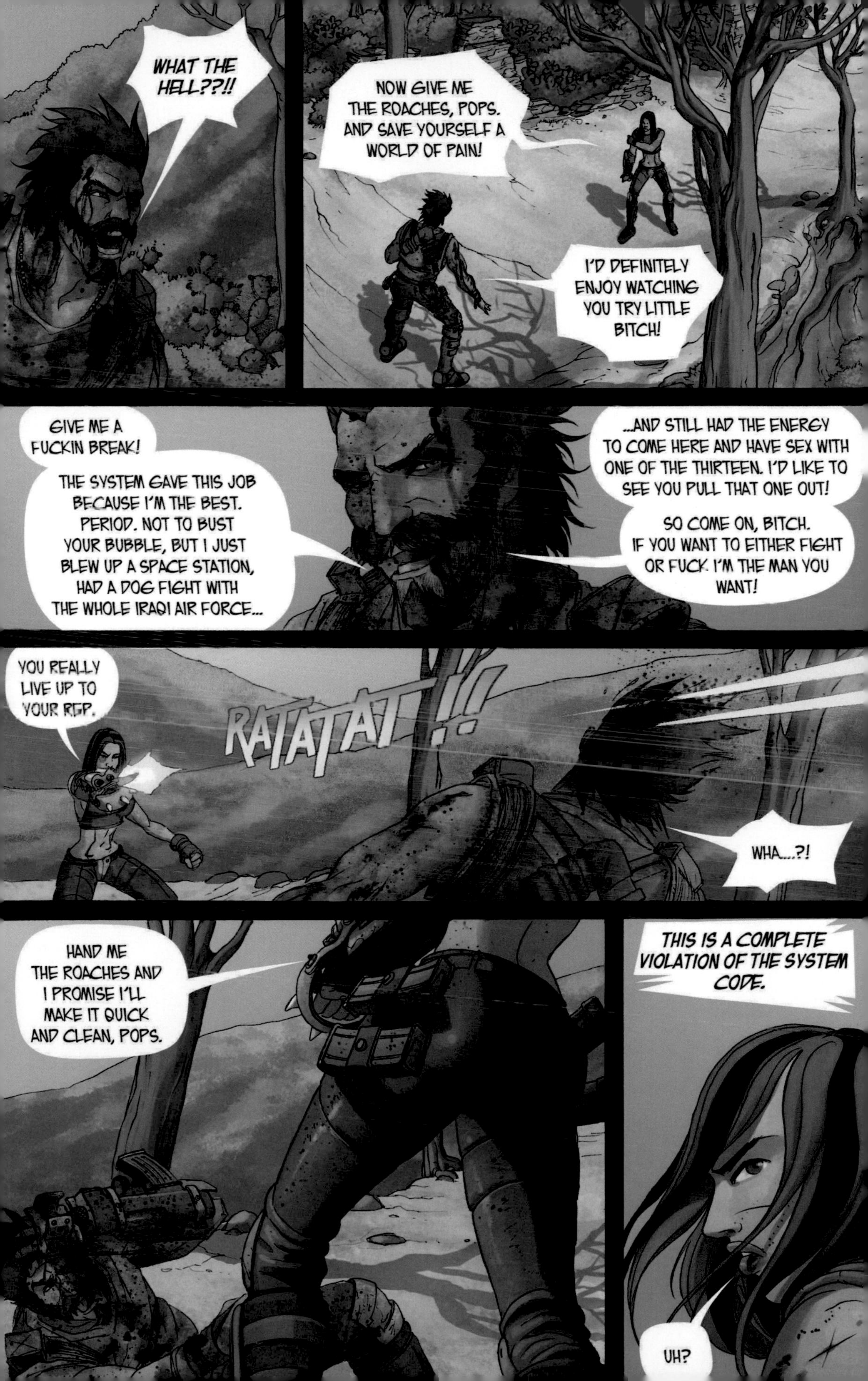
WHAT THE HELL??!!
NOW GIVE ME THE ROACHES, POPS. AND SAVE YOURSELF A WORLD OF PAIN!
I'D DEFINITELY ENJOY WATCHING YOU TRY LITTLE BITCH!
GIVE ME A FUCKIN BREAK!
THE SYSTEM GAVE THIS JOB BECAUSE I'M THE BEST. PERIOD. NOT TO BUST YOUR BUBBLE, BUT I JUST BLEW UP A SPACE STATION, HAD A DOG FIGHT WITH THE WHOLE IRAQI AIR FORCE...
...AND STILL HAD THE ENERGY TO COME HERE AND HAVE SEX WITH ONE OF THE THIRTEEN. I'D LIKE TO SEE YOU PULL THAT ONE OUT!
SO COME ON, BITCH. IF YOU WANT TO EITHER FIGHT OR FUCK. I'M THE MAN YOU WANT!
YOU REALLY LIVE UP TO YOUR REP.
RATATAT!!!
WHA...?!
HAND ME THE ROACHES AND I PROMISE I'LL MAKE IT QUICK AND CLEAN, POPS.
THIS IS A COMPLETE VIOLATION OF THE SYSTEM CODE.
UH?

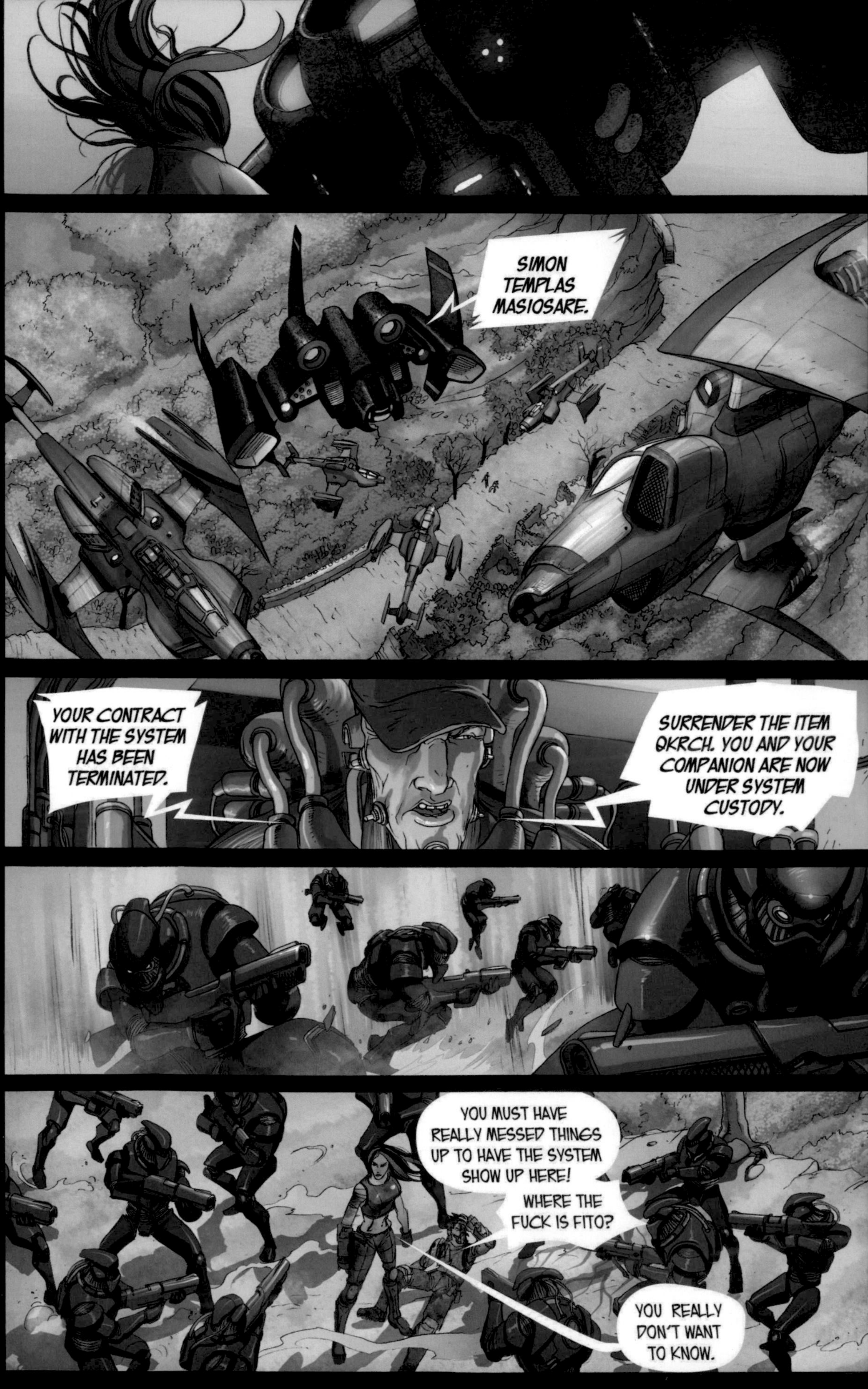
SIMON TEMPLAS MASIOSARE.
YOUR CONTRACT WITH THE SYSTEM HAS BEEN TERMINATED.
SURRENDER THE ITEM QKRCH. YOU AND YOUR COMPANION ARE NOW UNDER SYSTEM CUSTODY.
YOU MUST HAVE REALLY MESSED THINGS UP TO HAVE THE SYSTEM SHOW UP HERE!
WHERE THE FUCK IS FITO?
YOU REALLY DON'T WANT TO KNOW.

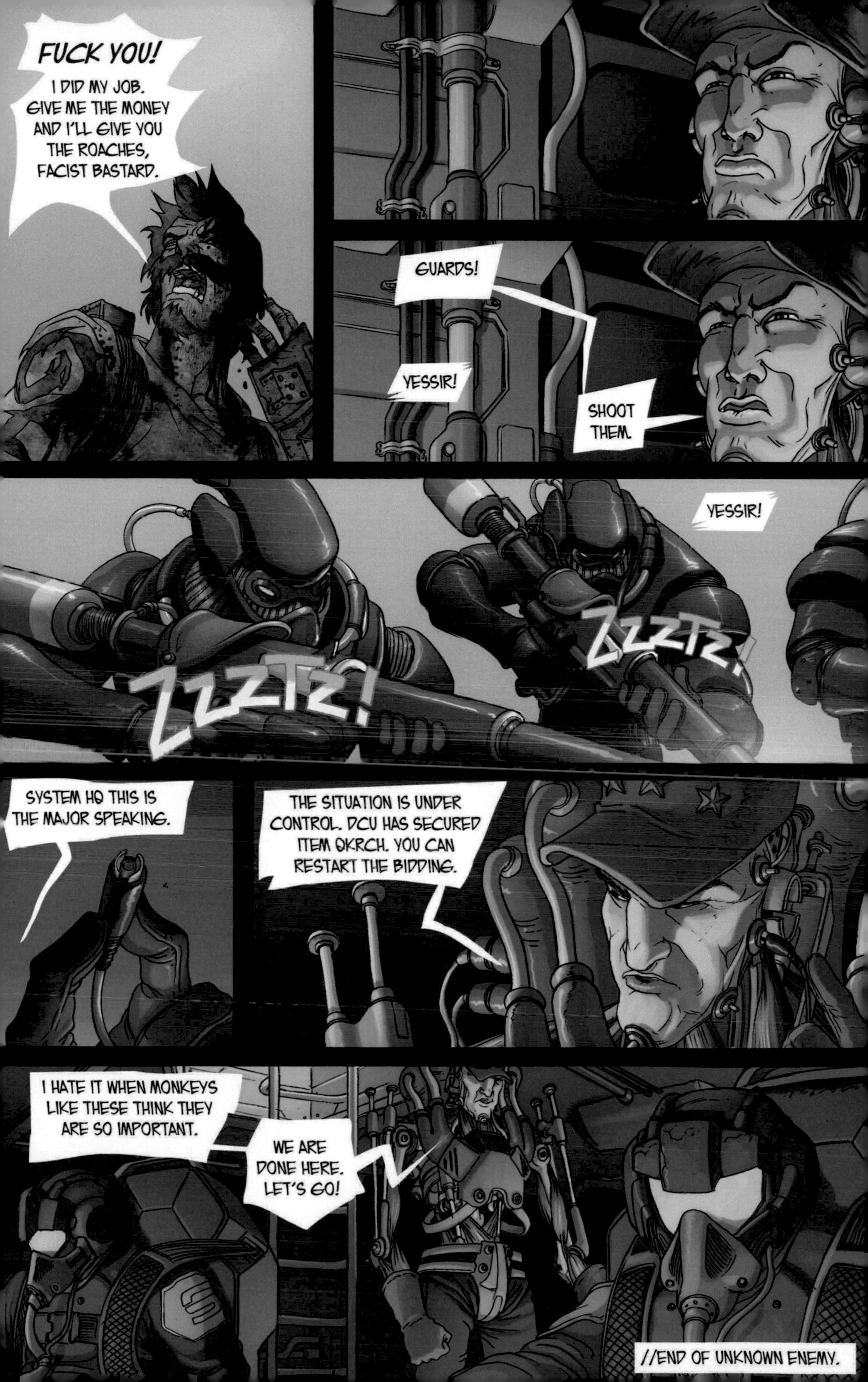
FUCK YOU!
I DID MY JOB. GIVE ME THE MONEY AND I'LL GIVE YOU THE ROACHES, FACIST BASTARD.
GUARDS!
YESSIR!
SHOOT THEM.
YESSIR!
ZZZTZ!
ZZZTZ!
SYSTEM HQ THIS IS THE MAJOR SPEAKING.
THE SITUATION IS UNDER CONTROL. DCU HAS SECURED ITEM QKRCH. YOU CAN RESTART THE BIDDING.
I HATE IT WHEN MONKEYS LIKE THESE THINK THEY ARE SO IMPORTANT.
WE ARE DONE HERE. LET'S GO!
//END OF UNKNOWN ENEMY.

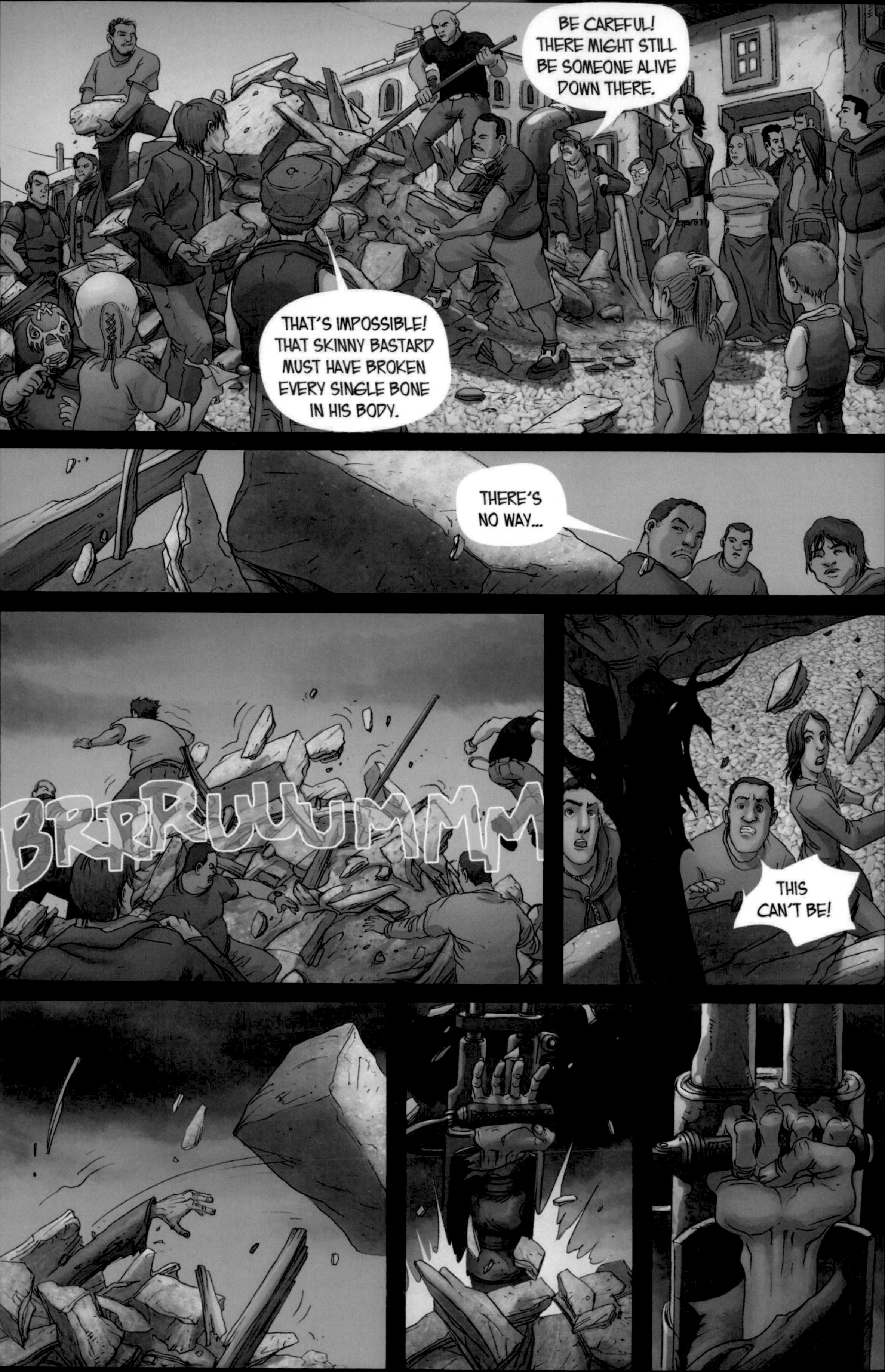
BE CAREFUL! THERE MIGHT STILL BE SOMEONE ALIVE DOWN THERE.
THAT'S IMPOSSIBLE! THAT SKINNY BASTARD MUST HAVE BROKEN EVERY SINGLE BONE IN HIS BODY.
THERE'S NO WAY...
BRRRUUUMMM
THIS CAN'T BE!

Zazil by
Raúl Treviño

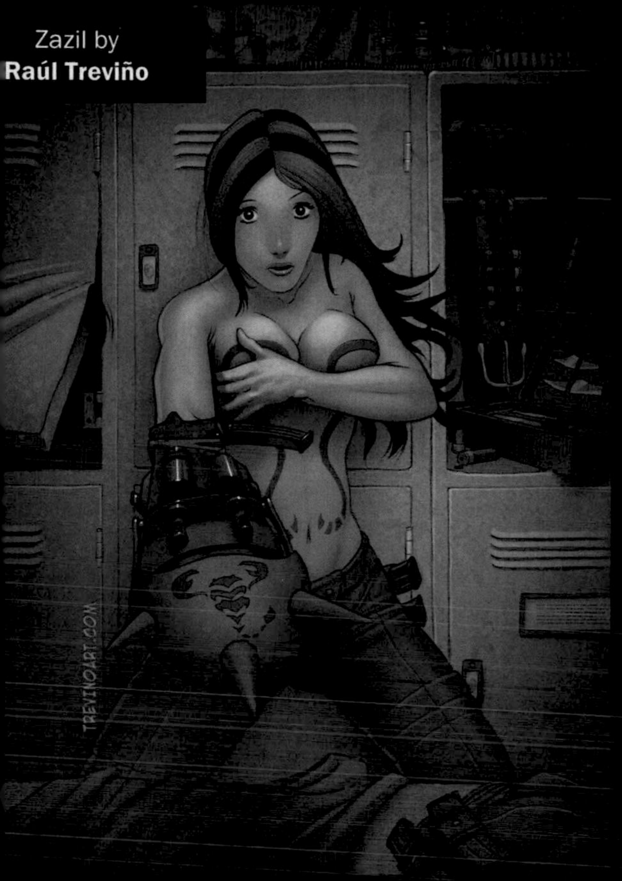
TREVINOART.COM

El Toque by
Jesús Aburto

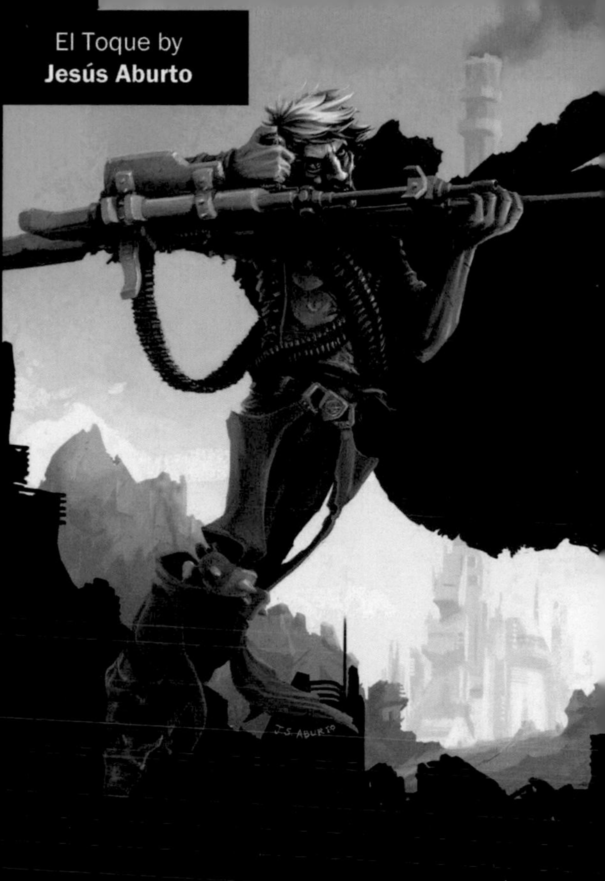
J.S. ABURTO

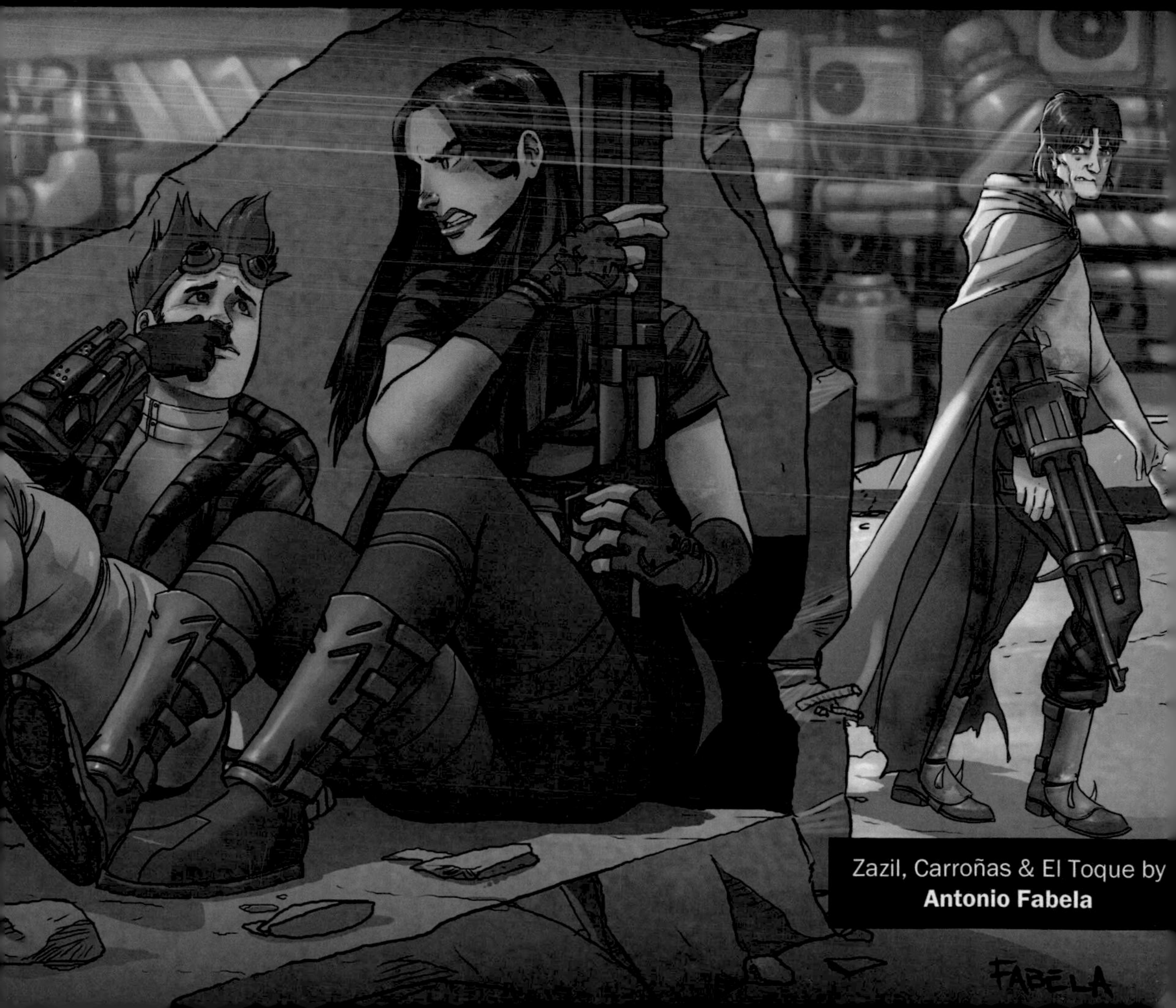
FABELA

Zazil, Carroñas & El Toque by
Antonio Fabela

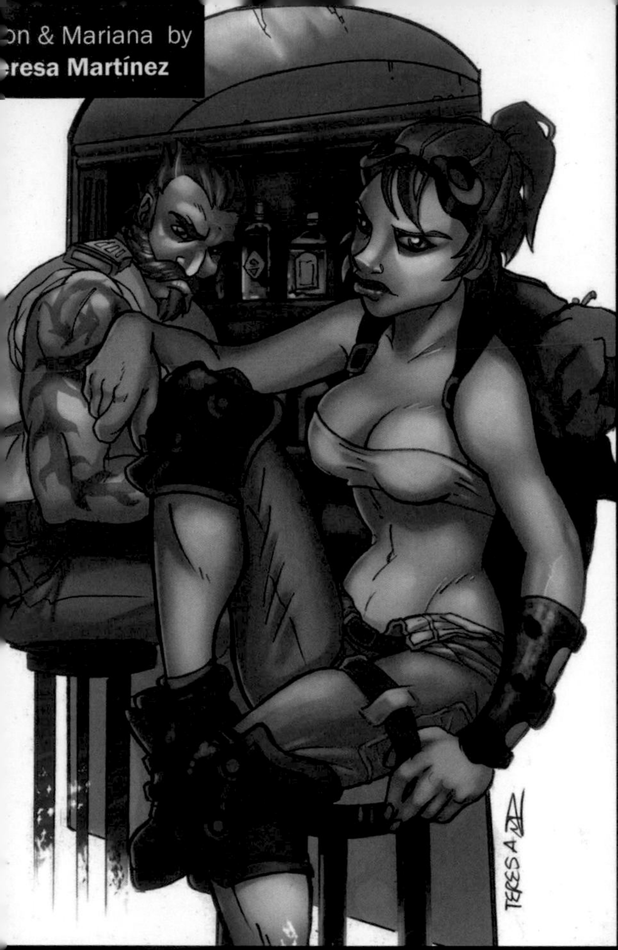

on & Mariana by
eresa Martínez

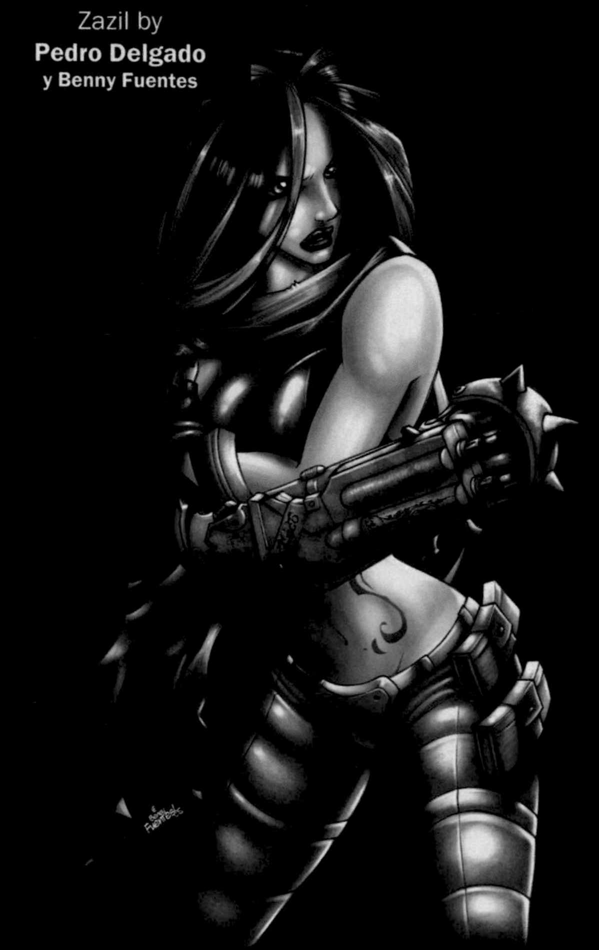

Zazil by
Pedro Delgado
y Benny Fuentes

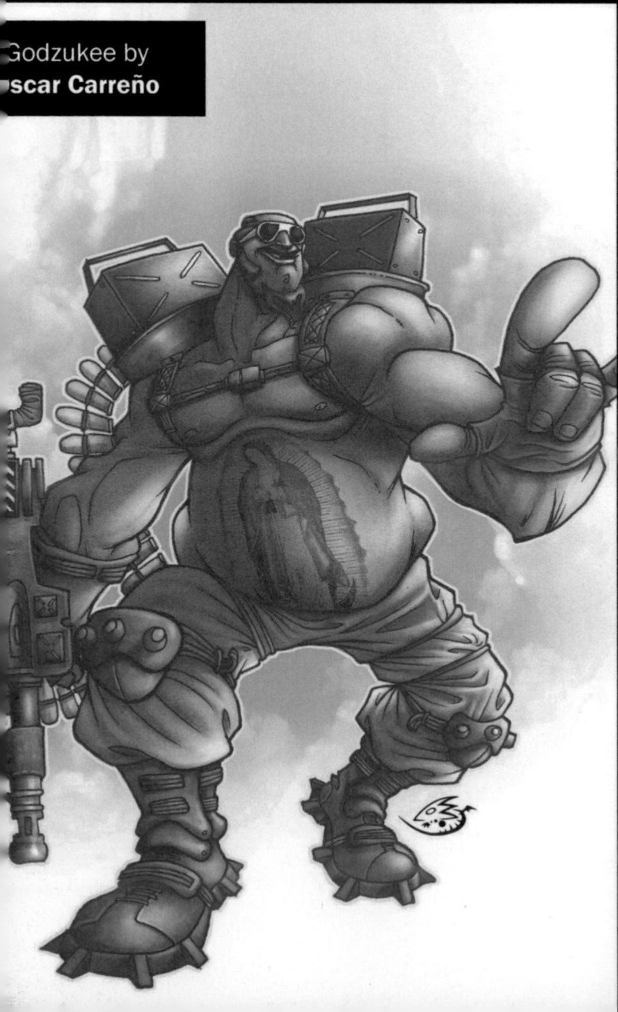

Godzukee by
scar Carreño

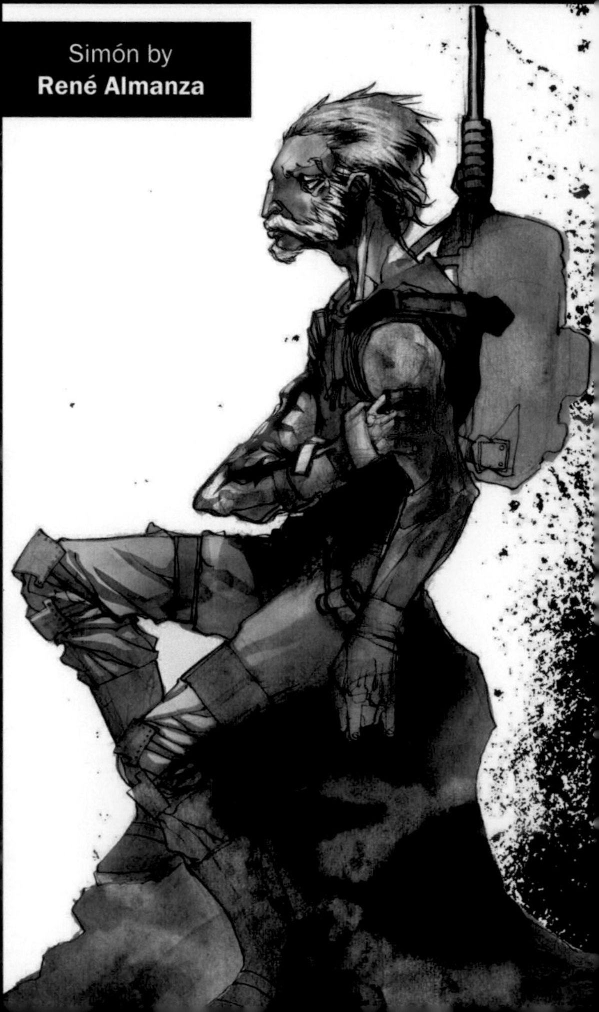

Simón by
René Almanza

SKETCHES & ADDITIONAL ART

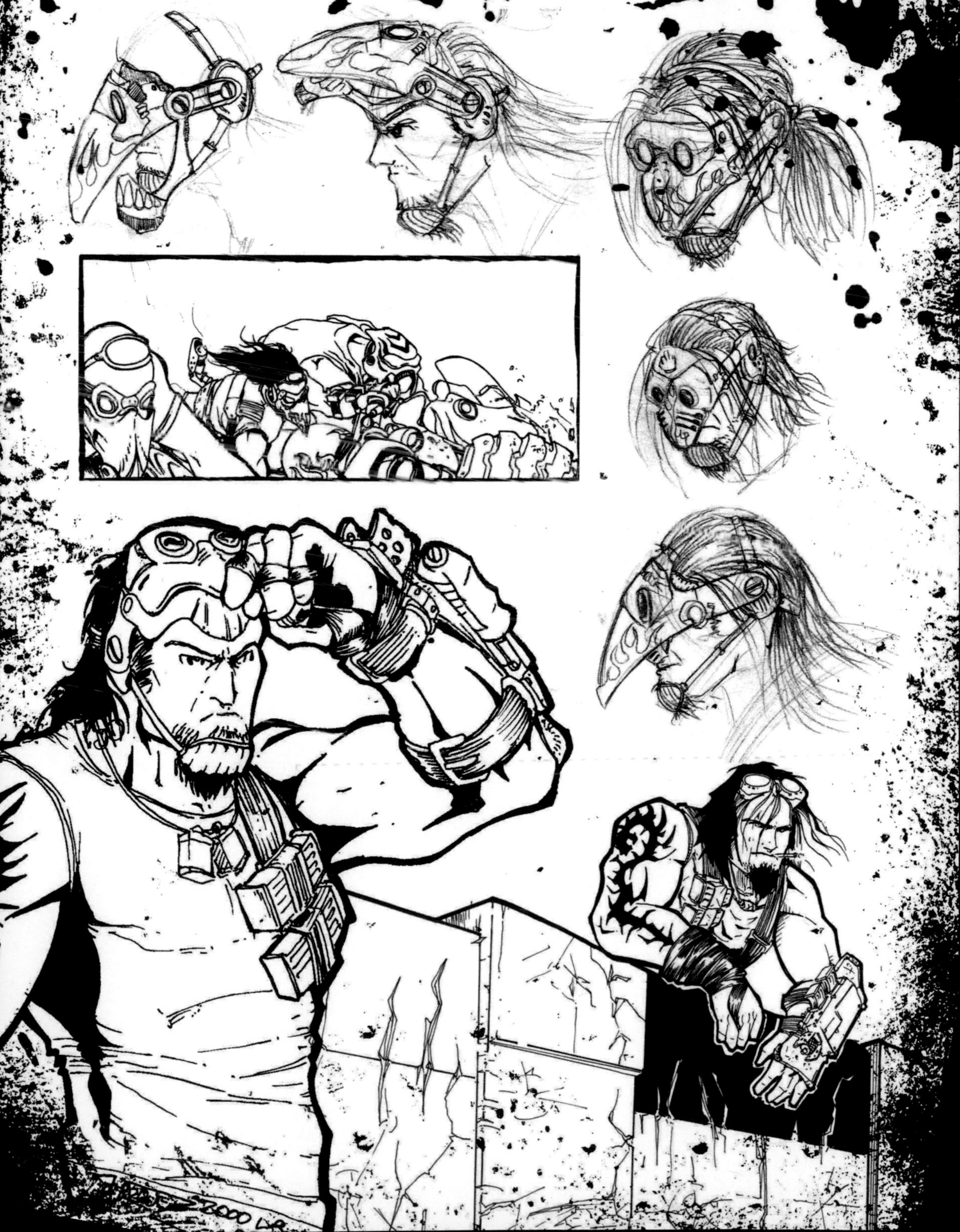

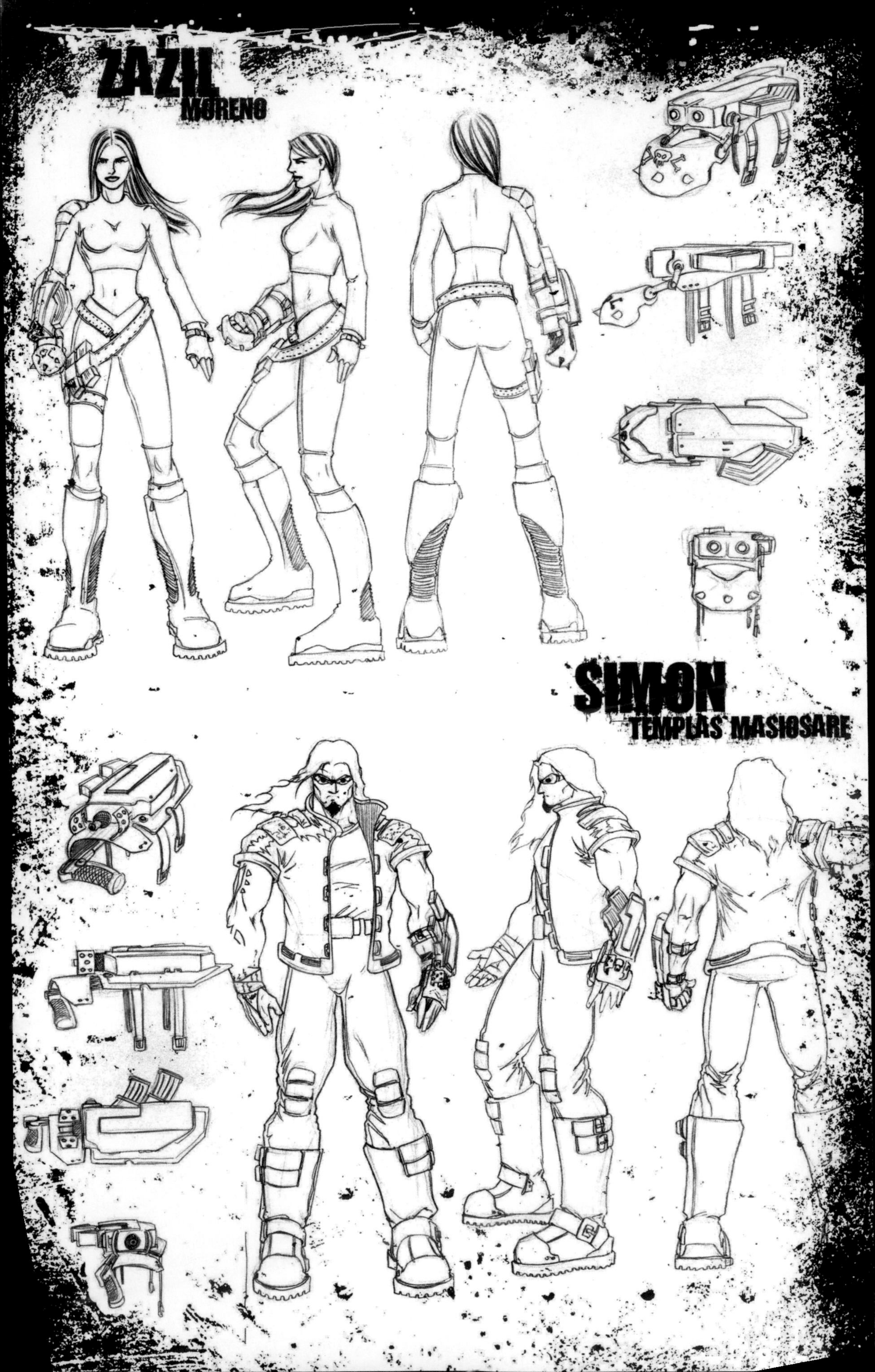
ZAZIL
MORENO
SIMON
TEMPLAS MASIOSARE

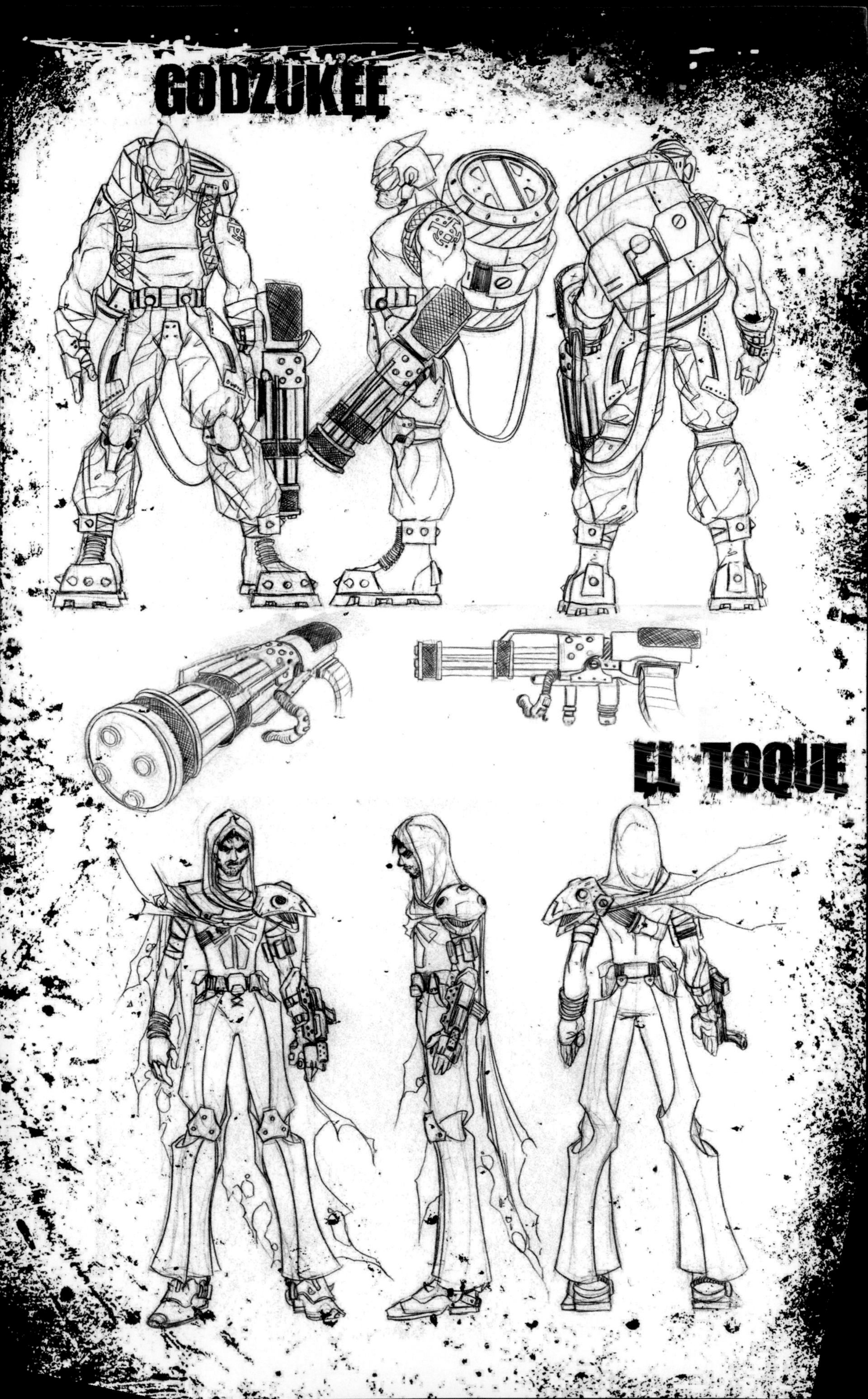
GODZUKEE
EL TOQUE

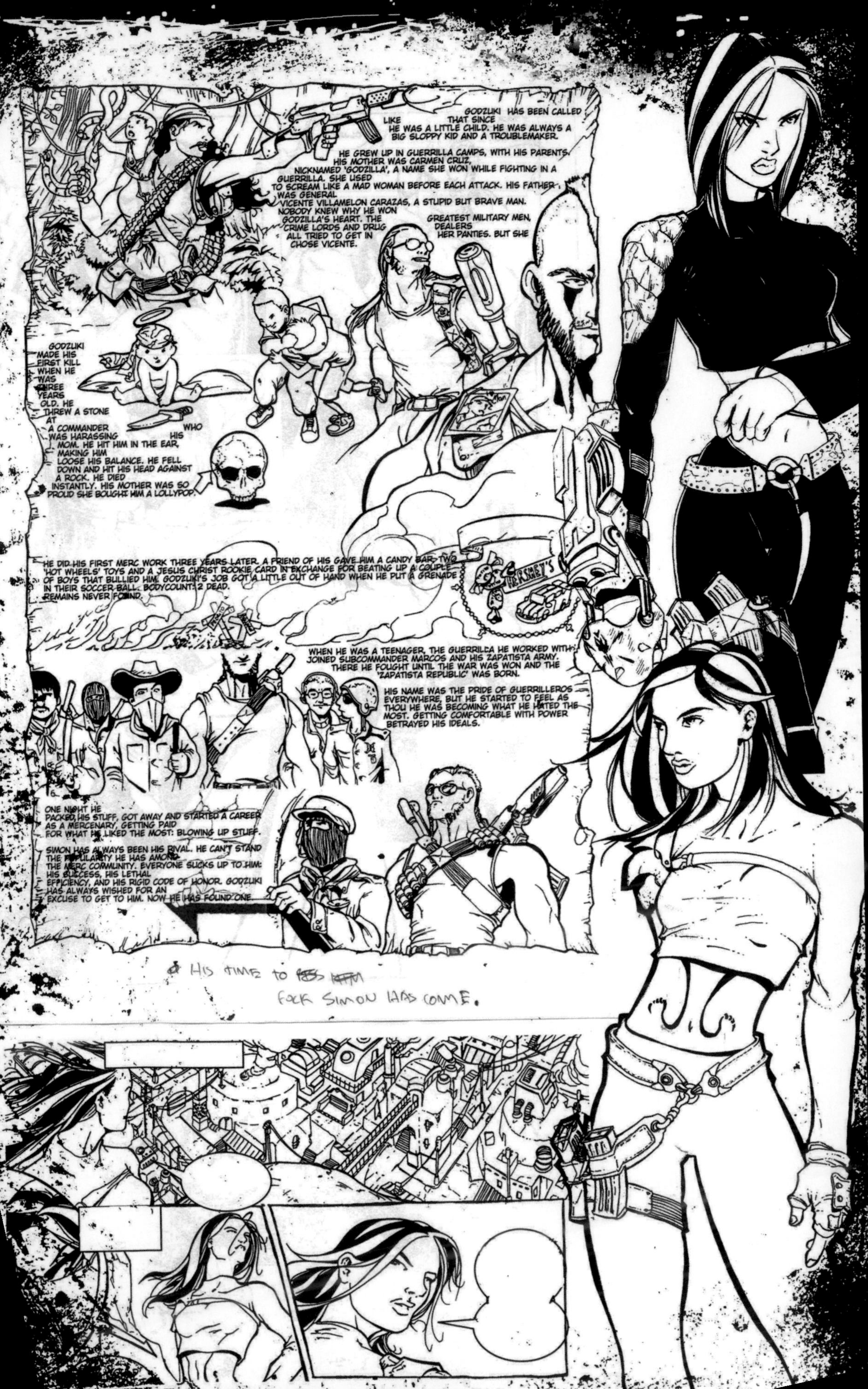
GODZUKI HAS BEEN CALLED LIKE THAT SINCE HE WAS A LITTLE CHILD. HE WAS ALWAYS A BIG SLOPPY KID AND A TROUBLEMAKER.
HE GREW UP IN GUERRILLA CAMPS, WITH HIS PARENTS. HIS MOTHER WAS CARMEN CRUZ, NICKNAMED 'GODZILLA', A NAME SHE WON WHILE FIGHTING IN A GUERRILLA. SHE USED TO SCREAM LIKE A MAD WOMAN BEFORE EACH ATTACK. HIS FATHER WAS GENERAL VICENTE VILLAMELON CARAZAS, A STUPID BUT BRAVE MAN.
NOBODY KNEW WHY HE WON GODZILLA'S HEART. THE GREATEST MILITARY MEN, CRIME LORDS AND DRUG DEALERS ALL TRIED TO GET IN HER PANTIES. BUT SHE CHOSE VICENTE.
GODZUKI MADE HIS FIRST KILL WHEN HE WAS THREE YEARS OLD. HE THREW A STONE AT A COMMANDER WHO WAS HARASSING HIS MOM. HE HIT HIM IN THE EAR, MAKING HIM LOOSE HIS BALANCE. HE FELL DOWN AND HIT HIS HEAD AGAINST A ROCK. HE DIED INSTANTLY. HIS MOTHER WAS SO PROUD SHE BOUGHT HIM A LOLLYPOP.
HE DID HIS FIRST MERC WORK THREE YEARS LATER. A FRIEND OF HIS GAVE HIM A CANDY BAR, TWO 'HOT WHEELS' TOYS AND A JESUS CHRIST ROOKIE CARD IN EXCHANGE FOR BEATING UP A COUPLE OF BOYS THAT BULLIED HIM. GODZUKI'S JOB GOT A LITTLE OUT OF HAND WHEN HE PUT A GRENADE IN THEIR SOCCER BALL. BODYCOUNT: 2 DEAD. REMAINS NEVER FOUND.
HERSHEY'S
WHEN HE WAS A TEENAGER, THE GUERRILLA HE WORKED WITH JOINED SUBCOMMANDER MARCOS AND HIS ZAPATISTA ARMY. THERE HE FOUGHT UNTIL THE WAR WAS WON AND THE 'ZAPATISTA REPUBLIC' WAS BORN.
HIS NAME WAS THE PRIDE OF GUERRILLEROS EVERYWHERE, BUT HE STARTED TO FEEL AS THOU HE WAS BECOMING WHAT HE HATED THE MOST. GETTING COMFORTABLE WITH POWER BETRAYED HIS IDEALS.
ONE NIGHT HE PACKED HIS STUFF, GOT AWAY AND STARTED A CAREER AS A MERCENARY, GETTING PAID FOR WHAT HE LIKED THE MOST: BLOWING UP STUFF.
SIMON HAS ALWAYS BEEN HIS RIVAL. HE CAN'T STAND THE POPULARITY HE HAS AMONG THE MERC COMMUNITY. EVERYONE SUCKS UP TO HIM: HIS SUCCESS, HIS LETHAL EFFICIENCY, AND HIS RIGID CODE OF HONOR. GODZUKI HAS ALWAYS WISHED FOR AN EXCUSE TO GET TO HIM. NOW HE HAS FOUND ONE.
HIS TIME TO
FOCK SIMON HAS COME.

HOW TO SWEAR LIKE A MEXICAN

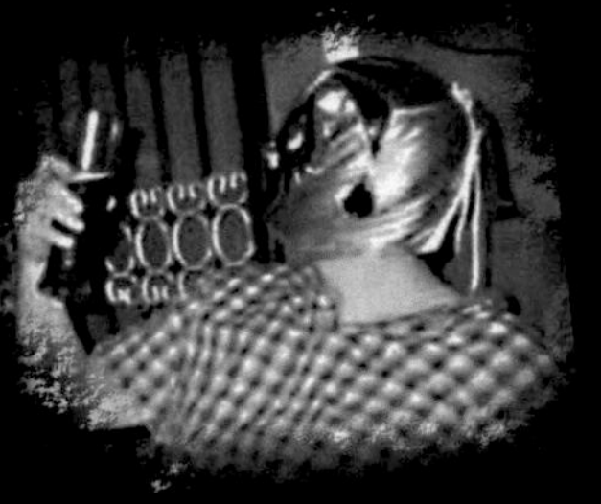

A LESSON IN SPANISH AND IN LIFE BY PROFESSOR MAFU FONTANA

Hello, kids. It's been a while since you've had the chance to learn something from me. Mexico has changed a lot in the last five years, but the secret to Swearing Like a Mexican remains the same. Listen closely, memorize and practice and you will be swearing like a Mexican in no time.

A la chingada (äl' e' shĭn' găd' ă): "A la" means "to the", as in a journey. "La chingada" refers here to the unknown, a motherless void that is the worst place of all. There are several ways to use this expression. The most common is when things are going bad or all resources to achieve a given goal have failed; then you are going to "la chingada". It is also used when someone gets on your nerves and you are either going to ignore him or shoot him in the head; ex. "a la chingada contigo". "La chingada" has hundreds, if not thousands, of uses and variations.

Cabrón (kăb' rŭn): n. Common expression to refer to a fellow man. On most cases "cabrón" is not sensed as an insult, except when it is said to you by a stranger; in such a case, physical confrontation is inevitable. It can also be applied to men who take advantage of the opportunities life presents to them in order to succeed, or that use its rivals weaknesses to beat him in fight or conflict. Ex: "salió más cabrón que bonito".

Cagüama (kă' hwăm' ă): n. Not really a swear word. Just a really big beer. Remember this word at all times when traveling to Mexico as it might proof useful. Recent advances in modern science have given Mexicans the "Cagüamón", which is just a bigger bottle of beer.

Chicharrón (shĕsh chär ŏn): n. A Mexican delicacy. There are two types of "chicharrón": Cooked pigs skin that is fried or dehydrated and used as a snack or an entrée, usually served with red salsa. And there's also a different cut that includes flesh and fat along with the skin and can be cooked in pig lard on a copper pot or stewed with different vegetables (like green tomatoes, onions, garlic, etc.) and an assortment of chili peppers. I know it sounds real nasty, but trust me, it's tasty as hell.

Chilango (shĭl an go): n. Many years ago this word was used to describe someone from any place of the Mexican Republic that had migrated to Mexico City in search of a better life. Now it is commonly used to name a person originating from Mexico City. Things to know about Chilangos: they are extremely paranoid, they smell funny, they usually try to take advantage of situations through slimy strategies and drive like stoned midgets on a go-kart ring.

Chingar (shĕn gär): v. Spanish equivalent of the verb "to fuck", used more commonly with all its variants in Mexico and Latin America. "Chingarse a alguien" ("to fuck somebody") may not only mean that you performed sexual intercourse with someone, but also that you took advantage, betrayed, cheated or victimized that person. Curiously, "chingar" is not usually used to say that you had sex with someone, but to indicate that you prevailed over an opponent in a competitive situation, or that you won something that was in dispute with one or many rivals. Probably the most offensive use of the verb "chingar" is in the phrase "chingas a tu madre", literally translated as "fuck your mother". Be prepared to face the consequences when you say these words while being In Mexico.

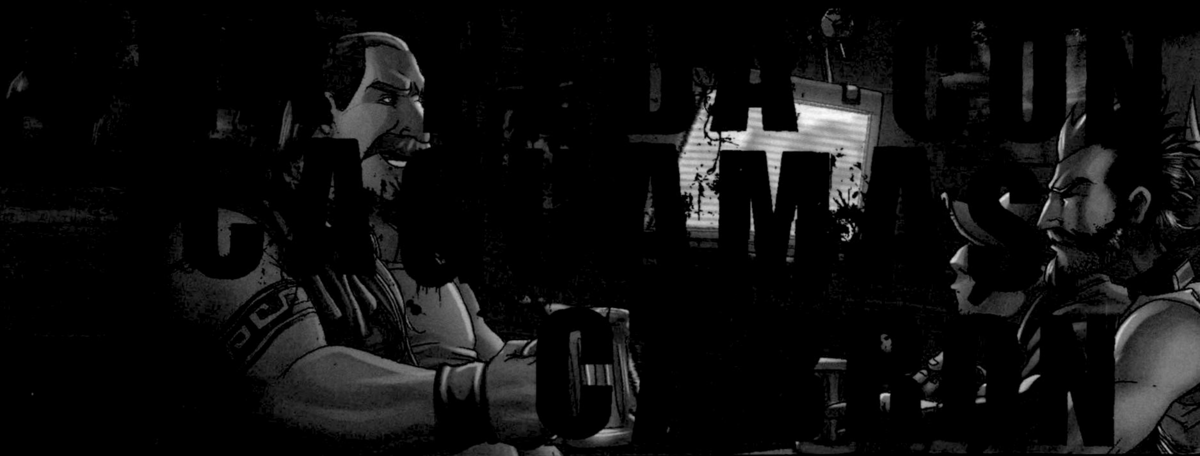

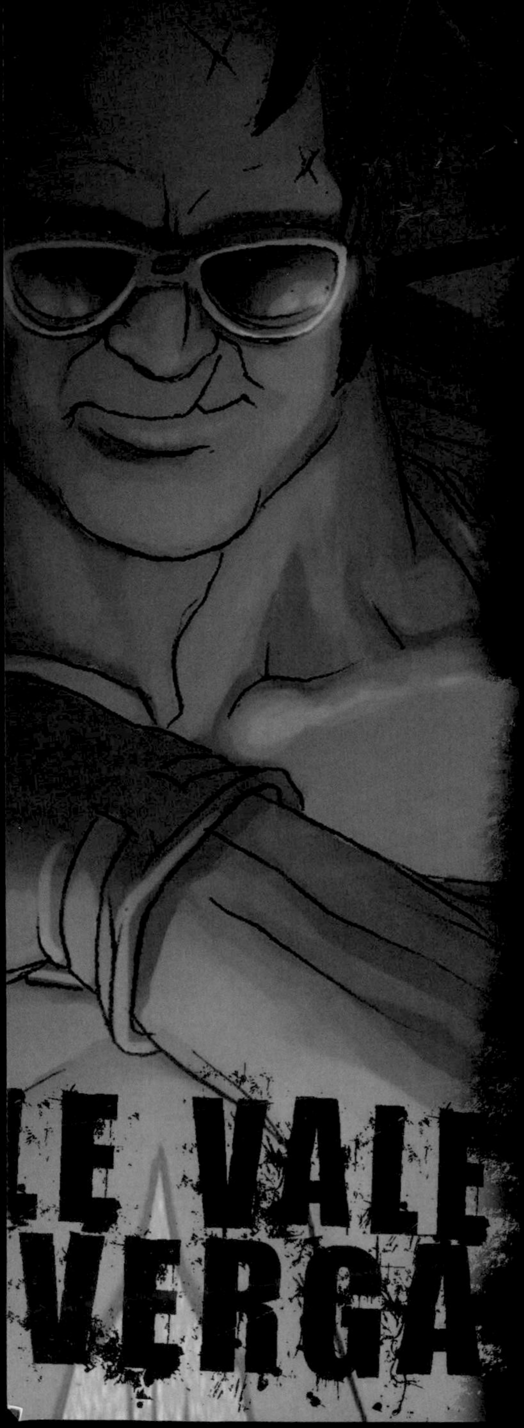
E VALE
VERGA

Culero (kool' er' o): adj. From "culo", or "asshole". Expression used for someone who is mean or treacherous. This word shows a lot of contempt for the person it is said to. Teachers and bosses are usually labeled as "culeros". Whatever you do, never trust a "culero" or he will fuck you in the ass given the right chance.

Desgraciado (thĭs gräw sä do): adj. Someone who lacks grace or that has fallen out of grace. Someone who is going through a period of bad luck, economic dismay or a non-existing love life. Someone who betrays a loved one. Usually follows the word "pobre", meaning "poor".

Gordo (gôrd o): adj. A fat person. "Gordo" is also a common nickname for husbands, boyfriends and loved ones. But don't go calling everyone "gordo" or you will receive a kick in the nuts in no time.

Gorilón (gôr ill ŭn): n. Not really a swear word, but can be used as an insult. Literally means "big gorilla". Usually used to describe thugs, bodyguards, bar bouncers and other kinds of brainless muscled beings.

Hijo de la Chingada (yĭ' hŏ dă lä shĭn' găd' ă): Vague equivalent of the expression "son of a bitch". By calling someone a son of "la chingada" you are telling that person that his mother is a whore. Or even worse: that he doesn't have (or ever had) a mother. The mother in Mexican culture is the utmost symbol of purity and goodness, and it's absence means that someone is evil, abusive and beyond repair. Nonetheless, very close friends (or passing acquaintances that get really drunk together) can call each other "hijos de la chingada", as long as it is in good character, without fear of insult or injury.

Joto (hôt' o): n. An effeminate man, or one that favors and practices sodomy. Common way of referring to someone that is unwilling to take risks in any facet of life, be in work, chance or love. Joto is also a commonly used word to yell at football referees or strikers that miss a clear goal. See also Puto and Maricón.

Macho (mătch' o): n. A big man. A man that does not fear confrontation, can drink for hours without losing his balance, wrangles woman like they are cattle and can eat the hottest chili peppers without flinching. You can prove how macho you are by arm wrestling, bragging about sexual adventures or enduring long periods of time on a "toques" machine, which consists of two metal tubes connected to a car battery. As you may have already noticed, macho-ness is not in any way related to intelligence.

Mamacita (mau' mau' sĭt' ă): Literally means "little mom", or "momma". It's a common word used in hopes of luring beautiful women to the arms of men; usually used by big, hairy, stinky guys that work on construction sites. Or intergalactic hitmen.

Mamar (măm är): v. From the latin "mammāre", or "to breast feed". The direct translation is "to suck". This is a very common word in every-day conversation. Some examples: A "mamón" is someone who is pretentious, pompous or that has excessive self-esteem (usually a result of being in a position of power or authority). A "mamada" is oral gratification, usually from a woman to a man. If something happens to you and it is "la mamada", it's usually something incredible or very good. For example, it would be "la mamada" if you received a "mamada".

Marrano (mär än' o): n. A pig. A filthy man or woman. Someone who cheats. Someone who practices weird sexual practices. A mexican politician or law-enforcer. As an adjective, "marrano" can be applied to refer to really big things. For example, "una torta marrana", meaning "a very big sandwich".

Pedo (pĕd ŏ): n. It literally means "fart", but this word has many different purposes in the spanish language. For example, "ni pedo" is something you would say to end a conversation without making a fuss about it. But if someone invites you to go to a "peda", then you are going to a party, or at least to a place where alcohol (usually beer) will be available in abundance. In that "peda" you are going to "agarrar el pedo" ("grab the fart", in it's literal translation), which is the action of ingesting large quantities of alcohol. Just don't let someone grab you while you are "pedo" (a vulgar way of saying someone is piss-drunk) or they'll probably start touching you in your private parts. This will no doubt "te sacará un pedo" (will scare you shitless) and then "se va a armar un pedote" (all hell will break loose). I hope you understood, because I'm not repeating this. Ni pedo.

Pendejo (pĕn' dä' hŏ): n. Used to refer to someone who is dumb. An individual is usually called a "pendejo" when he performs a dumb or clumsy action, or when he follows the rules and laws to achieve any given goal. Never let anyone call you a "pendejo", unless he has a good and valid reason; if you let him do it, you will be his "pendejo" for life.

Perro Aguayo, El: Legendary figure of the wrestling ring. Through his career he went through many facets, but was most remember for being a "rudo". He specialized in many moves, like The Arrow. When facing a difficult opponent he would use wild techniques, like biting their extremities of hitting them with chairs or pieces of wood. Fun fact: he cut his forehead with razor blades before fights so they would bleed easily when hit, for dramatic effects. He retired a few of years ago after 30 years of fighting. He is followed by his son, El Hijo del Perro Aguayo.

Pilinga Feliz™ (pĭl ingă fĕl is): A happy "pilinga", or happy prick. "Pilinga" is a very cutesy way of refering to a man's penis. "Pilinga Feliz" is a polular brand of condoms, lightly lubricated and thin enough to provide a more natural feeling for both partners. It features a specially contoured shape at the tip makes for a more comfortable fit on the penis. Comes in packs of 12, 24, 48 and 144 units. Also available in different flavors, the most popular being cola, malt, chico zapote, banana, sweet potatoe and horchata. "Pilinga Feliz" is a trademark of the Metesaka Oil & Rubber Corporation, based in Barranquilla, Colombia.

Pinche (pĭn' shă): "Pinche" is an expression of common use. It is an adjective that can be attached to almost anything and usually stands for poor quality or poor character. If someone calls you "pinche", it's usually to minimize or criticize you. Ex: "hijo de tu pinche madre".

Piruja (pĭr ŭgh äh'): n. An easy woman, or one with many sexual partners. Also used to refer to a female who performs sexual services in exchange for money. Very drunk men usually use this word to describe woman who reject them. Usually follows "pinche" in a sentence.

Puñetas (pŏŏh' nyet' äs): n. A puñetas is a man of limited intelligence and who deserves no respect. It is not a word of common use, but when applied it usually is to a weak, unthreatening person. Do not confuse with "Puñeta", which means "to masturbate".

Varo (văr ŭs): n. Dough, moolah, rhino, sponduliokc, bacon, bread, dough, cabbage, lettuce, kale, folding green, long green, ace, bean, boffo, bone, buck, bullet, case note, clam, coconut, fish, frogskin, lizard, peso, rock, scrip, simoleon, yellowback. Money, that is

Vato (văt ŭs): n. A common way to refer to a friend or acquaintance. It Mexico it is not used to refer to a woman ("vata"), but this use has become common among the Mexican population in the United States area. A vato loco hangin' with the raza may take a ride on his lowrider citing Cheech Marin and drinking a Tecate. May the Virgencita of Guadalupe have mercy on his soul.

Verga (bâr gă): n. From the latin "virga", or "wand". "Verga" is a vulgar name for the penis. If "the verga is taking you away" ("me lleva la verga"), then something must have gone wrong or you are in trouble. If you are going as fast as a "verga" ("echo la verga"), then you are moving very fast. But if someone tells you to go to the "verga" ("te me vas a la verga"), you should walk up to that person and punch him in the nose. That is, unless you have done something very bad or embarassing; then the best thing to do is to lower your head and walk slowly towards the exit.

Weyes (wă' yĕs): An ever more common way to refer to another person, be it a man or a woman. It's english equivalent could be "dude". It was first used in northern Mexico during the last half of the twentieth century, and it quickly spread across the country. It is never sensed as an insult, except by really uptight people who should either be ignored or kicked in a very painful place.

That's it, my gringo amigos. Now you are ready to party like and animal this spring break, or to visit downtown Los Angeles. And remember, kids, in case of doubt, visit your local taco stand (or approach anyone with a "Chivas" t-shirt) and ask.

EL ARSENAL

Simón by Francisco Ruiz-Velazco

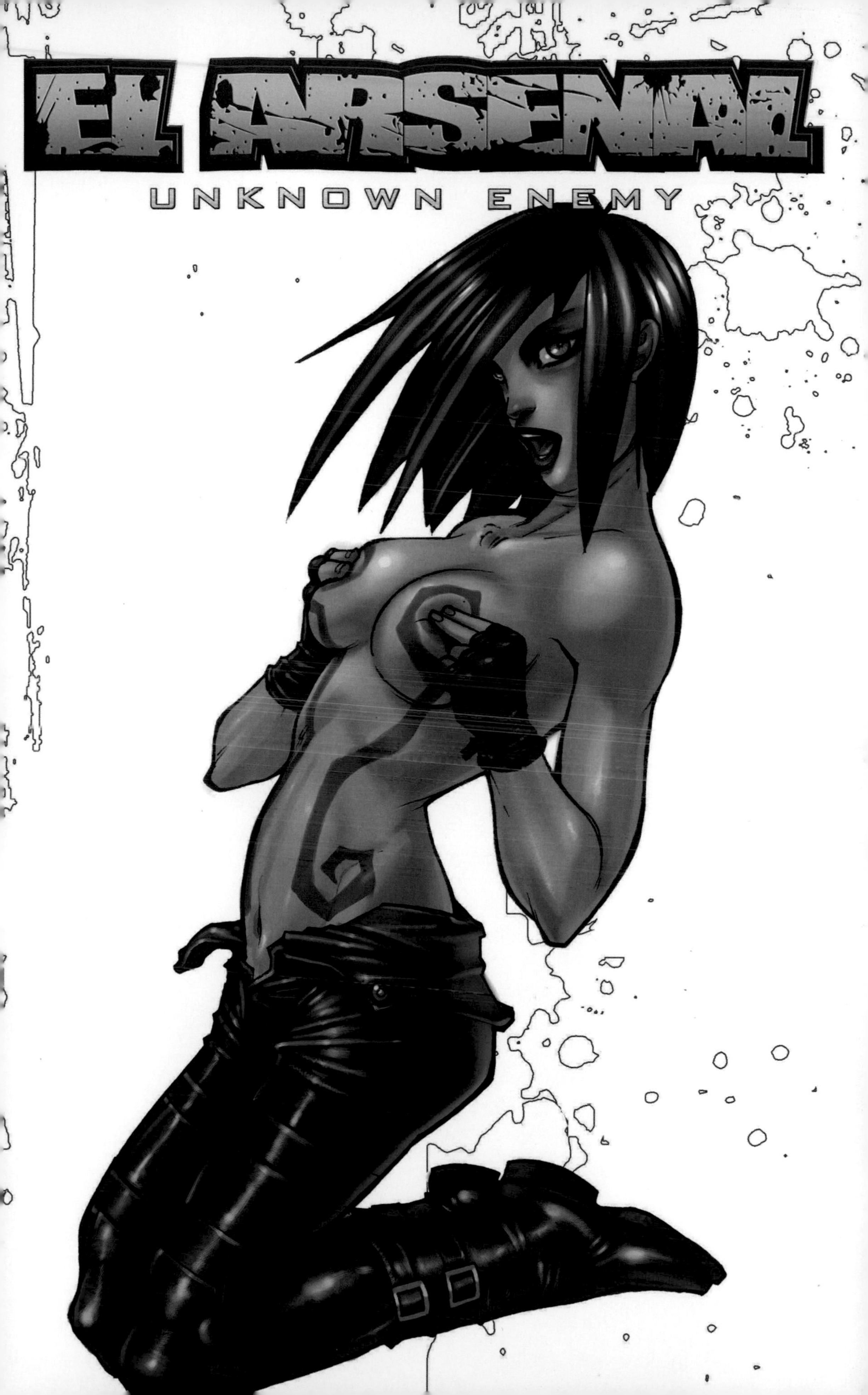
EL ARSENAL
UNKNOWN ENEMY

EL ARSENAL

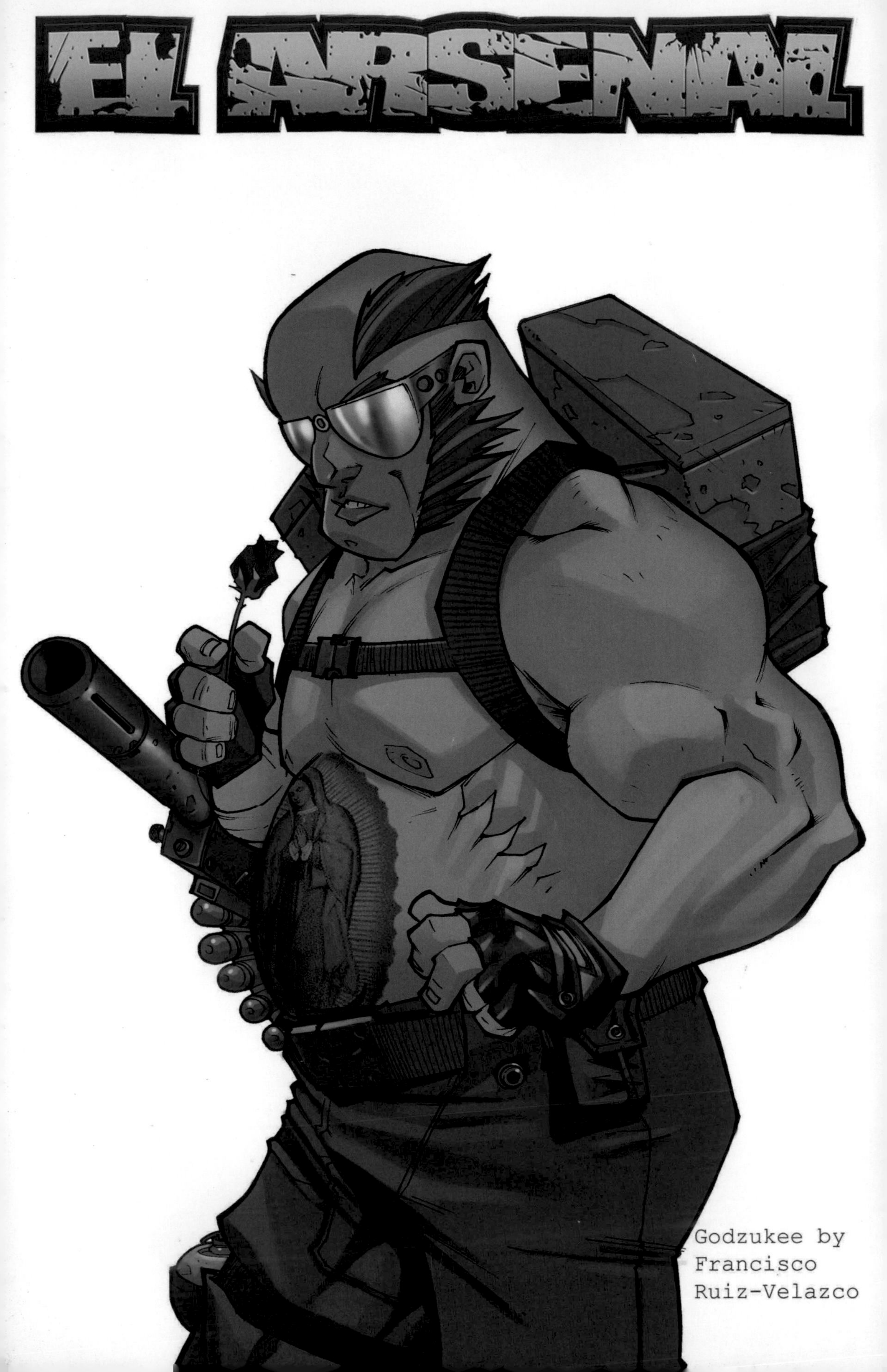

Godzukee by
Francisco
Ruiz-Velazco

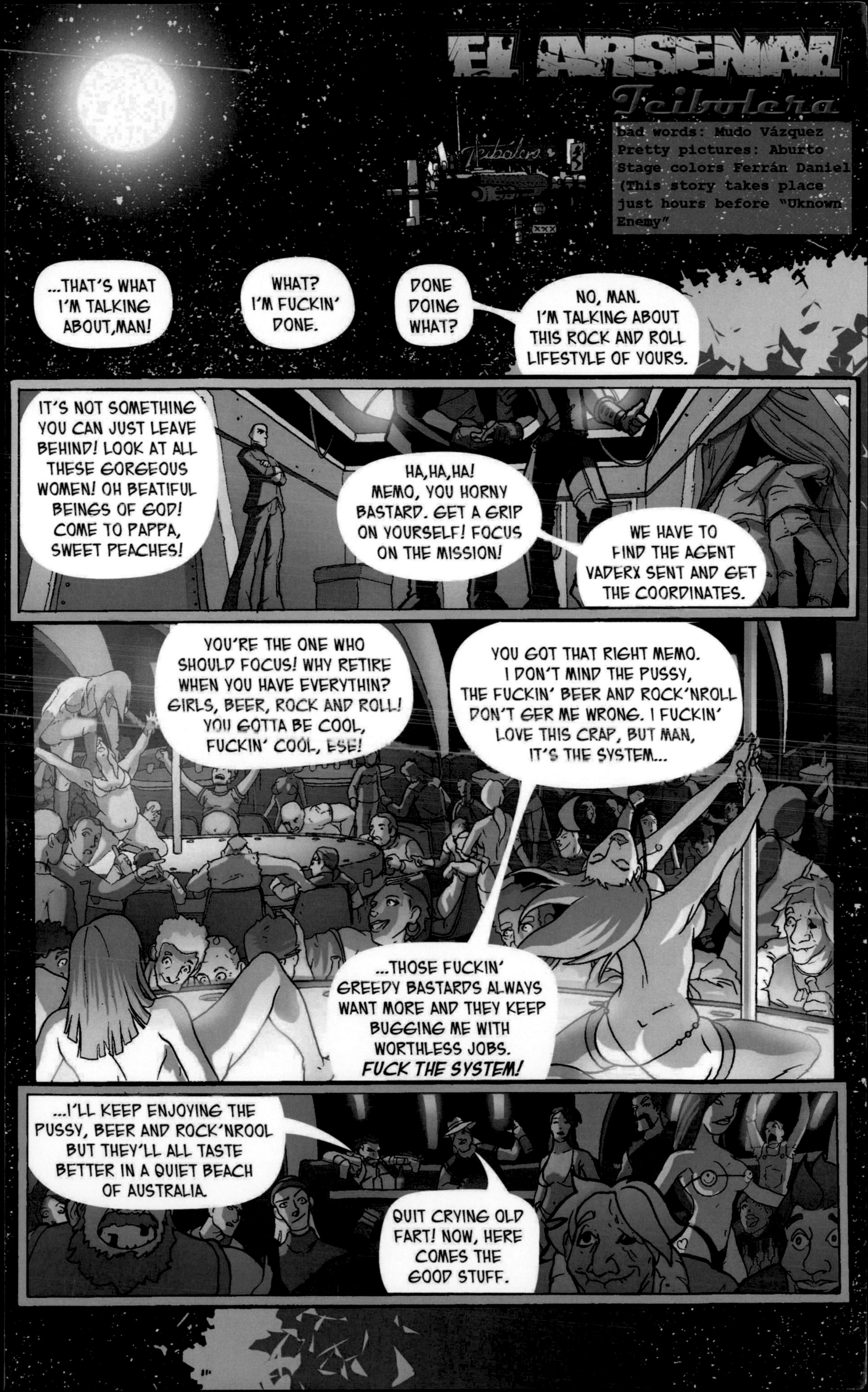
EL ARSENAL
Teibolera
bad words: Mudo Vázquez
Pretty pictures: Aburto
Stage colors Ferrán Daniel
(This story takes place just hours before "Uknown Enemy"
...THAT'S WHAT I'M TALKING ABOUT,MAN!
WHAT? I'M FUCKIN' DONE.
DONE DOING WHAT?
NO, MAN. I'M TALKING ABOUT THIS ROCK AND ROLL LIFESTYLE OF YOURS.
IT'S NOT SOMETHING YOU CAN JUST LEAVE BEHIND! LOOK AT ALL THESE GORGEOUS WOMEN! OH BEATIFUL BEINGS OF GOD! COME TO PAPPA, SWEET PEACHES!
HA,HA,HA! MEMO, YOU HORNY BASTARD. GET A GRIP ON YOURSELF! FOCUS ON THE MISSION!
WE HAVE TO FIND THE AGENT VADERX SENT AND GET THE COORDINATES.
YOU'RE THE ONE WHO SHOULD FOCUS! WHY RETIRE WHEN YOU HAVE EVERYTHIN? GIRLS, BEER, ROCK AND ROLL! YOU GOTTA BE COOL, FUCKIN' COOL, ESE!
YOU GOT THAT RIGHT MEMO. I DON'T MIND THE PUSSY, THE FUCKIN' BEER AND ROCK'NROLL DON'T GER ME WRONG. I FUCKIN' LOVE THIS CRAP, BUT MAN, IT'S THE SYSTEM...
...THOSE FUCKIN' GREEDY BASTARDS ALWAYS WANT MORE AND THEY KEEP BUGGING ME WITH WORTHLESS JOBS. FUCK THE SYSTEM!
...I'LL KEEP ENJOYING THE PUSSY, BEER AND ROCK'NROOL BUT THEY'LL ALL TASTE BETTER IN A QUIET BEACH OF AUSTRALIA.
QUIT CRYING OLD FART! NOW, HERE COMES THE GOOD STUFF.

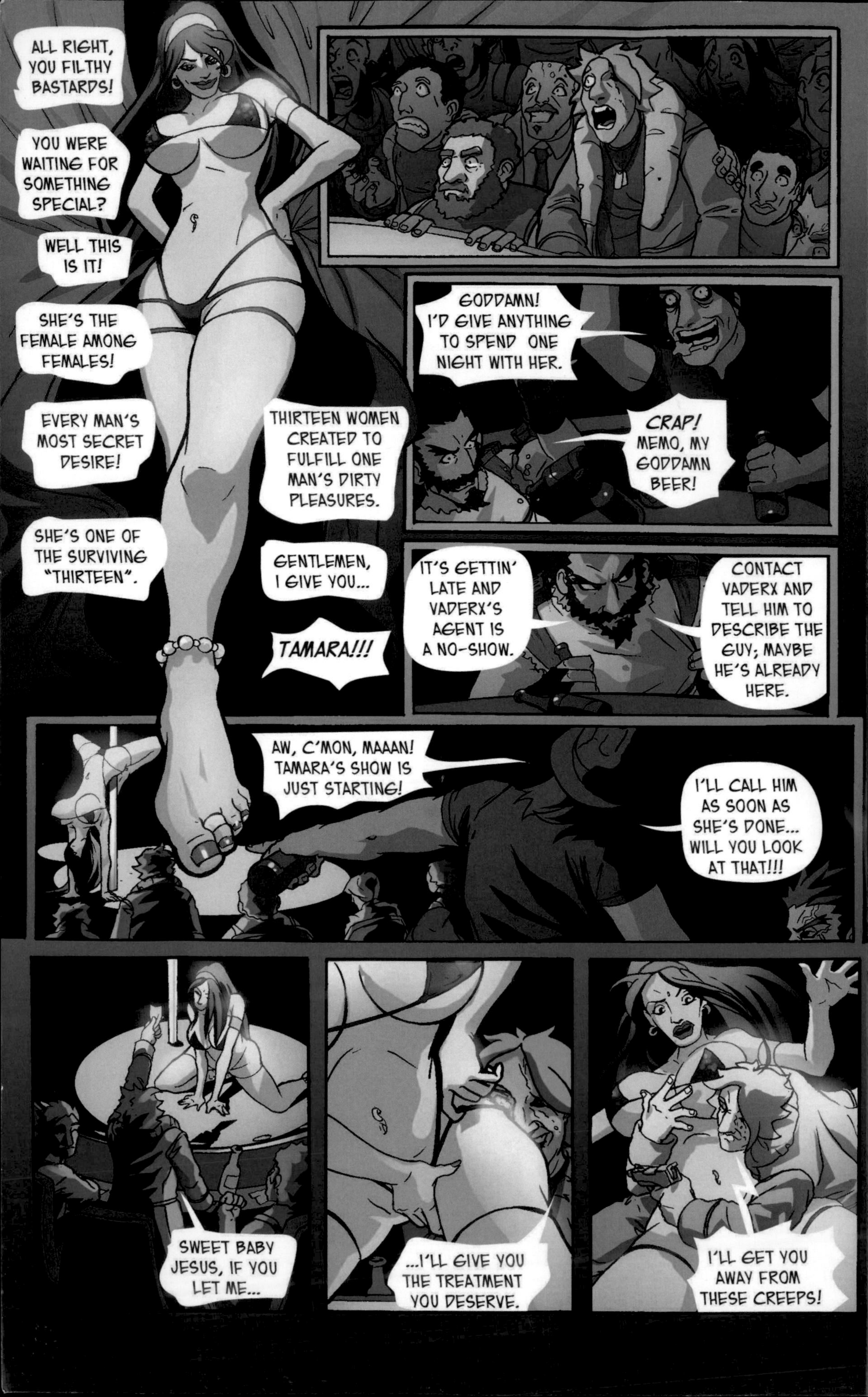
ALL RIGHT, YOU FILTHY BASTARDS!
YOU WERE WAITING FOR SOMETHING SPECIAL?
WELL THIS IS IT!
SHE'S THE FEMALE AMONG FEMALES!
EVERY MAN'S MOST SECRET DESIRE!
SHE'S ONE OF THE SURVIVING "THIRTEEN".
THIRTEEN WOMEN CREATED TO FULFILL ONE MAN'S DIRTY PLEASURES.
GENTLEMEN, I GIVE YOU...
TAMARA!!!
GODDAMN! I'D GIVE ANYTHING TO SPEND ONE NIGHT WITH HER.
CRAP! MEMO, MY GODDAMN BEER!
IT'S GETTIN' LATE AND VADERX'S AGENT IS A NO-SHOW.
CONTACT VADERX AND TELL HIM TO DESCRIBE THE GUY; MAYBE HE'S ALREADY HERE.
AW, C'MON, MAAAN! TAMARA'S SHOW IS JUST STARTING!
I'LL CALL HIM AS SOON AS SHE'S DONE... WILL YOU LOOK AT THAT!!!
SWEET BABY JESUS, IF YOU LET ME...
...I'LL GIVE YOU THE TREATMENT YOU DESERVE.
I'LL GET YOU AWAY FROM THESE CREEPS!

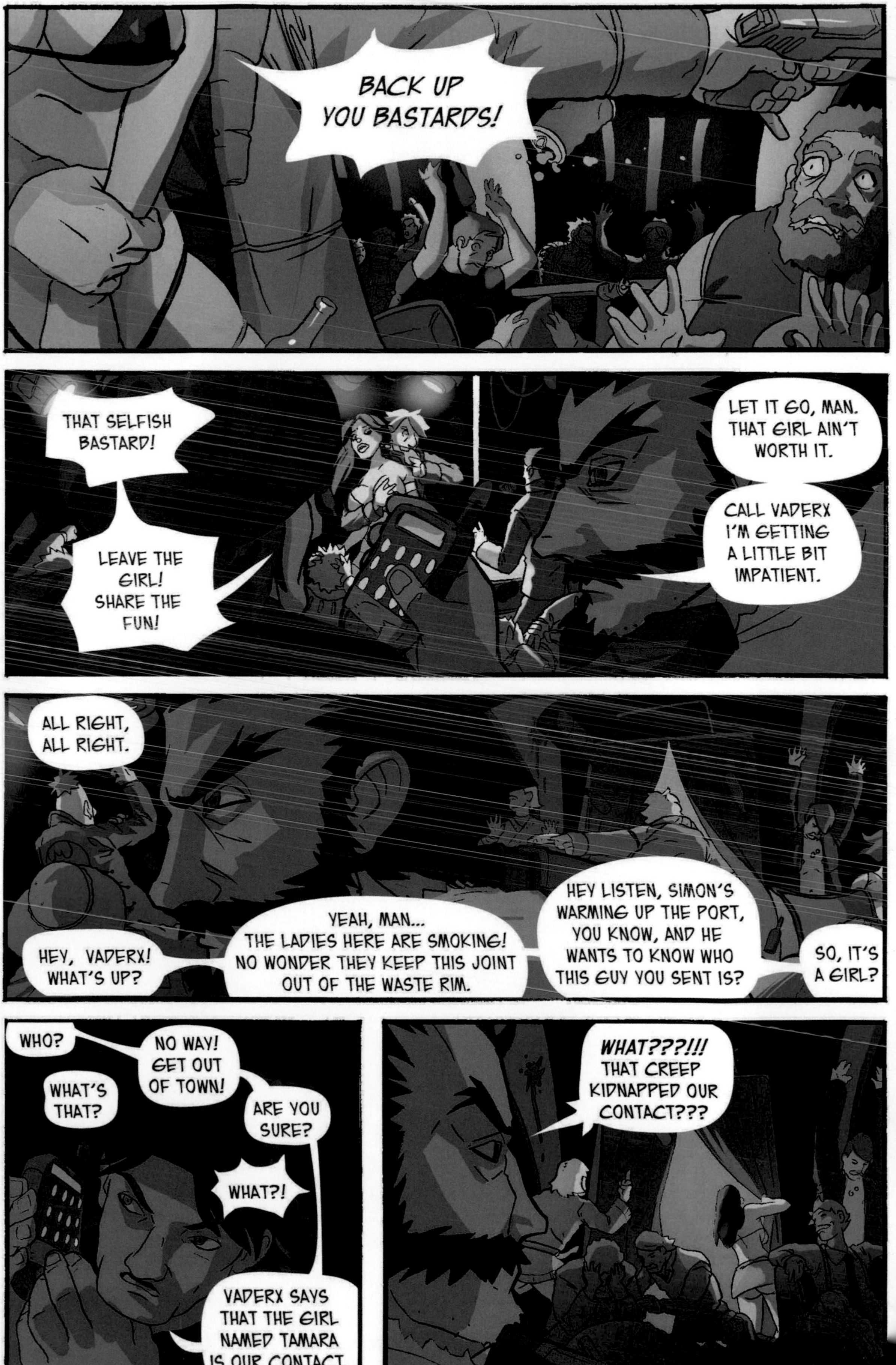
BACK UP YOU BASTARDS!
THAT SELFISH BASTARD!
LEAVE THE GIRL! SHARE THE FUN!
LET IT GO, MAN. THAT GIRL AIN'T WORTH IT.
CALL VADERX I'M GETTING A LITTLE BIT IMPATIENT.
ALL RIGHT, ALL RIGHT.
HEY, VADERX! WHAT'S UP?
YEAH, MAN... THE LADIES HERE ARE SMOKING! NO WONDER THEY KEEP THIS JOINT OUT OF THE WASTE RIM.
HEY LISTEN, SIMON'S WARMING UP THE PORT, YOU KNOW, AND HE WANTS TO KNOW WHO THIS GUY YOU SENT IS?
SO, IT'S A GIRL?
WHO?
NO WAY! GET OUT OF TOWN!
WHAT'S THAT?
ARE YOU SURE?
WHAT?!
VADERX SAYS THAT THE GIRL NAMED TAMARA IS OUR CONTACT.
WHAT???!!! THAT CREEP KIDNAPPED OUR CONTACT???

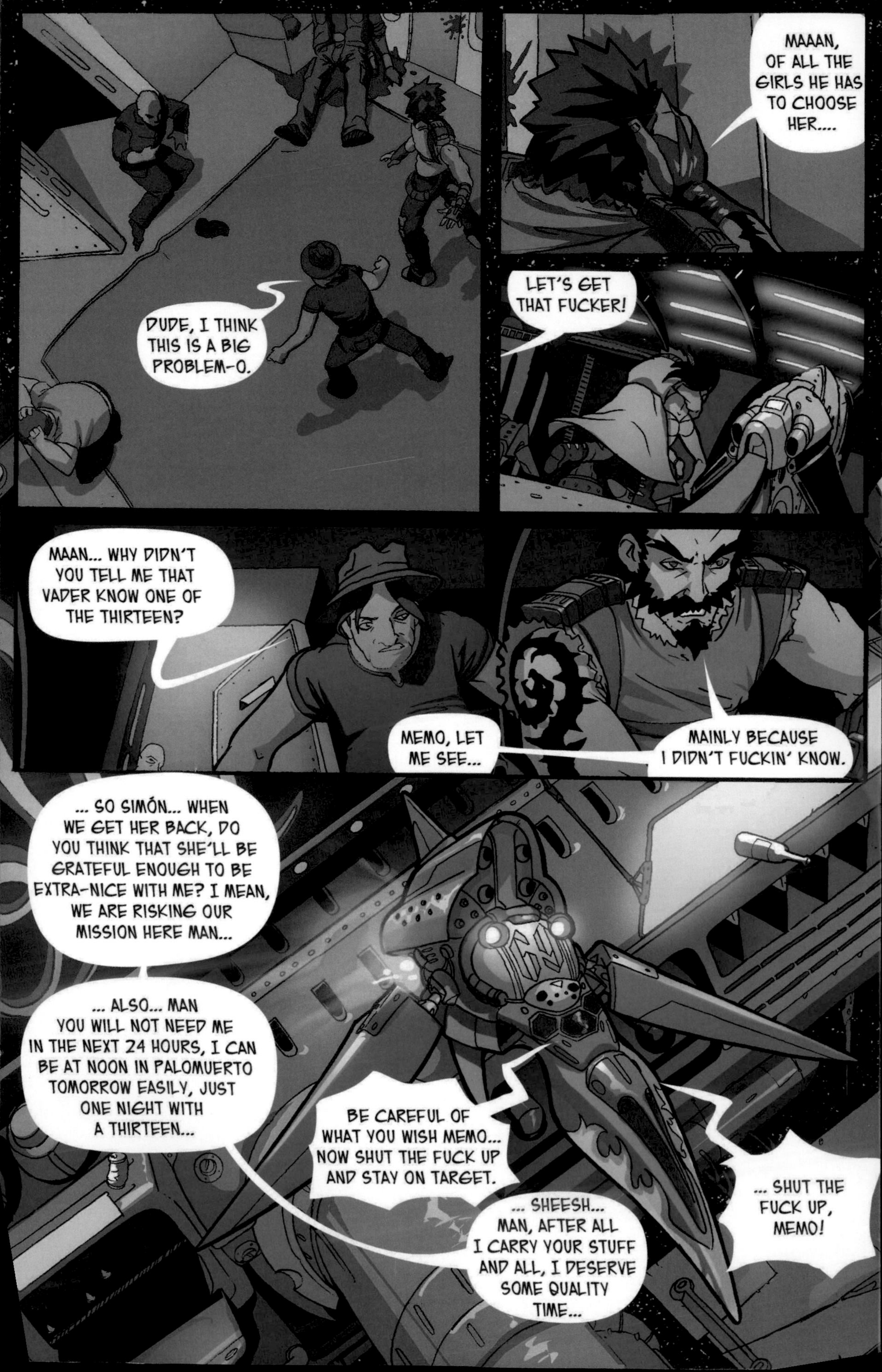
MAAAN, OF ALL THE GIRLS HE HAS TO CHOOSE HER....
DUDE, I THINK THIS IS A BIG PROBLEM-O.
LET'S GET THAT FUCKER!
MAAN... WHY DIDN'T YOU TELL ME THAT VADER KNOW ONE OF THE THIRTEEN?
MEMO, LET ME SEE...
MAINLY BECAUSE I DIDN'T FUCKIN' KNOW.
... SO SIMÓN... WHEN WE GET HER BACK, DO YOU THINK THAT SHE'LL BE GRATEFUL ENOUGH TO BE EXTRA-NICE WITH ME? I MEAN, WE ARE RISKING OUR MISSION HERE MAN...
... ALSO... MAN YOU WILL NOT NEED ME IN THE NEXT 24 HOURS, I CAN BE AT NOON IN PALOMUERTO TOMORROW EASILY, JUST ONE NIGHT WITH A THIRTEEN...
BE CAREFUL OF WHAT YOU WISH MEMO... NOW SHUT THE FUCK UP AND STAY ON TARGET.
... SHEESH... MAN, AFTER ALL I CARRY YOUR STUFF AND ALL, I DESERVE SOME QUALITY TIME...
... SHUT THE FUCK UP, MEMO!

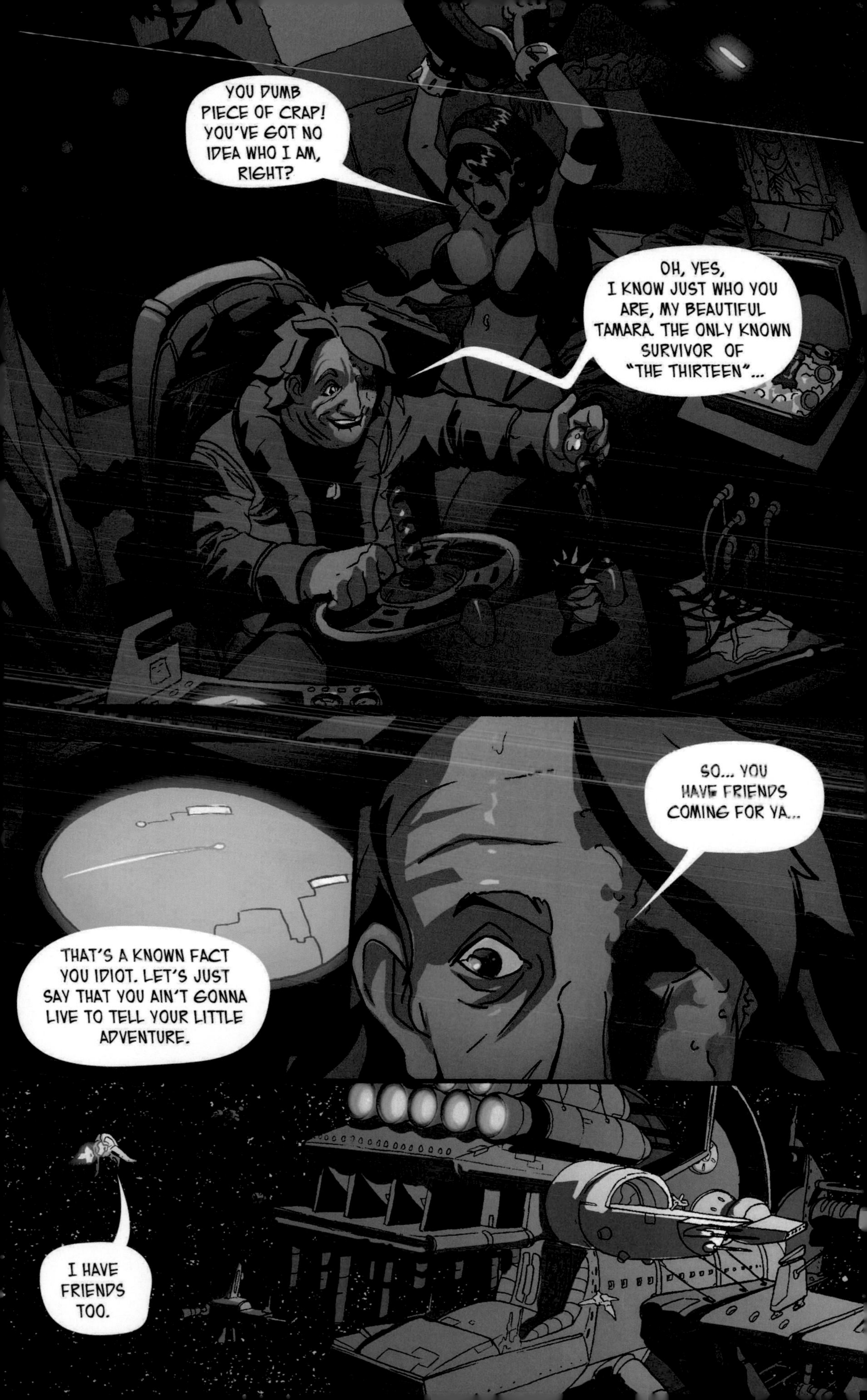
YOU DUMB PIECE OF CRAP! YOU'VE GOT NO IDEA WHO I AM, RIGHT?
OH, YES, I KNOW JUST WHO YOU ARE, MY BEAUTIFUL TAMARA. THE ONLY KNOWN SURVIVOR OF "THE THIRTEEN"...
SO... YOU HAVE FRIENDS COMING FOR YA...
THAT'S A KNOWN FACT YOU IDIOT. LET'S JUST SAY THAT YOU AIN'T GONNA LIVE TO TELL YOUR LITTLE ADVENTURE.
I HAVE FRIENDS TOO.

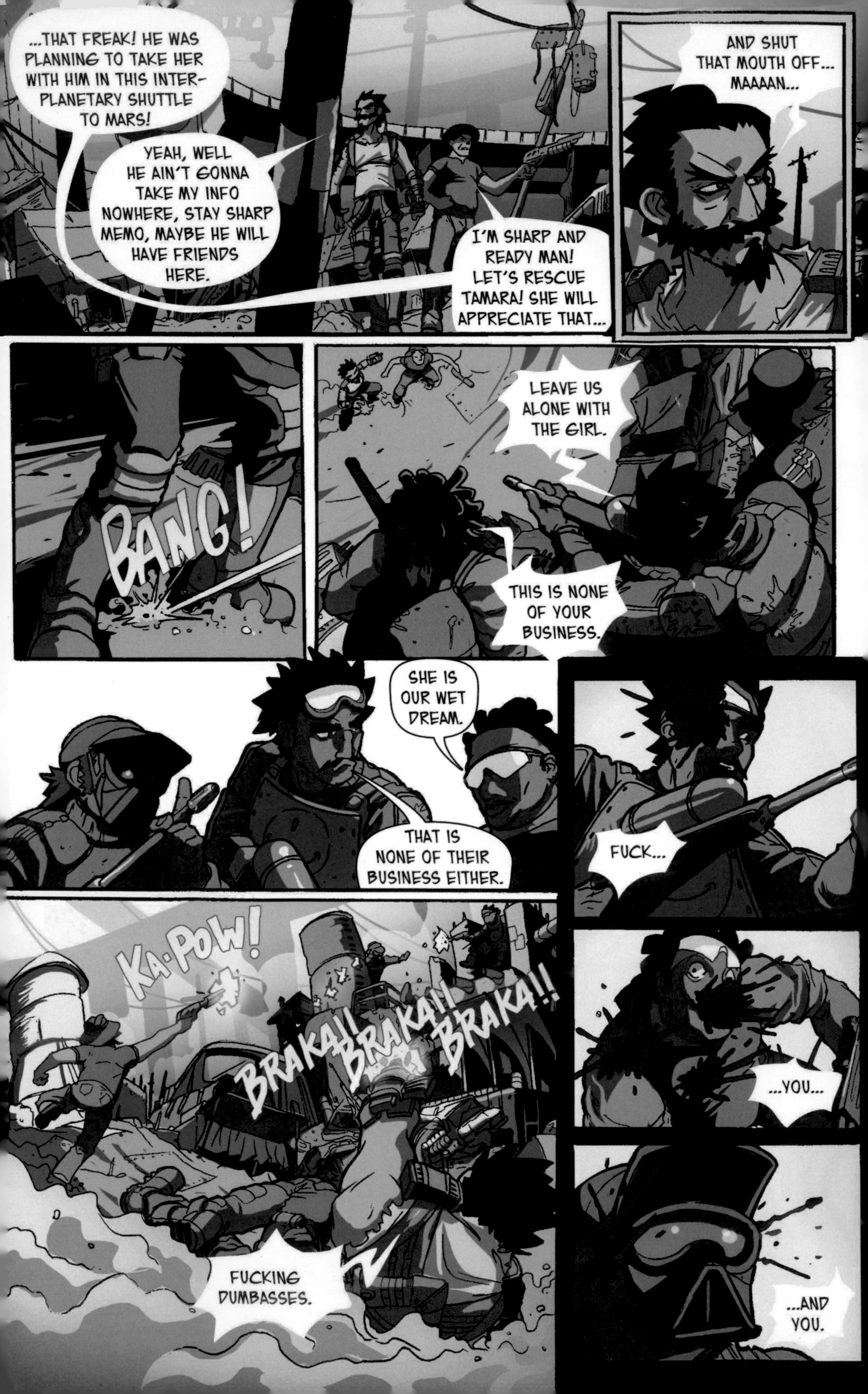
...THAT FREAK! HE WAS PLANNING TO TAKE HER WITH HIM IN THIS INTER-PLANETARY SHUTTLE TO MARS!
YEAH, WELL HE AIN'T GONNA TAKE MY INFO NOWHERE, STAY SHARP MEMO, MAYBE HE WILL HAVE FRIENDS HERE.
I'M SHARP AND READY MAN! LET'S RESCUE TAMARA! SHE WILL APPRECIATE THAT...
AND SHUT THAT MOUTH OFF... MAAAAN...
BANG!
LEAVE US ALONE WITH THE GIRL.
THIS IS NONE OF YOUR BUSINESS.
SHE IS OUR WET DREAM.
THAT IS NONE OF THEIR BUSINESS EITHER.
FUCK...
KA-POW!
BRAKA!! BRAKA!! BRAKA!!
FUCKING DUMBASSES.
...YOU...
...AND YOU.

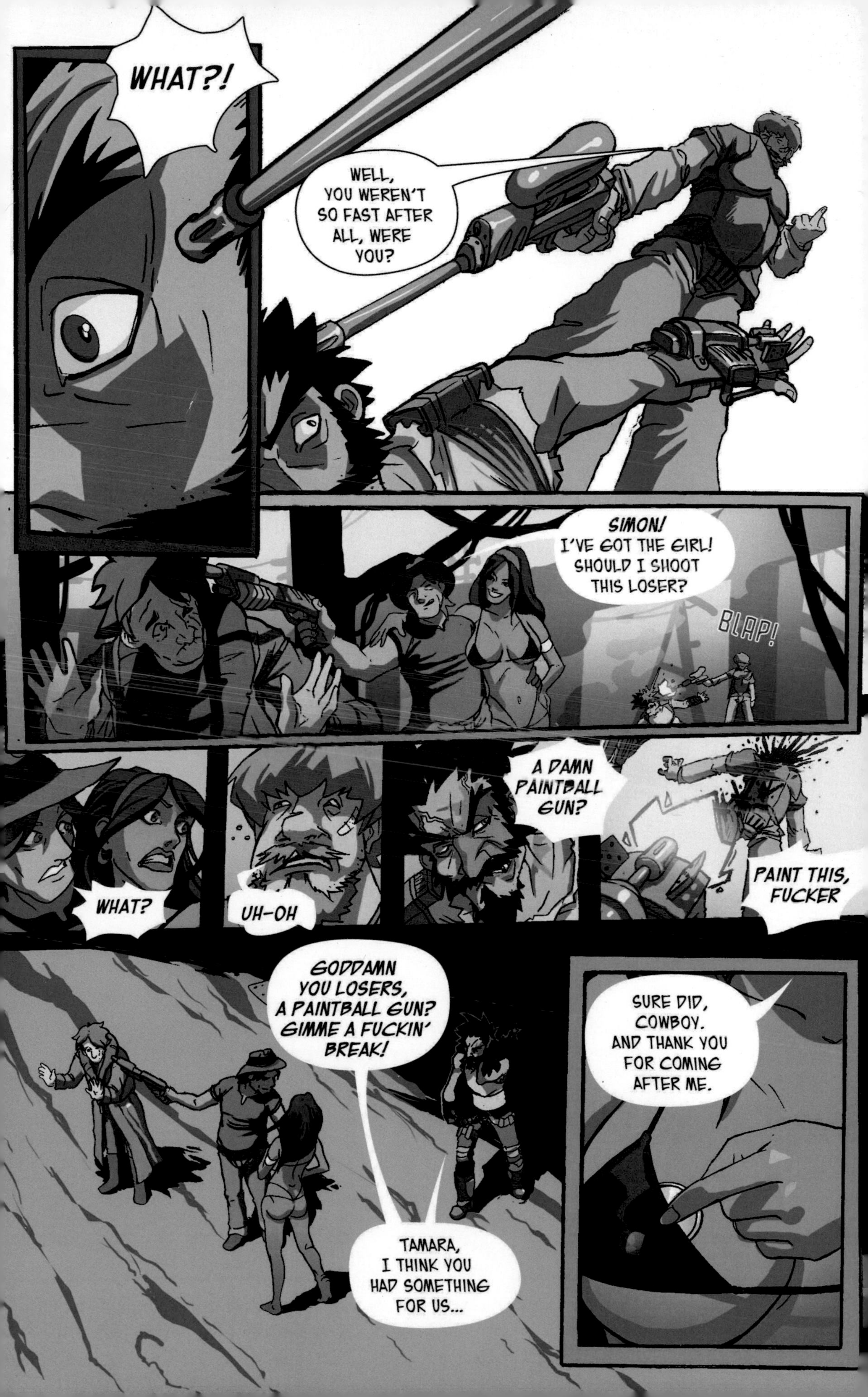
WHAT?!
WELL, YOU WEREN'T SO FAST AFTER ALL, WERE YOU?
SIMON! I'VE GOT THE GIRL! SHOULD I SHOOT THIS LOSER?
BLAP!
WHAT?
UH-OH
A DAMN PAINTBALL GUN?
PAINT THIS, FUCKER
GODDAMN YOU LOSERS, A PAINTBALL GUN? GIMME A FUCKIN' BREAK!
TAMARA, I THINK YOU HAD SOMETHING FOR US...
SURE DID, COWBOY. AND THANK YOU FOR COMING AFTER ME.

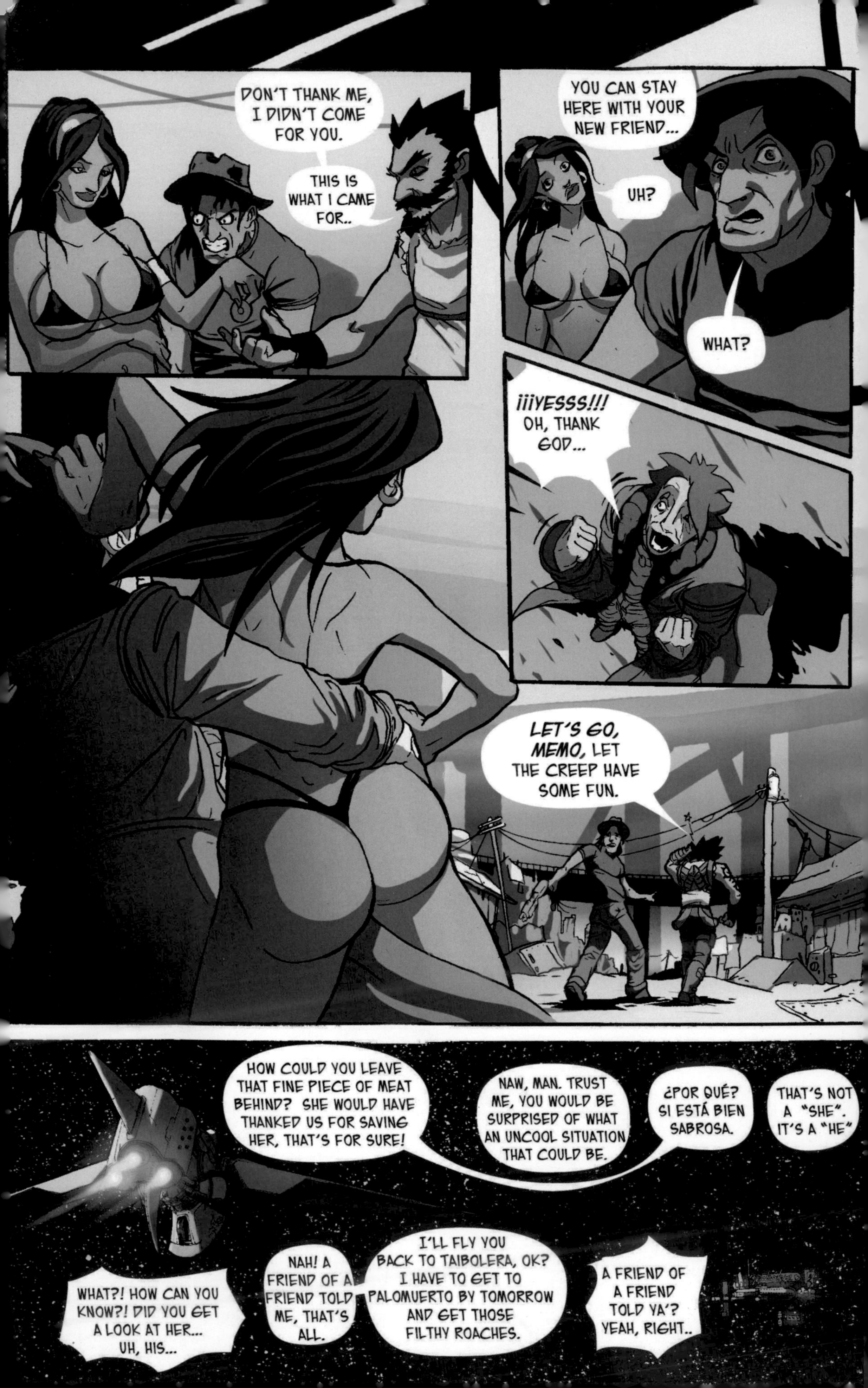
DON'T THANK ME, I DIDN'T COME FOR YOU.
THIS IS WHAT I CAME FOR..
YOU CAN STAY HERE WITH YOUR NEW FRIEND...
UH?
WHAT?
¡¡¡YESSS!!! OH, THANK GOD...
LET'S GO, MEMO, LET THE CREEP HAVE SOME FUN.
HOW COULD YOU LEAVE THAT FINE PIECE OF MEAT BEHIND? SHE WOULD HAVE THANKED US FOR SAVING HER, THAT'S FOR SURE!
NAW, MAN. TRUST ME, YOU WOULD BE SURPRISED OF WHAT AN UNCOOL SITUATION THAT COULD BE.
¿POR QUÉ? SI ESTÁ BIEN SABROSA.
THAT'S NOT A "SHE". IT'S A "HE"
WHAT?! HOW CAN YOU KNOW?! DID YOU GET A LOOK AT HER... UH, HIS...
NAH! A FRIEND OF A FRIEND TOLD ME, THAT'S ALL.
I'LL FLY YOU BACK TO TAIBOLERA, OK? I HAVE TO GET TO PALOMUERTO BY TOMORROW AND GET THOSE FILTHY ROACHES.
A FRIEND OF A FRIEND TOLD YA'? YEAH, RIGHT..